Living Ethically, Acting Politically

CONTESTATIONS

Cornell Studies in Political Theory

A series edited by
William E. Connolly

A complete list of titles in the series appears at the end of the book.

Living Ethically, Acting Politically

Melissa A. Orlie

Cornell University Press

Ithaca and London

First published 1997 by Cornell University Press

Printed in the United States of America

Cornell University Press strives to utilize environmentally responsible suppliers and materials to the fullest extent possible in the publishing of its books. Such materials include vegetable-based, low-VOC inks and acid-free papers that are also either recycled, totally chlorine-free, or partly composed of nonwood fibers.

Library of Congress Cataloging-in-Publication Data

Orlie, Melissa A.
Living ethically, acting politically / Melissa A. Orlie.
p. cm. — (Contestations)
Includes index.
ISBN 0-8014-3355-X (cloth : alk. paper) ISBN 0-8014-8472-3 (pbk. : alk. paper)
1. Political ethics. 2. Social ethics. 3. Ethics. I. Title. II. Series.
JA79.075 1997
320'.01'1—dc21 97-14935

Cloth printing 10 9 8 7 6 5 4 3 2 1

To Deborah Wuliger

Contents

Acknowledgments

In large measure, I came to write this book because of the emotional and material resources my families lent to my education. I am grateful to Edward and Frances Orlie, and to Christopher and Kathi Orlie. Without the faith and support of Luanne and Robert Dunlop, I would not have been able to write the dissertation that made me want to write this book instead. Since I love the life I live, their confidence and generosity means everything to me.

I have been blessed with exemplary teachers whose traces are manifest, if often invisibly, throughout this book: by Bettina Aptheker, Jim Clifford, J. Peter Euben, the late Rick Gordon, Donna Haraway, Ann Lane, Robert Meister, Hanna Pitkin, Jack Schaar, Gayatri Spivak, and Richard Wasserstrom at the University of California, Santa Cruz; by Sot Barber, George Kateb, Alexander Nehamas, Anne Norton, Alan Ryan, Jeff Tulis, Maurizio Viroli, and Sheldon Wolin at Princeton University. I am especially grateful to Peter Euben for his inspired teaching, which led me to political theory, and for the encouragement and friendship that helped me stay with what I learned to love in his classes.

At a crucial moment in the process, Bonnie Honig welcomed my thoughts and helped me see their significance in ways that affected their articulation long after the fact. Bill Connolly received my project with enthusiasm in its nascent stages, which gave my spirits a much-needed lift. Later he discerned the method in the madness of my third section and suggested a pattern for conveying it to others. By his example, I now have a better understanding of what Nietzsche calls a gift-giving virtue; he has a remarkable ability to care for a project as if it were his own, without claiming it for himself. George Shulman has often seemed to understand my work better than I do myself. His collaborative thoughts have freed me to say what I must. I am grateful to him and in awe of his grace: this book would have been much poorer without his powers of insight.

A number of people have read and responded to aspects of my work or inspired me with their conversation. I wish I could do more than list their names to express my thanks: Fred Alford, Amanda Anderson, Jane Bennett, Michael Bérubé, Dana Chabot, Mary Dietz, Carl Estabrook, Jim Farr, Belden Fields, Richard Flathman, Dilip Gaonkar, Peter Garrett, James Glass, Allen Hance, Sue Hemberger, Jeff Isaac, George Kamberelis, Bert Koegler, Ed Kolodziej, Jim Kuklinski, Mark Leff, Timothy Luke, Janet Lyon, Jenny Mansbridge, Sid Maskit, Kirstie McClure, Meta Mendel-Reyes, Richard Mohr, Sara Monoson, Gerry Munck, Dianne Pinderhughes, Paul Quirk, Mark Reinhardt, Dick Schacht, Jackie Stevens, and Laura Stoker. No doubt I have neglected to mention some who deserve my thanks.

Earlier versions of ideas developed here appeared as "Forgiving Trespasses, Promising Futures," in *Feminist Interpretations of Hannah Arendt*, edited by Bonnie Honig (University Park: Penn State University Press, 1995), 337–56, and "Thoughtless Assertion and Political Deliberation" *American Political Science Review* 88(3) (September 1994): 684–95. I am grateful to the anonymous reviewers of the latter, who gave my argument a chance and made helpful suggestions. Thanks to Barbara Carlile of the Marian Goodman Gallery and John C. Gilmour for their help in acquiring permission to reproduce the Kiefer watercolor.

It was my good fortune to come to the University of Illinois, whose people and practices inspire me as a scholar and teacher. I thank Peter Nardulli for helping to create such a wonderful environment for writing and teaching. Pete is the sort of department head that untenured faculty members dream of and are sure does not exist. His material and professional support were crucial to the realization of this project, as was the aid of the department's staff. I thank participants in the monthly colloquia and biweekly faculty seminars of the Unit for Criticism and Interpretive Theory for keeping my mind fresh. A faculty fellowship from the Program for the Study of Cultural Values and Ethics gave me release from teaching to complete the first version of the manuscript, and the Faculty Research Board provided funds for research assistance. Many of my themes were first explored in my graduate and undergraduate courses. I am grateful to all those students who approach thinking, their own thoughts and mine, with playful seriousness. I am especially indebted to conversations with Paul Hendrickson, Lisa King, Natasha Levinson, and Robert McCarthy. Lisa King was especially invaluable as anyone who uses the index will no doubt agree.

It has been a pleasure to work with people at Cornell University Press. I am especially grateful to Roger Haydon, Carol Betsch, and Barbara Dinneen for the care they have shown my ideas and words.

Jacqueline Madden fostered much of the invisible power infusing this book, and she knows better than anyone what writing it cost. Nick Burbules and Cheryl Cole kept me company during much of the final writing. While they sometimes read and commented on aspects of the manuscript, I most appreciate their willingness to converse with me for hours on end before I quit smoking. And to Cheryl I owe special thanks for asking me about limit-experience before I even knew that was what I was writing about; I look forward to other generative questions and more frequent trips to Chicago. Though, conventionally, we acknowledge only human things, I am indebted to my dogs, cats, house, and garden for opening me and keeping me open to energies that sustained me while I was writing. Lisa Jensen's friendship has provided an essential compass in my life. Finally, I dedicate this book to Deborah Wuliger, who has been my friend for over sixteen years, about as long as I have been trying to become a political theorist. She has seen me through everything. Without her, I could not have made this beginning.

M. A. O.

Abbreviations

BPF	Hannah Arendt. *Between Past and Future: Eight Exercises in Political Thought*. New York: Penguin, 1977.
CR	Hannah Arendt. *Crises of the Republic*. New York: Harcourt Brace Jovanovich, 1969.
CS	Michel Foucault. *The Care of the Self*. New York: Vintage, 1988.
CSPF	Michel Foucault. "The Ethic of the Care for the Self as a Practice of Freedom." *The Final Foucault*. Edited by James Bernauer. Cambridge: MIT Press, 1984.
DC	Thomas Hobbes. *De Cive*. Edited by B. Gert. *Man and Citizen*. Gloucester, Mass.: Peter Smith, 1978.
DP	Michel Foucault. *Discipline and Punish*. New York: Vintage, 1979.
E	Hannah Arendt. *Eichmann in Jerusalem. A Report on the Banality of Evil.* New York: Viking, 1964.
EL	Thomas Hobbes. *The Elements of Law Natural and Politic*. Edited by F. Tönnies. London: Simpkin Marshall, 1939.
FL	Michel Foucault. *Foucault Live*. New York: Semiotext(e), 1989.
FR	Michel Foucault. *The Foucault Reader*. Edited by Paul Rabinow. New York: Pantheon, 1984.
HC	Hannah Arendt. *The Human Condition*. Chicago: University of Chicago Press, 1958.
HSI	Michel Foucault. *The History of Sexuality. An Introduction*. New York: Vintage, 1990.
JP	Hannah Arendt. "The Jew as Pariah." *Jewish Social Studies* 6(2) (February 1944): 118–19.

L	Thomas Hobbes. *Leviathan.* Edited by C. B. MacPherson. New York: Penguin, 1968.
LCP	Michel Foucault. *Language, Counter-Memory, and Practice.* Ithaca: Cornell University Press, 1977.
LK	Hannah Arendt. *Lectures on Kant's Political Philosophy.* Chicago: University of Chicago Press, 1982.
LM	Hannah Arendt. *Life of the Mind.* Volume 1. New York: Harcourt Brace, 1978.
MC	Michel Foucault. *Madness and Civilization.* New York: Vintage, 1988.
OR	Hannah Arendt. *On Revolution.* New York: Penguin, 1965.
OT	Hannah Arendt. *The Origins of Totalitarianism.* New York: Harcourt Brace, 1973.
PK	Michel Foucault. *Power/Knowledge.* New York: Pantheon, 1980.
PPC	Michel Foucault. *Politics, Philosophy, Culture. Interviews and Other Writings, 1977–1984.* Edited by L. D. Kritzman. New York: Routledge, 1988.
RM	Michel Foucault. *Remarks on Marx.* New York: Semiotext(e), 1991.
SP	Michel Foucault. "The Subject and Power." In Hubert L. Dreyfus and Paul Rabinow, *Michel Foucault: Beyond Structuralism and Hermeneutics,* 2d ed. Chicago: University of Chicago Press, 1983.
TMC	Hannah Arendt. "Thinking and Moral Consideration." *Social Research* 38(3) (Fall 1971): 423–38.
TS	Michel Foucault. *Technologies of the Self.* Amherst: University of Massachusetts Press, 1988.
UP	Michel Foucault. *The Uses of Pleasure.* New York: Vintage, 1986.
VW	Phyllis Mack. *Visionary Women: Ecstatic Prophecy in Seventeenth-Century England.* Berkeley: University of California Press, 1992.

Living Ethically, Acting Politically

Anselm Kiefer, *Every Human Being Stands beneath His Own Dome of Heaven* (*Jeder Mensch steht unter seiner Himmelskugel*), 1970. Watercolor and pencil on paper. 15-3/4 × 18-7/8″ (40 × 48 cm). Private Collection.

Introduction

But I am one who can bless and say Yes, if only you are about me, pure and light, you abyss of light; then I carry the blessing of my Yes into all abysses. I have become one who blesses and says Yes; and I fought long for that and was a fighter that I might one day get my hands free to bless. But this is my blessing: to stand over every single thing as its own heaven, as its round roof, its azure bell, and eternal security; and blessed is he who blesses thus.

Friedrich Nietzsche, *Thus Spoke Zarathustra*

In this book I contest what is perhaps our most fundamental political faith (albeit a faith without hope), the inevitability and necessities of governance. I question what seems beyond question: first, the assumption that human beings must be ruled, whether by laws or by "men," the few as well as the many; second, the presumption that political bodies, and the common power that constitutes the political, must be sovereign. But I challenge these beliefs not in the name of "anarchy" but for the sake of ethical political action and alternative orders. If we are to live ethically and act politically, we must dispute this political faith and its necessities.

To contest the inevitability of governance and its necessities is to risk being called mad. Indeed, seventeenth-century religious enthusiasts suffered just this fate at the hands of Thomas Hobbes, among others. Perhaps the vitriolic responses the writings of Hannah Arendt and Michel Foucault sometimes provoke also may be understood in these terms. As a consequence of Arendt's and Foucault's challenges to governance and its powers, many of their interpreters have been perplexed and on occasion enraged by what they experience as sometimes unreasonableness, sometimes amoralism, in Arendt's and Foucault's perspectives. And the interpreters are right. Thinking that questions the inevitability and necessities of governance challenges what and who we *know* to be reasonable and mad.

In our time it is not especially novel to reimagine the relationship between madness and reason. The potential irrationality of the rational is a founding intellectual theme of the twentieth and the late nineteenth century and is this waning century's gravest and most unnerving practical lesson.[1] What I explore here in a preliminary and provisional way is how to live ethically—freely and responsibly—with this recognition and its dangers. To summarize my question, how are we to address and redress the harm that inevitably follows in the wake of even the good we would do?

In Anselm Kiefer's *Every Human Being Stands beneath His Own Dome of Heaven* I find one representation of our contemporary predicament. I have found Kiefer's watercolor arresting since I first saw it on exhibit at the Museum of Modern Art in New York City in summer 1989. The venue is significant because living in New York City crystalized for me ethical problems and political questions that have reached one culmination in this book. In short, I found my concerns transformed by the conditions in which I lived. On the one hand, I was awakened and enspirited by the concentration and multiplication of energies for which New York City is famous. On the other hand, social desperation and the limits of common-sense civility became visible to me in ways that a girl from the suburbs of Chicago and San Francisco and educated in the shelter of Santa Cruz and Princeton had not previously been able to see. In this context, the simultaneously pleasing and disturbing poetic quality of Kiefer's watercolor stirred my imagination. Coming to see in new ways my implication in my surroundings, I recognized within myself a longing for my own azure bell (in Nietzsche's phrase) and felt there was something both very right and very questionable about that desire.

I shall return to this question of desire, but, first, let me explain what I mean by my implication in my surroundings. Chapter 1 begins with a meditation upon our need to secure a home in the world (I mean a place to sleep and eat, not an ontological sense of belonging) and how this need implicates us in trespasses against others, specifically in processes that render others homeless. This claim is based upon observation, not speculation alone. Renting an apartment in a neighborhood undergoing gentrification was a constitutive experience for me and this book. When I moved into the then less-than-fashionable south end of Park Slope in Brooklyn, every building on my block was or was about to be in a state of renovation. But (don't tell my mother) crack sales and police sweeps were still the order of the day, and frequent auto break-ins infused capital into the underground economy. In 1991, when I left my Brooklyn neighborhood, the crack was pretty much gone, the buildings looked pretty, and the inhabitants of my apartment house were no longer elderly and working-class people of color but white upwardly mobile folks like myself. Progress? From one perspective, yes. But where did those other folks go? I have situations like this in mind when I speak in chapter 1 of a making from one perspective being an unmaking from another perspective. Good and harm are done simultaneously and in ways that perpetuate power relations that precede new activities. Such situations, manifest in the places we live, the food we eat, the clothes we wear, the other goods we use, and the activities we pursue, pose, I believe, the principal ethical and political challenges of our late modern time.

The catalogue description of Kiefer's print affords a suitable introduction to my themes and the ethical political predicaments I seek to think through.

> The saluting figure with the limited viewpoint imposed by the dome is set within a larger cosmos; his pose is pretentious, even silly, compared to the enormity of the earth. Nevertheless, the Nazi, or Roman, would have implicitly believed that the "dome of heaven" he concocted corresponded to a celestial vault, such as has been imagined in various religions. Keifer's comparison of spaces shows that true transcendence can only occur by passing beyond, or in the terms of Indian philosophy, by "shattering" the roof. Still, however arrogant, destructive, isolated, and limited, the figure has his worldview with which he understands and affects the universe.[2]

If only Nazis and Romans alone believed and lived thus! Among the real insights of this interpretation, we encounter the presumption that evil is always monstrous and evildoers malevolent. Kiefer's pretentious and silly yet apparently no less potent figure (for other heavenly domes have disappeared) could prompt us to reimagine evil.

Kiefer's vision is simultaneously reassuring and unsettling. The azure bell that the figure salutes *is* beautiful and for all we know even signifies virtuous or noble principles. We displace examination of our own conduct when we presume that only Nazi values so circumscribe the world. The sorts of harm which are the subject of this book are hard to see, in part because we make them so. By assuming that power is repressive, unthinking, and crude, we miss the more subtle forms of its exercise in which we participate. By presuming that evil is monstrous, we miss the constructive achievements and accompanying destructive effects of our own azure bells. In Part I, I explore the invisible, apparently unauthored character of modern power and the unintended harm and resentments that flow from it, arguing that they require us to rethink the explanation and meaning of evil as well as the generation and imagination of power.

Kiefer's figure appears isolated, thus pretentious and silly, even in his assertiveness. His isolation is a misperception, but a productive one. Predominant conceptions of power and conscience imagine an individual who is weak and at the same time inviolable and fundamentally untouched by power. In accordance with predominant understandings, the self-perception of Kiefer's figure would probably be that he is of little consequence: alone, he appears to make his own world, but he also appears to be ineffective, even in need of protection, given the enormity of his surroundings. The conscience of the modern individual, whose genealogy I proffer in Part 2, is free to affirm whatever it likes because, or as long as, the individual has little effect. But the azure bells we affirm are not of our making alone, though the social processes and relations with others that produce them are often invisible. Because these processes are invisible it seems that what the individual does or does not affirm matters little. The blue on the horizon suggests that there may be other domes of concern (we can even almost make one out to the left of his azure bell), but they are invisible, inaudible, out of his order.

Kiefer's print conveys the hidden and unexpected power of the apparently isolated individual: he has made the rest of the human world disappear. The perception of isolated inefficacy is deceptive. On the one hand, as Simone Weil notes, we live amid organizations organized by no one which systematically harm others. Thus, it would seem that no one is responsible for, nor free to alter, their effects. On the other hand, as Weil also notes (and Arendt and Foucault would concur), systemic power relations are sustained and elaborated by the daily, routine behavior of individuals.[3] The individual alone cannot make entire peoples and worlds disappear, but individuals who imagine that they are without power, and who are thus thoughtless of their power effects, participate in such disappearance. I am not saying that individuals acting alone, without the collaboration of others, can change the world. Indeed, one of the tragic characteristics of ethics is that living ethically entails acting politically, and the conditions of political action cannot be supplied by the individual alone. But neither can the conditions of politics be created without individual action.

I consider this contemporary "crisis of the subject," or our difficulties conceiving freedom and responsibility, both politically and ethically. Politically speaking, awareness of the social construction of selves ("subjects"), of increasingly constrictive social necessities, and of our manifold yet not always apparent participation in social processes which nevertheless seem out of our control make it difficult to identify human responsibility and generate profound doubt about human freedom. Ethically speaking, we experience a crisis because predominant ideas of intentionality and responsibility are ill-suited to addressing the harmful effects (what I call "trespasses" and at once "ordinary" and "ordered" evil) that inevitably follow not from our intentions and malevolence but from our participation in social processes and identities.

In contexts of ordered evil, we cannot approach dilemmas of ethical living alone; we must act politically. By connecting resistance against evil to reflections on the nature of power and political action, I reveal possibilities for the extraordinary within the ordinary. That is to say, I attend to the daily and common ways we exercise power, inflict harm, and show ourselves capable of action that transforms both selves and the world. In this light, we can see why ethical political action appears "miraculous." Like the seventeenth century Quakers I discuss in Chapter 4, Arendt and Foucault find political possibilities in what religious discourses meant by the powers they called "spirit" in the world and selves. By recognizing and actualizing these "invisible powers" within and among us, we see freedom where once only necessity was visible, possibilities for forgiveness where once only harm and resentments abounded, and new, ethical action where once there was only reaction.

I am not sure whether Arendt and Foucault are melodramatic, or whether I have made them so. Regardless, I think Peter Brooks's account of the "melodramatic imagination" captures the play of invisible powers in their writings and this book.[4] Foucault's and Arendt's writings are dramatic, as are the early Quakers' practices of the self, in that they create "excessive, hyperbolic, parabolic stor[ies] from the banal stuff of reality" (Brooks, 196). The hidden reality they reveal is the world of the "moral occult," or "the domain of operative spiritual values which is both indicated within and masked by the surface of reality" (Brooks, 199). This imagination appears melodramatic when it must find the spiritual in a context which seems to have been deprived of possibilities for transcendence (Brooks, 210). The desire for spiritual reality is born of a sense of ethical conflict, but can be satisfied only by constructing meanings and symbolic systems on, and over, a void in the absence of the justification afforded by a religious hermeneutic or universally accepted social code (Brooks, 211). In this context, ethical gestures often appear hyperbolic:

> the more difficult it becomes to put one's finger on the nature of the spiritual reality alluded to—the more highly charged is the vehicle, the more strained with pressure to suggest a meaning beyond. Melodrama may be a drama which is heightened, hyperbolic because the moral realm it wants to evoke is not immediately visible, and the writer is ever conscious of standing over a void, dealing in conflicts, qualities, and quantities whose very existence is uncertain. The violence and extremism of emotion and moral statement we find in melodrama may then derive from the fact that they are unjustified, unfounded emotion and ethical consciousness, qualities that cannot be shown to bear any imperative relationship to the way life is lived by most people. (Brooks, 204)

Only the exercise of a spiritualist imagination can bring this ethical sense into existence; and such an imagination is transgressive, not transcendent, "in a world which no longer recognizes any *positive* meaning in the sacred" (LCP, 30, my emphasis).[5]

In our time, is it enough for an impulse toward transcendence to recognize that it can only fulfill its desire by "passing beyond" and "shattering the roof" of what others mistake for celestial vaults? Or must we require something more than or different from this regulative ideal? What would enable Kiefer's isolated figure to cross the limits of his own azure bell? What would he have achieved were he to do so? I approach variations upon these questions in the third and final part of this book. Here, however, we can ask whether and if Kiefer's figure broke through his own dome of heaven, he would have any hope of comprehending the infinite expanse beyond. Foucault suggests not, when he says that "by denying us the limit of the Limitless, the death of God leads us to an experience in which nothing again may announce the exteriority of being." To "kill God" liberates life from the existence that limits it but also brings "it back to those limits that are annulled by this limitless existence" (LCP, 32). We can transgress, but not transcend, the limits of our being; we can exceed given ways of being, but only when we recognize that we always accede to another, limited way of being. When we acknowledge that we neither comprehend nor manifest the infinite possibilities of being—when every azure bell is a "nonpositive affirmation"—our transgression of limits opens us to the limitless. Transgression "serves as a glorification of the nature it excludes: the limit opens violently onto the limitless, finds itself suddenly carried away by the content it had rejected and fulfilled by this alien plenitude which invades it to the core of its being. Transgression carries the limit right to the limit of its being; transgression forces the limit to face the fact of its imminent disappearance, to find itself in what it excludes" (LCP, 34). Transgression is a parabolic experience that "transforms the present through the intervention of an unknown, free, and open future."[6] The longing for an azure bell one can affirm is born of dissatisfaction with the given and a spirited feeling that fosters hope in alternatives.[7] There are dangers as well, however, in the urge for transcendence, namely, that one's own limited azure bell will be mistaken for a celestial vault, or that the love of spirit will foster disregard or, worse, hatred for the earth. Arendt and Foucault are keenly aware of the dangers flowing from the desire for transcendence, but they also recognize promise in this desire, if transfigured, which informs their efforts to articulate a worldly spirituality.

Whereas the place of transgression in Foucault's work is widely recognized, readers may balk at my claim that Arendt's thinking is also transgressive. Typically, Arendtian thinking is a means of feeling at home in the world, of reconciling us to it. This reconciliation is the prescribed task of political judgment and might seem the most plausible account of Arendt's amor mundi. But I argue that judgment is an insufficient way to care for the world. Rather, thinking (in contrast to judgment) cares for the world by attending to the effects of the limits through which we constitute the world. I argue that Arendt, like Foucault, believes that these limits cannot be transcended; but she also believes, with him, that these limits must be transgressed if human plurality and natality are to be realized. Limits, though unavoidable, foreclose plurality and natality by fostering uniformity of being. We necessarily affirm limited being, whether we do so lovingly or not. But loving the world requires us continually to transgress those limits. This is the significance I find in Arendt's reflections upon promising and forgiving: they are spiritual political practices of overcoming, but as transgression, not as transcendence. More specifically, what I call forgiving promises are free and responsible ways of attending to the trespasses entailed by the homes we secure and the worlds we make; our azure bells may be things of beauty but are nonetheless implicated in the disappearance or absence of other ways of being.

My claim, then, is that both Arendt and Foucault believe that we find our selves, and others, through transgression. But what does it mean to say, in Foucault's words, that we find ourselves, our finitude, in what we exclude; that we find ourselves suddenly carried away by the content we have rejected and fulfilled by this alien plenitude that invades us to the core of our being (LCP, 34)? Arendt enables us to ask the question in a more straightforward way: what is the relationship between natality and plurality?

According to the social ontology I find in Hobbes, Arendt, and Foucault, every way of being trespasses against others, albeit to varying degrees. Transgressive thinking and action respond to these trespasses. When we respond to trespasses, we recognize that what the world and we have been made to be are not necessarily so. A recognition of this space of freedom within necessity reveals the plurality without us, the natality within us, and the intimate relationship between the two. Every belief and habit, even those that would do good, limit the plenitude of being. Through transgression, we experience that this particular limitation is not necessary; although limits are inevitable, their distinct instantiation is contingent. Plurality and natality are intimately related because only by affirming plurality—only by addressing and redressing our trespasses—can we actualize our capacity for new action. We both lose and create our selves in what we have excluded, because when we acknowledge other ways of being, we also create other possibilities within our selves. Becoming other than we are made to be—actualizing our natality, or our capacity to act anew as well as to be what we are made to be—can occur only when we affirm plurality, which is to say, when we respond freely and deliberately to our trespasses.

Natality is a paradoxical fact of human existence. On the one hand, the fact that we are born means that we do not create ourselves. There is mystery at the heart of our being, a dependence that renders us fundamentally nonsovereign. On the other hand, our individual birth is unprecedented and signifies our capacity for new beginnings. Just as there is no one exactly like us, we are capable of acting unexpectedly, in ways other than we are made to be. We are not only born, but we can also give birth to our selves and a new world if we accept and enact our nonsovereignty, the plurality within and without us. Why? An answer is suggested by the correlation between these two aspects of natality and the two senses I give to invisible powers. We can neither altogether discern nor control the external forces that make us, but we nonetheless guide those forces; thus freedom and necessity coexist as we freely exercise power amid necessity. Invisible powers within us, meanwhile, not only attach us to these external invisible powers but also may disrupt our relationship to them. In the absence of experience of the plenitude of being, however, we cannot become free, because we misapprehend our creative powers by failing to recognize both the role of others and ourselves in the generation of our azure bells. An intimate relationship links the recognition of plurality—alternative ways of being without us—and natality—energies for alternative ways of being within us.

If, as Peter Brooks writes, "the way the world is represented becomes the very process by which the moral occult is brought into existence" (209) then (to employ an old analytic distinction) both the form and content of this book seek to accomplish this task. Specifically, I enact the mutual transfiguration among different perspectives which I take to be a political form of transgression. In other words, there is a relationship between the style of interpretation I pursue—a mutual transfiguration among the perspectives of Hobbes, Arendt, and Foucault—and the ways of thinking and action I advocate.

Like melodrama, which is the tragic mode "for a world in which there is no longer a tenable idea of the sacred" (Brooks, 206), a novel tradition of political theory best suits our late modern time. Hobbes exemplifies an epic tradition of political theory for which the political, and its theorists, are sovereign.[8] In this tradition, the political is conceived as *monotheos*, theory is totalizing and finally aims at transcendence as the theorist seeks and advocates sovereign mastery over the world.[9] By contrast, the novel tradition of political theory I explore here conceives the political as *entheos*, theory is heteroglossic, transgressive, and aims at beginning powers and selves that are collaborative, not sovereign.[10] Mutual transfiguration, or what Bakhtin calls interillumination, may enable us to lose, then recreate, the habits of our minds and bodies at the limit of what we have excluded. Transgressing the limits made by our trespasses, we may begin principled politics, which is to say, we may live ethically and act politically.

PART I

THE CONTEMPORARY IMAGINATION OF POWER

What does it mean to live ethically today? We exist amid historical harm and wrongdoing, inherited or institutionalized advantages and disadvantages.[1] As a consequence, our relations with one another are suffused by collective and individual harms, both past and present. We do not, however, possess these powers that bring ill effects to others; we are constituted by and through them. How can we conduct ourselves ethically when we are conditioned by history and by the governing powers we carry as much as others are influenced or harmed by our effects? What does it mean to live freely and responsibly in such contexts?

At present these are vexing questions because it is difficult for us to envision freedom and responsibility in the concrete circumstances of our lives, let alone to find answers to the question of how to conduct ourselves ethically.

Harm and unfairness are inevitable and ubiquitous in human living, but contemporary power relations have transposed the "problem of evil." Although malevolent evil and malicious crime remain, "ordinary" evil is preponderant and more pressing in present contexts. Ordinary evil is the product of trespass, not sin; of thoughtlessness, not wickedness. Prevalent notions of ethical conduct—performing contracts, being reasonable, behaving predictably—do not necessarily diminish ordinary evil, but in fact often reinforce and extend it. Moreover, predominant rationalities often make us thoughtless rather than thoughtful agents of the governing powers that multiply trespasses. As a result, we face a "crisis of the subject" evinced, as Michel Foucault suggests, by our difficulty forming ourselves as ethical subjects of our actions and giving purpose to our existence (CS, 95). This political ethical crisis has two aspects. Responsibility becomes a problem when we find that we can neither recognize the harm brought to others by our imbrication in social rules and their governing ways of envisioning and making the world, nor imagine how to alleviate such harm.[2] Freedom becomes a problem as our own and others' actions are thwarted by constrictive social patterns and threatened by unthinking social behavior. These problems are intimately related, for our irresponsibility and calculability govern ourselves as well as others.

The predominant political ethos, or "social rule," of late modern states and the prevalent ways of thinking and acting that it promotes—what Foucault calls "governmentality"—are ill-suited to the ethical and political dilemmas posed by ordinary evil. In other words, this political ethos is a precipitant of the contemporary crisis of the subject-citizen. Interaction between relations of power and ways of thinking engenders particular impressions of power. These images of power imbue a broader political ethos that consists of the mutually interdependent relations among forms of association, rationalities, and ethical practices. A political ethos is conditional. Thinking and ethics are cultivated by the character and quality of "the political" or "common power." Changes in any of these elements may induce changes in a political ethos as a whole. Ineffectuality in any of them may strain the whole. On my reading, Thomas Hobbes offers a paradigmatic articulation of today's predominant experience of power. This imagination of power, which I call corporeal, sanctions a political ethos that preempts the political conditions required to live ethically amid ordinary evil. This political ethos occasions a crisis of the subject by obstructing the political bodies through which individuals might become thoughtful agents of the powers framing their conduct and through which they, in turn, shape others' actions (SP, 219–23).

Chapter 1 proceeds toward this conclusion by considering the poignant yet insufficiently appreciated understanding of power and evil that Hobbes initiates. In chapter 2, I sketch the conception of the political and governing discourse of power that Hobbes's political theory deems the most promising response to our predicaments. On my reading, Hobbes's ideal resonates with Michel Foucault's headless body politic permeated by disciplinary powers and Hannah Arendt's account of the rule of the social. To the extent that we read Hobbes either as the advocate of an absolute, ceaselessly interventionist state designed to protect us from ourselves and one another, or as the champion of individuality who theorized a minimalist state to preserve our freedom, I think that we misunderstand ourselves.[3] I further challenge our misreadings by considering how and why subject-citizens are swayed to authorize Leviathan's governing powers.

By provisionally answering the question of what it means to live ethically today, we presuppose a knowledge of where we are and what we are doing. In Part I, I situate myself and the reader amid contemporary ethical political predicaments.

CHAPTER I

Makings, Trespasses, and Ordinary Evil

Thought must consider the process that forms it and form itself from these considerations.

Michel Foucault, "Theatrum Philosophicum"

Thomas Hobbes articulates the bases of the contemporary imagination of power. His political theory makes presumptions about thinking and power, mind and body, and their interrelationships which continue to limit our political imaginations. Though I seek a critical purchase on the political rationality—specifically, the governmentality—infusing our impressions of power, my doing so does not entail a wholesale rejection of Hobbes's political theory. His insights into the conditions of modern power are indispensable. Moreover, and surprisingly, the social ontology of "making" he proffers is shared by two of his prominent contemporary critics: Both Hannah Arendt and Michel Foucault affirm Hobbes's transposition of the problem of evil. Each believes that as makers of our selves and our world, we inevitably "trespass" against one another.[1] As a result, evil becomes common and ordinary, resentment endemic, and war a constant threat. Hobbes's solution to this problem remains paradigmatic; Arendt and Foucault afford a much-needed revisioning of it. Reading Hobbes, Arendt, and Foucault together crystallizes contemporary political and ethical challenges.

Securing homes, making worlds

It is well known that Hobbes's "state of nature," that fictional starting point of social-contract theories, is indistinguishable from a state of war. Describing this state of "political nothingness," Hobbes penned his famous description of human life as "solitary, poor, nasty, brutish, and short."[2] In a state of war, we are all "invaders" equally able to kill one another. Even greater equality is found in our faculties of mind, "for prudence is but Experience; which equal time, equally bestowes on all men, in those things they equally apply themselves unto."[3] From our equality of ability "ariseth equality of hope in the attaining of our Ends" which makes us enemies of one another "endeavour[ing] to destroy, or subdue one another." We are contentious not only when we have the bad fortune to desire the same thing. According to Hobbes, we are always on the verge of battle (whether we recognize it or not) because competition and conflict are intrinsic to our pursuit of "felicity."[4] Hobbes believes that our pursuit of well-being unavoidably challenges others and evokes comparable challenges to our own endeavors. Self-preservation demands power, and in a state of nature conquest and dominion are perfectly reasonable because necessary. Human beings are predisposed to make war, however, not because we are naturally bellicose, though some of us are, but because our survival depends upon it (L, 13:183–86).

Hobbes identifies as a "generall inclination of all mankind, a perpetuall and restlesse desire of Power after power, that ceaseth only in Death." This ceaseless quest for power, which threatens order and presages war, is not due in any simple way (if at all) to insatiable desire. Rather, Hobbes maintains that we must exercise and increase our power simply to stay even, for "he cannot assure the power and means to live well, which he hath present, without the acquisition of more" (L, 11:161). Making a space for ourselves in the world demands the continuous exercise of power. If we face the aspirations of others without such power, Hobbes asserts, we cannot live.

What is this ceaseless quest for power and why does Hobbes believe it is unavoidable? My reading of Hobbes's social ontology of power rejects the most common answers to these questions. *Leviathan* is often considered a classic example of psychological egoism or mechanical physicalism. Critics of this outlook believe that Hobbes obscures or denies human interdependence and intersubjectivity. On their reading, Hobbes imagines an egoistic individual whose insatiable desires engender a hunger for power to acquire what he wants, a craving he seeks to satisfy by dominating others. But Hobbes's assumption of a ceaseless quest for power, these critics maintain, unjustifiably presumes that human beings are preoccupied with only their individual (usually economic) interests. In short, many readers have taken Hobbes to be the ideologist of an emerging bourgeois order. Hannah Arendt puts it this way: "Power, according to Hobbes, is the accumulated control that permits the individual to fix prices and regulate supply and demand in such a way that they contribute to his own advantage. . . .[I]f man is actually driven by nothing but his individual interests, desire for power must be the fundamental passion for man" (OT, 139). In Arendt's view, the presumption of a ceaseless quest for power is founded upon the contestable assumption that human beings are driven by nothing but their individual interests. Thus, to challenge Hobbes's political theory we need only establish that his conception of human nature is untenable and his related ideas about the character of language, learning, institution-building, and the like equally baseless. On this understanding, the strife Hobbes assumes inevitable may be quelled by better understanding the basis of human communication and by fortifying the sociality it promises.[5]

I read Hobbes's argument as ontological. But this does not mean, as the foregoing view supposes, that he advances a specific conception of "human nature."[6] Whether we are egoists or altruists, communicatively virtuous or hopelessly inept, our character is not determinative for human struggle and strife. Hobbes believes that both sorts of human beings exist, and many others besides. What engenders the materiality of the world is that all of us are shaped by and give shape to the world in ways that open it, and our selves, to certain possibilities while foreclosing others.[7] Even the "altruist"—one who acts in the interests of others—creates and blocks alternatives, for both herself and others.[8] Hobbes does understand power as something like "accumulated control" in relation to individual self-constitution and preservation, but not in the sense Arendt means. On my reading, Hobbes conceives power as a relationship, not a quantity (e.g., EL, I.viii.4:34). Power is manifest and registered in its effects; it is not a possession we hold or, strictly speaking, an instrument we use to control others. The economic metaphors of "price" and "supply and demand," while apt in some cases, unduly limit the scope of Hobbes's reflections. All other ambitions flow from power, not because power enables us to "buy" what we want per se, but because the satisfaction of our ambitions flows from (or is blocked by) the order of the world.[9] These makings and unmakings, and not the individual passions and interests that succeed them, are the key to understanding what Hobbes means by "our perpetual and restless desire of power after power."

Hobbes is a political theorist of man the fabricator. In his view, we find ourselves in a universe full of energy but short on certain shape and meaning. What we find there, we make ourselves.[10] From the first line of *Leviathan* to the last, Man the fabricator assumes the place of God the artificer. Because God is humanly incomprehensible (L, 3:99), for political purposes God is all but dead. We name, build, fashion our selves and our world with neither reference nor access to transmundane powers, or at least this is what Hobbes would teach us to do. Our makings compete and conflict because there is no given, universal order to guide them. Each of us desires to make our way in the world, and in this respect our passions are similar. We are not made, however, by either God or Nature to pursue identical, or even compatible, makings, and thus the objects of our passions differ (L, Intro:82–83). Prior to human artifice, the universe does not *naturally* favor some makings over others. After human fabrication, social order *artificially* favors some makings and discourages or confounds others.

Our continual quest for power, then, does not mean that we all possess a will to dominate others for the sake of domination itself, though some of us may.[11] Rather, Hobbes's social ontology assumes a multiplicity of makers and makings with unavoidable and divergent effects. We regard the world and find our bearings within it according to differentiating perspectives rooted in our bodies and their distinct histories. Our bodies are an effect of experience, the product of "artifice" as much as "nature." We are conditioned by our efforts to make the world and by others' like efforts, with the result that the constitution of our body is in "continuall mutation" (L, 6:120). Our quest for felicity—to satisfy the perceived needs and desires of our bodies—affects others. In this respect, all of our activities, including our thinking, are vehicles of power. In fact, "differences of Wit" may be attributed to "more or lesse Desire of Power." Diverse bodies produce disparate desires for power, engendering contrary thoughts. Every thought, opinion, or judgment is laced with power, our pursuit of it, our conniving to retain it, or our envy at another's holdings, for "the Thoughts, are to the Desires, as Scouts and Spies, to range abroad, and find the way to the things Desired" (L, 8:139). Our thinking, words, and deeds are bound to our different bodies and their contingent interests, and to our quest for power. We endeavor to secure and maintain social spaces in a manner conducive to our body/mind's pursuit of felicity.[12] As we do so, we exercise power. If we cease to do so, we're dead, both because we are no longer fulfilling the conditions necessary to staying alive and because we are liable to be killed by others in full pursuit of their felicity.

According to Hobbes's social ontology, diverse persons' views and habits cannot naturally coexist, or rarely so, and certainly not across the expanse of a body politic, because we seek to make the world in our own felicitous image. This is the case whether we are egoists or altruists, liberals or communitarians, or, as in Hobbes's time, Presbyterians or Diggers. Consciously and not, we all endeavor to shape the spaces in which we make our way in "manners" that confirm and affirm our opinions and habits.[13] In doing so, we have disparate effects that duel with others' efforts to do the same. You would cultivate the commons for food, where I would build a factory. You would rent the apartment I would convert into a condominium. You would teach my children evolutionary theory, I would have them know that God created them in His likeness.

Thus, we now see the predicament Hobbes confronted: If every human activity, including the expression of opinion, has power effects upon others, then every word and deed is potentially "seditious," an obstacle or threat to social and political order. If all ideas manifest our efforts to make the world—and to rule it in accordance with our particular makings—then social and political discourse may be as treacherous as the fields of military battle or a street fight, because it may lead to them. The quest for power, and the unending challenges to it if power is gained, is "such a warre, as is every man against every man." More precisely, human making, without the mediation of some "common power," is an act of war.[14] Lacking common power and knowledge to arbitrate among our contesting and diverse makings, and bent on thoughtlessly asserting our own truths and the way of life they secure, we will inevitably fall into war with one another. In such a state of war, natural or civil, "nothing can be Unjust. The notions of Right and Wrong, Justice and Injustice have there no place" (L, 13:188). Good and evil are thereby expressions of passion, matters of opinion, not knowledge. Private opinion regarding good and evil reigns in such a state because there is no sovereign authority to produce the knowledge and power necessary to keep us in awe (L, 13:185). Opinion is always seditious in the absence of sovereignty, Hobbes concludes, because it promises the dissolution of a commonwealth and our devolution into war.

The political death of God

The earthly absence of a transcendent or natural source of sovereignty—the political death of God—defines "modern" conditions. Our makings inevitably clash and forebode conflagration because no absolutely authoritative theological or ontological source exists (or is available) to arbitrate disputes among our makings. A humanly discernible, natural order would enable us to determine the legitimate origins of power, the source of the efficacy of makings, and the reasons for their success or failure. On my reading, however, Hobbes does not invoke this preordained structure. If God could reveal to us knowledge of good and evil, we might simply open our ears to the Word of God and know which among all those in the competition of makings should be affirmed and which condemned. But Hobbes believes that God's Word is not directly available to us. If Hobbes had recourse to these ontotheological resources, he would not have a political problem, and we would not have ethical predicaments. The political death of God precludes easy answers, and the question of how we are to live together becomes increasingly treacherous and pressing, in part because dead gods are so manipulable.

According to Arendt, the absence of ontotheological sources starkly reveals the political function of an "absolute." Political founders and theorists have felt the need for an absolute from which to derive the authority of law and power. They have sought a source of law which would bestow legality upon posited, positive law. They have sought an origin of power which would bestow legitimacy on the powers that be. The foundations of the modern body politic are inherently unstable, and modern governance is dubious, because no such absolute source is forthcoming (OR, 158–62). It would seem that without a transcendental source, power and law are simply arbitrary, the product of what might makes right.[15] How can the legitimacy of a body politic be assured without the sanction of religion? How can peace be secured given the dubious, contingent foundations of all modern claims to rule? How are we to arbitrate contests among diverse ways of making the world? It is Hobbes's insight, and Arendt's as well, to conceive these as questions about the constitution of the political.

Given Arendt's perspective on Hobbes's political theory, it may seem odd to enlist her aid for a sympathetic elaboration of the struggles endemic to human making. But fabrication is as crucial to Arendt's social ontology as it is to Hobbes's.[16] For Arendt, necessity and compulsion persist wherever human life is sustained. Harm and grievances are therefore an ineluctable effect of human living. The satisfaction of human needs for food, shelter, and leisure entails compelling nature, oneself, and others to bear the burdens of life. The world of human artifice which enables us to satisfy these "needs" is fabricated. Such making (as principally a matter of poeisis) masters necessity by means of strength, force, and coercion toward nature and other human beings. Because making a world and forging locations in it master our selves and others, an element of violation—and potential violence—inheres in all fabrication (HC, 31, 129–30, 140). Our activities engage us in a weblike world; our words and deeds may make that world, reinforce it, or initiate something new within it (HC, 8–9,188). But nothing we do is free of harmful effects. When we make our way and pursue our felicity, we trespass against others.[17]

According to Arendt, trespasses inevitably inhere in all human activities because as we locate ourselves in the world we establish new relationships (HC, 190–91, 240–41). We can neither undo trespasses ourselves nor prevent them: They occur under circumstances where we did not or could not have known what we were doing (HC, 239–40). Trespasses are unavoidable because they flow not from our intentions per se but from makings and unmakings as they constitute and condition us. We trespass against others when we pursue a living and create a home. Furthermore, at least potentially or some of the time, we are trespassed against. Every way of making the world conflicts with some other ways of living in it, each of which precludes or circumscribes others. In the early modern period, for example, the livelihood of some people was tied to the cultivation of common lands, a way of life threatened by enclosure. From another perspective, however, the privatization of land and its results (among them, the emergence of socially dislocated, "free" laborers) facilitated a process of economic development which culminated in the building of factories. Cultivating the commons and building factories represent competing ways of ordering the world.

In my view, Hobbes would invoke the ordinance of neither God nor Nature to explain why the building of factories overcomes the cultivation of the commons.[18] In fact, as I explain in chapter 2, Hobbes's notions of what is "true" or "real" are far more pragmatic than such explanations would allow. Enclosure of the commons and the eventual building of factories, while efficacious from one perspective, have obvious negative consequences for others. Hobbes would not deny that "masterless men" and fundamental individual insecurity become commonplace with this way of making the world (OT, 124–47). Indeed, he regards this fact as constitutive of the modern problem of order. Many ways of making the world are fundamentally incommensurable. The social dislocation so pronounced in Hobbes's time has its correlate today, for instance, each time an apartment is converted into a condominium—the denial of affordable housing to some is the condition of a home for others. To be modern, in Hobbes's sense, is to be without any transcendent source for resolving the conflicts between these ways of living. Recognition of the arbitrariness or contingency of prevailing ways may breed resentment among the perceived losers and fuel their will to continue war to reverse their fortunes. Hobbes seeks to discipline both losers and winners and, thereby, to quell resentment in the face of trespass and the will to make war trespass often induces. As we shall see, Hobbes would teach us to revere an earthly authority, our Mortal God, so that we can live in peace.

For all their differences, Hobbes and Arendt share the conviction that when we make our way in the world—create a home, pursue a living—we often violate others by threatening their homes and livelihood. This is not, as Arendt's reading of Hobbes suggests, because we naturally desire to dominate others. Rather, an element of force and violence inheres in our unavoidable efforts to master necessity and to forge a location in the world (HC, 31). Subtlety and near invisibility are distinguishing features of modern forms of rule. Most often we prevail when our ways and manners give shape to human artifice. Ordinarily, our success is accomplished not by domination or physical force but by the preponderance of opinion and habit. Nonetheless, a perpetual and restless exercise of power is an unavoidable consequence of every world-making and home-securing effort. Hobbes seeks to reconcile us to this fate and uses it to teach peace.

Ordered evil

Hobbes's and Arendt's social ontology of making defines evil as ordinary. Arendt coined the phrase "the banality of evil" in her effort to understand Adolph Eichmann, who demonstrated to her that ordinary, thoughtless evil could be as, if not more, potent and destructive than its "radical" forms. Arendt's conclusion upon reflecting on the horrors of this century was that "no wicked heart [. . .] is necessary to cause great evil" and that "the sad truth of the matter is that most evil is done by people who never made up their mind to be either good or bad" (TMC, 438). Understandably, Arendt was still tempted to name Eichmann's evildoing radical, but she believed that traditional ways of understanding extreme evil had become hopelessly inadequate.[19]

Trespass does not include crime and willed evil (HC, 240), but its harmful effects are no less potent for that. Trespasses originate not in a recalcitrant will, but in the pursuit of living. The fact that trespasses are not always intended does not lessen their weight and efficacy. Trespasses are the harm brought to others by our participation in governing ways of envisioning and making the world. The trespasser is the "lawful citizen" who, because well-disposed toward the law, daily becomes the agent of injustice.[20] To paraphrase Thoreau again, when we speak of trespass, we speak not of far-off foes but of those who, near at home, cooperate with and do the bidding of those far away; without the former, the latter would be harmless.[21] Trespassers are not the active, hands-on instruments of wrongdoing, but the "responsible," well-behaved, predictable subjects of social order who reinforce and extend its patterns of rule. From the perspective of trespass, evil is not a mysterious force without us, nor an obstinate element deep within us. In its most common, modern forms, evil is rarely intended and seldom the product of malice, but it is an effect of living our locations and pursuing our felicity. Everyday evil does not originate in sin, and in its most usual forms it is not pathological, though it may be manifest in practices that pathologize others. Ordinary evil arises from and rests upon the surface of beings and things.[22]

According to naturalistic mythologies evil is an external force assailing men and women from without. By contrast, Euripides was among the first to represent human beings confronting the mystery of evil as part of their own being, just as Medea experienced passion as a force possessing her.[23] In this case, the problem of evil is encapsulated in a servile will. Paul Ricoeur argues that symbolization alone can convey the paradoxical coincidence of free will and servitude in the same body/mind: The servile will yields itself to evil but in doing so in some measure reigns over itself.[24] Both theodicy and anthropodicy seek to illuminate the enigma of a free will that makes itself a slave. Discourses of willful evil assume more and less theological or secular forms. As we move from the religious to the medicalized, we move from theodicy to anthropodicy.[25] In any case, projection of evil as mysteriously entrenched in the recesses of our being (as opposed to evil arising from and resting upon the surface of beings) is typically understood to have catalyzed a deep, confessing subject who interrogates him or herself to uncover and convert its intractable, evil-generating parts.

Given Hobbes's preoccupation with human passions and the threat their infusion of our activities poses to civil order, it is understandable that we often associate a deep, interiorized conception of evil with Hobbes's view.[26] I think we are at least partly mistaken, however, in doing so.[27] We need not have recourse to original sin or its secularized equivalents to conceive evil as inherent in our being. Rather, we can understand evil ensuing with the traces we leave on the surface of all to which our bodies/minds and activities relate us. To restate, we exercise power and engender its effects—make, unmake, trespass—whether we build a factory or cultivate the commons, rent an apartment or convert it into a condominium, teach creationism or preach evolutionary theory.

Impressions of power and understandings of evil are interdependent. When evil is conceived as an external, alien force, we inhabit a naturally ordered universe. Such order can be more or less chaotic, more or less comprehensible—an animistic world or a great chain of being—but either way its power suffuses human lives and their surroundings in ways that are more or less mysterious. In such cases, theodicy emphasizes natural rather than social or human evil; or human evil is understood to be engendered by a natural order or to be the consequence of violations of it.[28] Power is a natural force and mystery, and human efficacy partakes of that force and mystery.[29]

By contrast, human beings who confront evil as a passion or possessing force most often regard evil as manifest in a will to impose upon others. In this case, power is imagined as a repressive force that negates, dominates, or oppresses the other. Evil is believed to originate in uncontrollable or recalcitrant passions deep within the self. A reading of human "origins" determines whether evil is regarded as exceeding human control or as educable pride and stubbornness. For example, both the early Christian and Rabbinic traditions interpret Gen. 1–3 as a story of human freedom, of our capacity to deliberately direct our passions and powers to foster and protect human equality and freedom. By contrast, Augustine's doctrine of original sin bars freedom of choice to do good or evil. Indeed, such willfulness is a sign of Adam's rebellion and the mark of fundamental human disobedience. In Augustine's view, human beings are incapable of ruling themselves (thus, his apologia for temporal powers).[30] On either account, however, we inhabit a domain of sin, willed evil, and wickedness. The power that confronts or expresses this evil is negative and pressing, whether repressive or oppressive. Both theodicists and anthropodicists may inhabit this universe. As human beings replace God as the principal interlocutors and accountants of evil, however, we witness a corresponding movement from religious to medical discourse, from sin to pathology, from theodicy to anthropodicy.[31]

Trespasses are evil of a different order, sort, and origin. Trespasses are not willed wickedness, but inadvertent, unthinking, often unknown or invisible harms. Artificially originated and ordered, they come in the wake of the political death of God. In the absence of transcendentally authorized sovereign order, every human making actuates some ways of living while it impedes others. Thus, every manner of living involves trespass. Trespasses are "ordinary" in multiple senses of the word. "Conforming to order; an effect of regular and methodical behavior." "Customary." "Frequent." "A common occurrence." "Usual; not singular, exceptional, nor extra-ordinary."[32] Trespass is the predominant conception of evil in a normalizing society where power is a productive force permeating the social body.[33]

On my reading, Hobbes mainly conceives evil—harm and wrongdoing—as a matter of trespass, not of sin or wickedness. In effect, Hobbes secularizes and externalizes the problem of evil. To say that Hobbes secularizes the problem of evil is not particularly controversial, and although some may regard the language of evil as anachronistic in Hobbes's case, the concept of evil is applicable whenever we seek to discern and attribute responsibility for harm and wrongdoing.[34] Thus, Hobbes remains engaged with the problem of evil, though he is a "secular" thinker. It may be more controversial, however, to claim that Hobbes externalizes the problem of evil, at least from a perspective that believes Hobbes calls forth a deep, confessing subject. I have downplayed Hobbes's attribution of social and political disorder to insatiable desires or deep interiors. To be sure, there are persons for whom such explanations will be especially apt. But they will be only one sort among many others. The point is that even those with moderate desires and calm, shallow interiors must make their way in the world. In doing so they will leave traces upon other beings and things, and they will be similarly marked by the ways of those others.

We are not only makers and unmakers, we are also made and unmade.[35] We are not only trespassers, we are also trespassed against. Indeed, our trespasses against others are often the effect of aspects of what we are made to be, of things that we apparently did not "choose." Structural advantages or disadvantages that accrue to one's "race" or "gender" are illustrative examples in contemporary contexts.[36] We do not possess these powers that make us while bringing ill effects to others; we are constituted by them. Arendt explains:

> Men are conditioned beings because everything they come in contact with turns immediately into a condition of their existence. . . . The things that owe their existence exclusively to men nevertheless constantly condition their human makers. Whatever touches or enters into a sustained

> relationship with human life immediately assumes the character of a condition of human existence. This is why men, no matter what they do, are always conditioned beings. (HC, 9).

Much of what we are made to be, and many of the happenings in which we are implicated, exceed our agency; they certainly are beyond our mastery. Human beings may make their fate, but they are also captives of it. We suffer at the hands of forces and aspects of existence that we did not produce and can do little to alter. Our inventive fiddling within these confines appears limitless, but our effective control is not, for everything we fabricate to reshape our existence becomes a condition of that existence. Each inventive liberation is, from another perspective, a new confinement.

The fact that we conceive of ourselves as makers and yet are also made sets in motion dynamic cycles of resentment which become all the more vexed as human artifice expands. As the weight of what we are made to be grows heavier, our capacities as makers (let alone actors) feels increasingly constrained. In this context, Hobbes's notorious determinism does not seem so farfetched. As the world of human artifice expands and is augmented, the resources for making ourselves and our world are progressively circumscribed. The increasing weight of the world fosters a deterministic outlook as we make our way through increasingly restrictive limits on self-made accomplishments. The makings that precede and constitute us bind what we are capable of doing. The contours and rules of the human artifice surrounding us discipline how and what we can make, or at least the probabilities of which makings will succeed. Hobbes would cultivate a skeptical conversion that reconciles us to this fate.

As human makers, we expect to be powerful, but, in the face of the accumulation of human artifice, we feel weak. We know we must make our own way, but the competition and conflict between our own and others' makings leaves us feeling vulnerable, not only because of our potential failures, but also because of the harm that may come our way as a result of others' projects. The physical vulnerability we feel as embodied creatures, and the fundamental insecurity of this situation, may leave some of us feeling and acting meek. Hobbes suggests, however, that meekness is not likely to be an effective strategy for living. To forswear a perpetual quest for power—to simply let others' opinions and habits prevail over one's own—is to forsake the "course," which is to die. Indeed, to abjure this perpetual quest for power is impossible. Some may feel that they exercise no power, but from Hobbes's perspective this simply means that they never win, that their makings rarely prevail on their own terms. They are made more than they make. They are trespassed against more than they trespass. They are profoundly wounded; they are even defined by their wounds.[37]

In the absence of a natural order of things, the perpetual contest among our makings and unmakings initiates an apparently insatiable will to control our circumstances and fosters increasing resentment as a result of our failures to do so.[38] We identify others to blame for our suffering. Indeed, our vulnerability, our weakness and wounds, may make us all the more determined to control others. In contexts of pervasive trespass, the precariousness of our claims to rule more readily fosters dogmatism than humility. In a fabricated world, our value and possessions are measured by what piece of that world we can carve out for ourselves. The successes of others, unless our makings are similar, signify our own failure. As a result, we may be increasingly inclined to make war against one another in covert and overt ways. Hobbes accepts this tendency toward war. Making and trespassing are endemic to social life. How are we to respond to this situation—trespasses, the resentments they rouse, and the figurative and sometimes literal war they presage—in a way that secures not only our survival but also "commodious living"? Given the ordinariness of evil, what must "common power" be?

A textbook interpretation of Hobbes proceeds from an imminent threat of war to the creation of an absolute sovereign with authority and power to protect us from one another. "Natural individuals" transfer their rights to a unified agent ("king" or "head") resting atop the body politic and the sovereign's prohibitions determine right from wrong (thus clarifying our freedoms and duties) and its sword keeps us obedient by punishing transgressors. Under these civil conditions we cannot successfully make war because we are certain of the sovereign's retribution, and therefore we will not do so. Where and when the sovereign is not bearing down upon us, however, we are free to do as we like.

This representation of power and the body politic in general, and of Hobbes's *Leviathan* in particular, is the touchstone for Michel Foucault's well-known critique of "sovereign" theories of power and the "repressive hypothesis." Foucault believes that, as heir of Hobbes, we "moderns" are still preoccupied with the concentration of power in, and flowing from, one place. We still search for the origin of power and wish to measure its force. As long as we continue to do so, Foucault claims, we shall never comprehend contemporary power relations, because we thereby neglect the fact that "power is constructed and functions on the basis of particular powers, myriad issues, myriad effects of power" as they disperse and multiply among the institutions and practices that figure a body politic (PK, 188). Individuals, circulating through the social body, are the primary vehicles of power, and that social body itself is formed through "the materiality of power operating on the bodies of individuals" (PK, 55). In its capillary form, power "reaches into the very grain of individuals, touches their bodies and inserts itself into their actions and attitudes, their discourses, learning processes and everyday lives" (PK, 39).

Our bodies are "made" by techniques of power. As we move through social space, we carry with us the effects of these modes of power. Individuals, vehicles for wider powers, struggle against one another in their mutual relations. Political theory, Foucault claims, has tended to conceal these battles. Its obsession with personified sovereignty has deflected attention from local power effects and the subjugations to which they attest, while furthering them by legitimating the institutions and practices through which such power is masked.[39] In other words, Foucault believes that we are still preoccupied with finding the "head" of a body politic which now, for all intents and purposes, is headless. If we are to understand power, we must cease to think of it in terms of sovereignty, law, and an original, unified agent. Yet, Foucault says, for the most part "in political thought and analysis, we still have not cut off the head of the king" (HSI, 88–89; PK, 121).

Foucault's rejection of sovereign theories of power and the social contract tradition led him to conceptualize power in terms of battles, strategies, and tactics. Once you detach the question of power from law, he explains, you are led to ask the question whether power is not a generalized sort of war. In fact, he hypothesizes that politics is war continued by other means (PK, 90). This inversion of Clausewitz's formulation has a triple significance, each of which Foucault elaborates throughout his middle works.[40]

First, politics sanctions and upholds the disequilibrium of forces that are displayed in war. If, to employ the Hobbesian formulation, we authorize sovereignty to get ourselves out of a state of war, it is Foucault's view that civil society perpetuates disparities in power and forms of domination present in those earlier battles. Second, sovereign theories of power mislead because they obscure the perpetuation of war in civil society. The essential function of discourses of right, Foucault claims, has been to efface the domination intrinsic to power. He wants to invert this pattern and give due weight to the fact of domination (PK, 95). This goal is most insistently pursued in *Discipline and Punish*, in which he argues that a military model of strategies and tactics provides a fundamental means of preventing civil disorder (DP, 168). Such a "microphysics of power" inhibits outright warfare in civil society as it informs disciplinary practices (DP, 167–68). The necessity of combat and rules of strategy provide whatever coherence or unity these mechanisms of power possess. War is the logic of power. "In this central and centralized humanity, the effect and instrument of complex power relations, bodies and forces subjected by multiple mechanisms of 'incarceration,' objects for discourses that are themselves elements of this strategy, we must hear the distant roar of battle" (DP, 308).

The third significance of Foucault's hypothesis is that history is the "hazardous play of dominations." All outcomes are the effect of war, the products of a contest of strength, and finally decided by a recourse to "arms" (LCP, 148; PK, 91). This remains an immensely influential formulation for contemporary genealogists of power relations. Heirs of Foucault understand systems of meaning and value as the product of continuous struggle, "false arrests," "arbitrary fixings and impositions," even "violent practices."[41] Who is at war with whom in the headless body politic? Foucault hazards another hypothesis: "It's all against all. . . . Who fights against whom? We all fight each other. And there is always in each of us something that fights something else" (PK, 208). Foucault, and "poststructuralists" generally, relocate Hobbes's "state of nature." We (I include myself) find battles, sometimes outright war, traversing "civil society" and its subjects. Disciplinary tactics and mechanisms secure social order by containing and concealing these battles, even as such strategies further the effects of war. A simultaneously individualizing and totalizing mode of power orders this "carceral society" as each of us conceives ourselves in ways that incorporate us into a social totality. Political integration is not accomplished, however, by a sovereign agent who forces our subjection, specifies rules and roles, and delimits our activity by prohibition and punishment. Instead, we are incorporated into this totality as we become subjectified by its political rationality (TS, 143–162). The headless body politic is permeated by agonistic power relations in which we all partake and are implicated. If we are to analyze and contest these relations, Foucault says, we must eschew the model of Leviathan in the study of power (PK, 102). From this perspective, Hobbes is of little contemporary relevance, even a deceptive influence.

My reading of Hobbes as a theorist of makings and trespasses suggests that Foucault is wrong about Hobbes. To begin with, Hobbes is keenly aware of just how pertinacious war is.[42] Like Machiavelli before him, Hobbes believes that all states are founded in conquest and therefore that "scarce a Commonwealth in the world, beginnings can in conscience be justified" (L, R&C:722). Likewise, a state of war always looms in international relations. But Hobbes's teaching about the intransigence of war is more thoroughgoing still. He sensitizes us to the persistence of war in "civil society," particularly to two aspects of it. First, Hobbes judges it impossible to transform or discharge the actualities of making and trespass.[43] Our disparate desires and divergent thoughts cannot and should not be leveled.[44] Life always remains a race (and battle) in which outcomes are relationally determined with assymetrical effects. My value and worth are contingent upon your granting or respecting them, fostering a proto-Hegelian struggle for recognition. The ramifications of such contests are not purely psychological, however, for struggle among various ways of imaging our selves and our world influences what that world is made to be and the beings and things to which it either recurs (e.g., factories, condominiums, evolutionary theory) or resists (e.g., subsistence agriculture, affordable housing, creationism). Second, Hobbes's positing of an unrenounceable right to life under any government may be read as tacit admission that individuals are in a state of war vis-à-vis the life- and liberty-threatening projects of the social totality into which they are incorporated. Just as individuals, alone and in association, would remake us in ways that serve their interests and purposes, so too governments, even "democratic" governments in whose collective projection we partake, would use us for purposes other than our own. Like Foucault, Hobbes sees war within and beyond selves, struggle, and strife folded into "civil" conditions.

From another perspective, however, my narrative has progressed with a deceptive air of inevitability. Far from establishing their common contemporary relevance, what Hobbes and Foucault share would suggest to some their pernicious influence. From this perspective, my discussion of Arendt's objection to Hobbes's perspective hardly touched upon the relevant matters, if I am right that she, like Foucault, shares Hobbes's social ontology of making. According to my reading, Hobbes, Arendt, and Foucault are theorists of ordinary evil who believe that we unavoidably trespass against others as we make and unmake our selves and world. From the perspective most notably evinced in the work of Jürgen Habermas, however, this account suffers from a fundamental confusion, albeit a common one: the conflation of instrumental and communicative rationality, making and understanding a world. Habermas's early essay, "The Classical Doctrine of Politics in Relation to Social Philosophy," culminates with this critique of Hobbes, more familiar in the cases of Hegel, Marx, and Weber.[45]

I read Hobbes's account of the state of nature as a figuration of his ontological projections. By contrast, Habermas reads Hobbes more literally, regarding his state of nature as a nonethical, "purely physicalist account of the human species prior to all sociation." Hobbes "deals solely with the apparatus of sensation, with instinctive reactions, with the animal motion of biological entities, with the physical organization of men and their causally determined modes of reaction." In Habermas's view, this account presents Hobbes with a problem, as it will all others who share Hobbes's confusion. Hobbes "demanded of the causal order in the state of nature those norms he required for the foundation of his civil state. But the wholly mechanistic understanding of nature had actually inherited these norms from a prior transference of normative categories, which it thereupon suppressed."[46] Thus, Habermas believes, Hobbes's theory of natural law conceals the communicative rationality inherent and necessary to all world-making efforts.[47]

Yet Habermas attributes to Hobbes a "pure" nature that he never imagined. For Hobbes, the organic and artificial are always already mixed so that pristine nature is not accessible to us. On my reading, Hobbes's state of nature makes no claim to find a unitary human nature (i.e., we are not all beasts with a will to make war) but describes a social condition and projects a social ontology.[48] This social ontological perspective displaces a conundrum of Hobbesian interpretation. If, as Habermas claims, Hobbes's account is a description of human nature, it is difficult to imagine how we ever enter society, contractually or otherwise. Hobbes's principal concern, however, is to secure and legitimate social order and governmental rule in the absence of absolute or transcendent sources of authority, whether God or His created Nature.[49] Hobbes does not, as Habermas claims, transfer and then suppress normative premises; rather, Hobbes recognizes the problem for order posed by the artificiality and contingency of all such norms.

In this respect, Hobbes shares with Arendt and Foucault a social ontology that challenges Habermas's own teleological social ontology.[50] All three recognize (though they draw disparate political conclusions about) the inevitable and ubiquitous trespass inherent in even communicatively rational norms. For each of them, the normative is always to some degree normalizing, which is what recommends to Hobbes popularly authorized norms of rationality as a resource for solidifying the dubious foundations of modern governance. For their part, Foucault and Arendt do not conflate instrumental making and communicative action, but seek to recover the possibility of acting anew in response to the trespasses and exclusions embedded in every world-making and -understanding effort. No doubt communicative ethicists like Habermas would not accept this social ontology, but it poses a "discursively redeemable" shift in the grounds and terms of debate. Ontological matters themselves, however, are finally not logically or argumentatively decidable.[51] Instead we must ask how social ontological projections—the conception of the political they favor, and the rationalities and ethics they cultivate—extend, discern, and respond to the trespasses in which they implicate us.[52]

If I am right that Hobbes externalizes the problem of evil—regarding trespass and war to be the product not of original human sinfulness but the unavoidable effects of makings and unmakings in a world without a preordained order—how would he explain and alleviate the suffering, political dissolution, and social disorder our human condition seems to forebode? The intricacies of Hobbes's solution, his political theodicy as it were, is the subject of the next chapter. But I can sketch the situation and solution in brief.

Human fabricators are inclined and in fact need to make themselves a home in the world. In the wake of the political death of God, however, the stakes of our makings are inordinately raised, to such an extent that figurative, sometimes literal, war is often part of what we make. There seems nothing but the force of makings themselves to decide the matter. The succession of makings and unmakings perpetually escalates our anxiety and desire for control. In Hobbes's view, this will to make and control, and the anxieties it induces, are reasonable, especially in a "state of nature." Nevertheless, assertively pursuing our makings in the absence of a common power (and a state of nature is any situation where there is no such power to which, in awe, we willingly submit) is finally self-defeating, for it inevitably perpetuates war-making. Only sovereign power can secure our selves and our homes by arbitrating among and managing our makings. To prevent war, to secure social order and a home for ourselves within that order, we must will what we are made to be by the governing powers and knowledge sovereignty produces. Our conformity to governing truths sustains social orderliness and thus solidifies the dubious foundations of modern governance. Ordinary evil becomes ordered and, thereby, governable.

But that is not all. Hobbes seeks to preserve and even to cultivate individuality. How does social rule contribute to an ethic of individuality? Conforming to social rule increases our efficacy (and that of the state as a social totality), and, to the extent that we learn to discipline our selves, Hobbes's political discourse and the silence of its laws grant us freedom to make our living and home as we see fit. How the norms and "invisible powers" of governing discourses are originated, authorized, and extended, however, remains a mystery. To this task of political theological illumination I turn in the next chapters.

Hobbes's wish to have us examine and redress the roots of war to attenuate its likelihood or ferocity does differentiate him, however, from many contemporary genealogists with whom he shares a social ontology. He theorizes "common power" and interrogates individual conduct—political and theoretical vocations that have become suspect in some theoretical and political circles. Hobbes's strategy is not without its dangers, but it does have the virtue of highlighting ethical questions posed by the individual's participation in power relations. In contrast, Foucault's middle works often do not politically theorize the subject's relationship to the body politic so much as represent that subject as a discursive *effect* of tactics and strategies. As Foucault himself later acknowledges, this approach (however ironically or inadvertently) sustains a negative, repressive model of power to the extent that it conceives subjects as targets rather than agents of power and represents common power (no matter its form, quality, or character) as equivalent to domination.

In other words, when we envision power as domination—and we do so whenever we speak of power becoming inscribed in or pressing upon an object—we tend to elide subjects' participation in governing powers. Though circumstances of domination do exist where individuals are so forcefully contained that the freedom of a response is denied them, such situations increasingly seem atypical within late modern states, even as we continue to use language that belies this professed understanding.[53] When we document wars over truth, meaning, and value without theorizing the subject's perpetuation of governing relations, we inflame rather than interrupt a politics of resentment. The exercise of power is inevitable, but contemporary representations of power too often neglect how and to what extent individuals may direct its effects, and overlook the political preconditions of their doing so. As a result, it is not surprising that today many persons are overcome, like the middle Foucault, by the impression of politics and culture as an inevitable, if highly mediated, war of all against all.

Genealogies document "wars of truth" many sovereign theories conceal, including in its own distinctive way Hobbes's own.[54] But too often we do not query the roots of war or the imagination of power that informs our impressions. Even if we are persuaded by genealogical critiques that such wars exist and that theories such as Hobbes's obscure the "roar of battle," resources for conceiving how we participate in or perpetuate these battles (and thus how we may politically moderate them) are too often wanting. From a genealogical perspective, we are ordinarily the victims of war, rarely its instigators.

While Foucault's middle works would have us "cut off the head of the king" in the interest of documenting and intervening in battles, the theorist of *Leviathan* entreats us to interrogate our predilection to make war in hopes of alleviating it. If the problem of evil arises with our being in the world, Hobbes proffers both an ethics of individuality to temper those effects and governing powers sagacious enough to cultivate the political ethos that sustains them. Interpreters of Hobbes who have emphasized the prowess and pervasiveness of the Leviathan state often miss the crucial role of free individuality and popular authorization in the development and deployment of its governing powers. Likewise, interpreters who find in Hobbes a champion of individuality often underestimate the role of the scientific regulation of political discourse and governing powers in the cultivation and claims of individuality. As I show in the next chapter, Hobbes's brilliance and contemporary relevance consists in his articulation of a governmentality and political ethos of social rule, for he thereby provides the basis for a "free" individuality and conscience that sustain social order. Hobbes's political theory does not resolve our ethical and political predicaments, but reading him does help crystallize the sources of our confusion.

CHAPTER 2

Subject-Citizens and Corporeal Souls

The one remaining "embodiment" of the altogether dispersed sovereignty of the people is in those rather demanding forms of subjectless communication that regulate the flow of the formation of political opinion and will so as to endow their fallible results with the presumption of political rationality. Discourses do not govern. They generate a communicative power that cannot take the place of administration but only influence it. This influence is limited to the procurement and withdrawal of legitimation.

Jürgen Habermas, "Further Reflections on the Public Sphere"

The symbolism of the king's body and the physiology of the body politic are shifting terrain. Historically, they have been fields where political and theoretical contests are acted out, and they remain so.[1] To associate Hobbes's political theory with the vision of a unified, all-powerful sovereign, as Foucault and so many others have done, is not wholly inaccurate. Hobbes is indeed a theorist of absolute sovereignty and of the art by which "is created that great LEVIATHAN of greater stature and strength" than the natural man for whose protection and defense it was intended (L, Intro:81). Yet Hobbes's figuration of the body politic reveals hitherto overlooked aspects of his conception of sovereignty and its governing powers, as well as revealing unexpected significance in Foucault's admonition that the time has come to "cut off the head of the king." Hobbes deems his ideal body politic, and its governing discourse of power, the most promising response to both ordinary evil and the dubious foundations of modern governance.

Corporeal souls

In *De Cive* Hobbes refigures the body politic:

They who compare a city and its citizens with a man and his members, almost all say, that he who hath the supreme power in the city is in

> relation to the whole city, such as the head is to the whole man. But it appears by what hath already been said, that he who is endued with such power . . . hath a relation to the city, not as that of the head, but of the soul to the body. (DC, 6.19:188)

In *Leviathan* Hobbes retains the metaphor naming sovereignty "an Artificiall Soul giving life and motion to the whole body" (L, Intro:81). Hobbes's anatomy of the body politic, when coupled with his doctrine of a corporeal soul, suggests that he did not conceive governing powers as simply prohibitive or repressive, or their effects as only centrally generated. On the contrary, Hobbes imagined productive governing powers permeating the social body.

On my reading, the body politic Hobbes envisioned resonates with the regimes of power Foucault depicts in *Discipline and Punish*. But reading Hobbes and Foucault together calls us to query Foucault's oppositions between theories of sovereignty and a "military dream of society," between spectacle and surveillance. The "fundamental reference" of the military dream of society, Foucault says, "was not to the state of nature, but to the meticulously subordinated cogs of a machine, not to the primal social contract, but to permanent coercions, not to fundamental rights, but to indefinitely progressive forms of training, not to the general will but to automatic docility" (DP, 169).[2] Foucault too readily opposes what, I believe, we must learn to think together. Hobbes's image of a corporeal soul proves an apt figure for modern governing powers and the subject-citizens who bear them, while his account of the popular authorization of sovereignty demonstrates how "automatic docility" can be democratically [if invisibly] controlled (DP, 207). Hobbes's ideal body politic appears, and as a result becomes, "headless."

Hobbes refashions the soul to rationalize biblical teaching and to dispel the "dark doctrines" that undermine political authority. For the sake of their immortal souls dissenters often proclaim that salvation demands their disobedience to worldly political authority. This politically dangerous conclusion rests on an erroneous belief in incorporeal substances which Aristotle allowed and "the Schoolmen" supported. But to speak of incorporeal substances, Hobbes claims, is "an absurdity of speech" (EL, 1.11:56). "By the name of the spirit we understand a body natural, but of such subtilty that it worketh not on the senses; but that filleth up the place which the image of a visible body might fill up" (EL, 1.11:55). Our conception of spirit, Hobbes says, is of "a figure without colour." But the notion of a figure implies dimension, and thus a spirit is something that has dimension, however difficult it may be to discern. It is common, Hobbes admits, for people to speak of spirits as incorporeal—"as without dimensions and quantity"—but to do so contradicts Scripture and is indicative of a fundamental misunderstanding: "It is said of the spirit, that it abideth in men; sometime that it dwelleth in them, sometimes that it cometh on them, that it descendeth, and cometh and goeth; and that spirits are angels, that is to say messengers: all which words do consignify locality; and locality is dimension, is body, be it ever so subtile." (EL, 1.11:55–56). Hobbes concludes that Scripture favors those who hold spirits, and the soul (which is a form of spirit), "for corporeal, than them that hold the contrary" (EL, 1.11:56). To think otherwise is "but a false opinion concerning the force of imagination." From Hobbes's perspective, the soul, like any other nonimaginary part of the universe, is body; it occupies some place and is subject to change because it inevitably suffers the effects of contiguous bodies (L, 46:689). "That which is not Body, is no part of the universe," but a figment of an absurd imagination (EL, I.11:56). To Hobbes's mind, discourses of the incorporeal attribute powers to the imagination it does not have and see things that do not matter.

The corporeal soul functions on two registers in Hobbes's political theory, signifying both the character of the individual soul and the governing powers that constitute the subject-citizen with a soul. The subject-citizen's soul is corporeal, and sovereignty is like a corporeal soul. This doctrine of a corporeal soul facilitates Hobbes's response to the problem of evil in two ways. As I have already noted, Hobbes denies authority to those who seek to defend their political disobedience and social disruptions by reference to the health of their immortal soul. The soul's corporeality is crucial to this criticism. Like our bodies/minds, our soul manifests and advances our particular felicity; it reflects how we have been made and unmade, and how we would make and unmake others in turn. If our soul registers our beliefs about good and evil, then its pronouncements, like those beliefs, express our particular appetites and aversions (L, 6:120). If ungoverned souls, and the consciences they inspire, were allowed to reign over the sovereignty that alone can arbitrate disputes between competing ways of seeing and making the world, then war would be our fate. This Hobbesian position is widely recognized.

But the political theoretical implications of Hobbes' dismissal of discourses of the incorporeal have not been sufficiently appreciated.[3] In Hobbes's time, religious and political dissenters invoked invisible and incorporeal powers to materialize their own apparently absent power and to represent patterns of power they wanted to change. "Knowing together,"[4] these political actors materialized their impressions of previously invisible powers, generated political meanings to comprehend them, and devised political strategies to alter them. Denying the existence of incorporeal substances, Hobbes deauthorizes such political discourse and rules it out of order as the figment of absurd imaginations. The significance of Hobbes's detheologization of power becomes apparent when we see that governing powers become as difficult to conjure as a soul (EL, 1.11:55–56). Like the fear of invisible powers Hobbes deems the seed of religious sentiment (L, 11:168) governing powers inspire awe and reverence for the body politic they manage. When political bodies appear, then become, headless, governance is solidified and ordinary evil ordered.

The soul is Hobbes's preferred figure for sovereignty, and its corporeality suggests the distinctive character of governing powers. By reference to the soul, Hobbes suggests that sovereignty possesses quantity and dimension or "locality," however subtle it may be or however difficult to discern (EL, 1.11:55–56). Yet the soul, unlike the head, also suggests a force that permeates the organism rather than inhabiting a single place—it gives life and motion to the whole body. A sovereign soul does not move along a single, prescribed path, from the top down as it were, but is manifest and expressed throughout the social body. Sovereignty's effects, as befits the corporeal, are material. We can expect sovereignty's governing powers, like a corporeal soul, to be material as well as pervasive and productive.

Hobbes's more literal renderings of the character, ends, and effects of governing powers confirm that he found the corporeal soul an apt figure for those powers.[5] Foucault associates theories of sovereignty like Hobbes's with a conception of law as prohibition, or with that which says "no" (e.g., DP, 57; PK, 119). For Hobbes, however, civil laws do not primarily prohibit. They direct subjects and produce effects; they mold more than they suppress their object. "A good Law is that, which is Needfull, for the Good of the People, and withall Perspicuous. For the use of Lawes, (which are but Rules Authorised) is not to bind the People from all Voluntary actions; but to direct and keep them in such motion, as not to hurt themselves by their own impetuous desires, rashnesse, or indiscretion, as Hedges are set, not to stop Travelers, but to keep them in the way" (L, 30:388).

As Hobbes specifies earlier in the same chapter, the "good of the people" is their safety, by which "is not meant a bare Preservation, but also other Contentments of life, which every man by lawfull Industry, without danger, or hurt to the Commonwealth, shall acquire to himselfe" (L, 30:376). Civil laws procure the commodious living impossible in a state of nature. They do so by regulating "plenty"—the distribution of materials conducive to life—and through "the conveyance of it by convenient conduits to the public use" (L, 24:294–95). Civil laws create conditions under which persons may nourish themselves and live more contentedly (L, 17:227). For example, when women and men become unable to maintain themselves through their labor, they ought not to be left to the uncertain charity of private persons but should be provided for by the laws of the commonwealth, just as the idle may rightly be compelled to work by the same laws (L, 30:387). The goal of the latter, compulsory laws (as of all discipline or punishment) "is not revenge and the discharge of choler" but correction both to benefit their object and to secure the peace of the commonwealth. Crimes, especially those that spring from contempt of justice or equity, "provoke indignation in the multitude" (L, 30:389). Such resentment is always to be avoided, for a people's prosperity, no matter what their form of government, is increased by discipline and concord among them (L, 30:380).

In Hobbes's ideal commonwealth, specific laws responsive to the needs and capacities of the people are the product not of imposition but of a heightened attentiveness to the grievances and demands of "each Province." Hobbes only requires that such demands not contravene sovereignty or contest the constitution of "common power" (the political). Like corporeal souls, governing powers are productive, materially manifest, and localized. Emanations of sovereignty are not incorporeal substances or spirits without body. Indeed, Hobbes says that power exists only when specific, material effects—like walls, chains, hedges—are evident. And there will be such effects. Subject-citizens may name them, even air their grievances, as long as the effects they criticize are and do matter. In fact, Hobbes submits that governing powers are generated by listening to and learning from such local pronouncements: "The best Counsell, in those things that concern not other Nations, but onely the ease, and benefit the Subjects may enjoy [. . .] is to be taken from the generall informations, and complaints of the people of each Province, who are best acquainted with their own wants, and ought therefore, when they demand nothing in derogation of the essentiall Rights of the Soveraignty, to be diligently taken notice of" (L, 30:393).[6]

Leviathan advocates the regulation of political discourse predicated upon the responsive management of subject-citizens' needs and desires as they are facilitated by civil order and the local institutions that assure it. In Hobbes's commonwealth, freedom is measured by the "silence of the laws" and it increases in proportion to our self-discipline. The form political power assumes, Hobbes maintains, is irrelevant to freedom. Rather, the liberty of subjects is measured by the degree to which their activity remains, at least apparently, unregulated by artificial bonds or covenants (L, 21:266).[7] If there are no theoretical limits to what sovereignty can regulate, there are practical ones, for "there is no Commonwealth in the world, wherein there be Rules enough set down, for the regulating of all the actions, and words of men." Where the laws do not speak, "men have the Liberty, of doing what their own reasons shall suggest, for the most profitable to themselves." Subjects are free "to buy, and sell and otherwise contract with one another; to choose their own abode, their own diet, their own trade of life, and institute their children as they themselves think fit."[8]

Hobbes imagines, or at least hopes, that the "silence" by which we measure our freedom will be extensive. Indeed, the breadth of freedom Hobbes envisions is startling, given his understanding of the inherent dangers posed by our competing opinions and makings. Once we recognize the local, productive character of governing powers, however, Hobbes's presumption of extensive freedoms becomes explicable. Citizens who participate in governing powers and knowledges subjectify themselves and thereby become "freely" subject (subject-citizens).

Resorting to overt prohibition of habits or repression of opinion are last resorts that signify an inept regime or an especially obstinate citizenry. By contrast, Leviathan's subject-citizen formulates her fears and aspirations and continually relearns the necessity of her own discipline and conformity to the social rule embodied in civil codes. She thereby incorporates and emboldens what governing powers deem the best means of securing her health and happiness. The productivity, health, and happiness of the population ("commodious living") are the goals of civil codes. Primarily, these goals are not achieved by sovereignty's "right of death" but by a "life-administering" power that optimizes the aptitudes, desires, and efficacy of subject-citizens while at the same time assuring their governability, "concord," and prosperity.[9] For instance, ideally, civil laws are not "applyed to Individualls, further than their protection from injuries" but function "by a general Providence, contained in publique Instruction, both of Doctrine, and Example" (L, 30:376). In *De Cive*, Hobbes claims that compacts and promises are not sufficient to make men safe from mutual harms and that "we must therefore provide for our security, not by compacts, but by punishments" (DC, 6.3–4:175–76). In *Leviathan*, however, Hobbes adds that "terrour of legal punishment" is not enough to protect the rights of sovereignty and to secure the obedience and discipline of its subject-citizens. The grounds of these rights and their obedience "need to be diligently, and truly taught" (L, 30:377). The threat of punishment is not enough to secure order; the people must understand and participate in governing knowledges and live in accordance with their truths. Political sciences of the laws of social cause and effect facilitate the constitution of sovereignly authorized political bodies.

Hobbes's science of sovereign politics would govern public discourse so that we become reasonable subjects of its political rationality in accordance with social necessities of cause and effect. This governmentality produces truths sufficiently potent to prevent our degenerating into war, even when laws are silent and even when governing powers are invisible. Repressive power is not this truth, for such power, as Foucault teaches and Hobbes knew, is inefficient and obstructs commodious living. The arbitrariness of tyrannical power represents no great improvement upon a state of nature. Sovereignty is absolute, but it also must be logical, bound by the knowledge (if not by the subjects) it produces.

Hobbes's political science generates power for commodious living. Likewise, governing powers produce knowledge, because truth and falsehood do not inhere in objects but in words. Moreover, conventional links between language and the world are the product of makings and unmakings (L, 4:109). Governing powers generate knowledges that necessarily and authoritatively define meaning and making and thereby manage disputes arising in the breach between language and world (L, 6:120).

Geometry furnishes the perfect model for fabricated public reason because its proofs are undeniable but "man, the most subjective of all creatures, has nonetheless willed the existence of geometry and freely chosen its starting point."[10] Recall Ricoeur's formulation of the problem of theodicy: how does a free will make itself a slave of evil? Correlatively, Hobbes's political theodicy seeks to explain the popular authorization of social necessities by justifying the ways of political and social power to subject-citizens. Hobbes formulates a solution to the puzzle of free subjection and in the process inverts the explanatory direction of theodicy. Traditionally, theodicy has asked how we are to understand the world, especially the evil in the world, given who we believe God to be. Hobbes inverts this formula to ask and answer, in effect, given the way the world is, in what sort of God must we believe.[11]

Norms of social behavior enlarge the opportunities for individuals' exercise of power while controlling the harmful social and political consequences of conflict among divergent ways of seeing and making the world. "*Liberty* and Necessity are Consistent" because all acts proceed from "causes in a continuall chaine" of "necessity" (L, 21:263). When public reason establishes logical, then causal, connections, it reproduces the systems of power that secure social order (L, 5:115). More specifically, public reason governs our multiplicitous opinions by remaking the bodies/minds that hold them. A conscience reformed by public reason chastens the idiosyncratic and contradictory leadings of our bodies/minds by enabling us to observe that certain behaviors (e.g., dress, speech, and other manners of bearing) cause certain effects (L, 11:160–61). By our conformity to reasonable patterns of social behavior we accrue social efficacy, but in each case our identification of and with the cause grants its given power.[12]

As subject-citizens incorporate social powers, they engender and elaborate governing effects and become sovereign, individually and collectively, which is to say, they increasingly become one and uniform. By this method of popular authorization, the conventional is made essential and the freely subject produce social necessities. As a consequence, competing and conflicting bodies/minds are made governable. Ordinary evil ceases to be a visible problem to the extent that it is ordered. That is to say, popular authorization of governing power and knowledge institutes uniformity among subject-citizens to the degree necessary to constitute a cohesive, if not always coherent, collectivity—a Mortal God.

Hobbes's political science induces lawful, rule-governed behavior. But Hobbes is agnostic about the form of rationality best suited to regulate political discourse. Like the question of the public religion best suited to a commonwealth, it is largely a historical and cultural matter. As long as political rationality is sufficiently rigorous to identify and manage the "irrationalities" that "derail" social interaction and precipitate war, any form of public reason will do.[13] Indeed, the general characteristics and aims of Hobbesian political rationality are shared by discourses that we might place at opposite ends of the contemporary spectrum. Though "rational choice theory" and "communicative rationality" are not the same (and the differences between them matter) both would be functional political rationalities from Hobbes's perspective. Each seeks to explain and facilitate lawful, rule-governed behavior. In other words, each theory is an account of rationality which demands logical, defensible, consistent, and noncontradictory discursive rules that prescribe and justify the performance of contracts, reasonable conduct, and predictable behavior. Both rational choice and communicative rationality proceed from logical claims. These claims establish "causal," or socially efficacious, connections that retrace systems of discursive power. Both approaches maintain, however, the impartiality of their methodical rules vis-à-vis particular substantive "value" claims. In this way, both can fulfill Hobbes's requirement of political rationality to produce truths that can manage by transcending individuals' and groups' contesting and contestable claims. Governing rationalities address ordinary evil by displacing the problem.

Governing discourses induce and secure the performance of implicit and explicit social contracts not only by emphasizing what our nonconformity will cost, but also by highlighting the benefits and pleasures our conformity promises. As a consequence, competing and conflicting bodies/minds are made governable. Subject-citizens authorize the governing powers that discipline them and are educated so that "individuall persons may apply [to] their own cases" the good laws made and executed by sovereignty (L, 30:376). As they incorporate these powers, subject-citizens carry and engender their governing effects. Subject-citizens authorize governing powers and thereby make their own corporeal souls.

Governing powers

Michel Foucault calls *Discipline and Punish* "a correlative history of the modern soul and of a new power to judge" (DP, 23). His discussion helps us more fully imagine how corporeal souls are made and the character of the governing powers that make them. Moreover, Foucault illuminates the multiple valences of a body politic constituted in the image of a corporeal soul. The play of the corporeal/noncorporeal, visible/invisible in Foucault's story is complex and ambiguous. As we shall see, the movement of these binaries is even more overdetermined in the contemporary imagination of power. Corporeal souls are made by invisible powers that render their objects permanently visible; governing powers themselves are increasingly effective *and* invisible to the extent that they constitute the facticity of their objects. This fluid movement of visibility/invisibility and corporeality/noncorporeality is crucial to the specific productivity of modern powers, because corporeal powers and souls constitute "headless bodies."

The new modes of power studied by Foucault initiate a distinctive relationship to body and soul. The opening pages of *Discipline and Punish* are justly famous for their contrast of the public execution of the regicide Damiens with the prison time-table. These pages graphically convey what Foucault characterizes (at least initially) as the slackening hold of punitive measures upon the body (DP, 10). As we move from torture to more gentle ways of punishment, the target of power seems no longer to be the body, but the soul or mind.[14] Foucault asks whether this shift means that we have entered the age of noncorporal punishment (DP, 101). He never directly answers his question, but the story he tells suggests an answer.[15] The soul, Foucault says, is real, even today. At the same time, the soul is "the present correlative of a certain technology of power over the body" (DP, 29). Modern souls are born within and manifest "ordered evil."

> It would be wrong to say that the soul is an illusion, or an ideological effect. On the contrary, it exists, it has a reality, it is produced permanently around, on, within the body by the functioning of a power that is exercised on those punished–and, in a more general way, on those one supervises, trains and corrects, over madmen, children at home and at school, the colonized, over those who are stuck at a machine and supervised for the rest of their lives. This is the historical reality of this soul, which, unlike the soul represented by Christian theology, is not born in sin and subject to punishment, but is born rather out of methods of punishment, supervision, and constraint. (DP, 29)

The modern soul is produced by norms that are elaborated and extended through ordinary, methodical behavior in accordance with social rules of cause and effect. We shall have to consider how governing powers "discipline" the body to "make" a soul before we can assess to what degree that soul and the powers that produce it are corporeal or noncorporeal.

The pages of *Discipline and Punish* are full of startling claims. Foremost among them is Foucault's conclusion that the soul has become the prison of the body: "The man described for us, whom we are invited to free, is already in himself the effect of a subjection much more profound than himself. A 'soul' inhabits him and brings him to existence, which is itself a factor in the mastery that power exercises over the body. The soul is the effect and instrument of a political anatomy; the soul is the prison of the body" (DP, 30). How does power invest the body to create a soul that itself becomes the prison of the body? How are corporeal souls made?

Disciplinary power reaches the soul by means of the body (DP, 16). The prison, and other disciplinary institutions that borrow its techniques (DP, 138), seek to transform conduct:

> The cell, that technique of Christian monachism, which had survived only in Catholic countries, becomes in this Protestant society [England] the instrument by which one may reconstitute both *homo oeconomicus* and the religious conscience. Between the crime and the return to right and virtue, the prison would constitute the 'space between two worlds,' the place for the individual transformation that would restore to the state the subject it had lost. (DP, 123)

The "classical age" discovered the body as a target of power. The goal, Foucault says, is not to procure renunciations, as in monastic practices, but to manipulate, shape, and train the body so that it obeys, responds, and becomes more skillful and efficacious. A body is docile when it can be perpetually subjected, used, transformed, and improved. A productive, healthy, and happy body is a useful one. Beginning in the seventeenth century, a new "micro-physics of power" reached ever broader domains to cover the entire body politic (DP, 139) and to afford "a closer penal mapping of the social body" (DP, 78).

Mechanisms of power, then, frame the everyday lives of individuals to create docile and useful bodies (DP, 77). The scale, object of control, and modality of power constitute a new relationship to the body, which is no longer treated en masse, but individually. The economy, efficiency of movement, and internal organization of the body is the object of control. A subtle coercion is exercised upon the body to obtain a hold upon it "at the level of the mechanism itself—movements, gestures, attitudes and rapidity: an infinitesimal power over the active body." The modality of these new techniques executed "an uninterrupted, constant coercion, supervising the processes of activity rather than its result" through the codification of time, space, and movement. In such disciplinary regimes, the human body enters a machinery of power which explores it, breaks it down, rearranges, and remakes it (DP, 138).

But how do disciplinary powers engender a soul? What does it mean for the body to be imprisoned by the soul? In short, how are *subject-citizens* made? The body/mind's incorporation of governing powers—our compliance with the necessities of social cause and effect—brings a "normalizing" soul into existence. The individual thereby becomes the vehicle of her own subjection. Disciplines compare, differentiate, hierarchize, homogenize, and exclude by reference to the norm. An individual who can be described, judged, measured, and compared also can be trained or corrected, classified or excluded. We might think of disciplines as social scientific laboratories for the production of necessities of cause and effect. The soul is both an effect of normalizing judgment and its instrument, a means of inculcating individual calculability and its expression. The individual is subjectified by the visibility and facticity of what disciplinary powers document her to be, and the soul is the tool of this subjection. The soul, itself constituted by the grip of power upon the body, aligns the body with extant norms in the interest of avoiding more punitive measures. This "corporeal soul" pursues, coaxes, secures, and perpetuates bodily discipline and conformity.[16] Bentham's Panopticon provides the now infamous image of the functioning of normalizing powers within the subject's soul and upon his body: "He who is subjected to a field of visibility, and who knows it, assumes responsibility for the constraints of power; he makes them play spontaneously upon himself; he inscribes in himself the power relation in which he simultaneously plays both roles; he becomes the principle of his own subjection" (DP, 202–3). In short, he becomes a prisoner of his own soul.

Discipline "makes" individuals (DP, 170), in two senses. First, the individual subject observed and trained by disciplinary powers is fabricated, not found. Second, the individual we come to know is an invention. Disciplinary powers prescribe the facticity of individuals by rendering them analyzable, describable, and, thereby, calculable objects. The individual who conforms to the causes and effects of social norms prescribed by governing powers—the body reformed by a normalizing soul—behaves in predictable ways; if she does not, then proximate bodies/minds' exercise of governing powers may be redoubled or recourse made to more overtly punitive measures. To the extent that our corporeal souls make our bodies/minds, however, we appear to be found, not fabricated. To the extent that governing norms become our own, their enactment appears to express our individuality, rather than to be invented through a corporeal soul's hold upon our body/mind.

The "calculable man," whose soul imprisons his body, is first recognized and then perpetually reinscribed by means of a permanent visibility. Yet the powers that render the individual visible are themselves increasingly invisible. An invisible power "imposes on those whom it subjects a principle of compulsory visibility. In discipline, it is the subjects who have to be seen. Their visibility assures the hold of power that is exercised over them. It is the fact of being constantly seen, of being able always to be seen, that maintains the disciplined individual in his subjection" (DP, 187).

Disciplinary powers are at once absolutely indiscreet and discreet: indiscreet because they are everywhere, always alert, and registered materially as they grasp and shape the body; discreet because they function permanently, invisibly, and largely in silence.[17] The visible effects of power upon the body make it docile and useful, but the invisibility of power guarantees order (DP, 200). Ideally, the panoptic effects of disciplinary power within the individual induce a state of consciousness (or governed conscience) which secures the automatic functioning of power (DP, 201). Indeed, disciplinary power becomes invisible by rendering its object visible. As governing powers constitute the visibility and facticity of their object, they become increasingly invisible. First, they become invisible in their effects, for what is socially produced is now taken to be a "natural" fact. Second, they become invisible in their activity, for as power's object becomes power's vehicle and assumes its place, power's object becomes a power in its own right. Consequently, citizens exercise the governing powers that constitute them as subjects and authorize the necessities of cause and effect to which they subject themselves.

A "carceral society" of visible, calculable subjects is formed as mechanisms of discipline gradually extend throughout the social body (DP, 209, 298). "Disciplines function increasingly as techniques for making useful individuals. Hence their emergence from a marginal position on the confines of society, and their detachment from forms of exclusion or expiation, confinement or retreat" (DP, 211). Disciplines not only correct abnormal, marginal individuals, they also make normal subject-citizens when "massive, compact disciplines are broken down into flexible methods of control." Bentham dreamed of transforming disciplines practiced in relatively enclosed places like barracks, schools, and workshops "into a network of mechanisms that would be everywhere and always alert, running through society without interruption in space and time" (DP, 209). Bentham's dream "makes" social reality when this microphysics of power infiltrates all other forms of power (DP, 216) until "society is penetrated through and through with disciplinary mechanisms" (DP, 209).

"Networks of surveillance" systemically integrate disciplinary power and organize it into a multiple, automatic, anonymous power: "Although surveillance rests on individuals, its functioning is that of a network of relations from top to bottom. . . . [T]his network 'holds' the whole together and traverses it in its entirety with effects of power that derive from one another: supervisors, perpetually supervised" (DP, 176–77). Disciplines make possible relational powers that are sustained by their own mechanisms and replace the spectacle of public events with the "uninterrupted play of calculated gazes" (DP, 177). As modes of surveillance reveal all, the powers that institute surveillance themselves become increasingly invisible. A "faceless gaze" (i.e., a headless body) transforms "the whole social body into a field of perception: thousands of eyes posted everywhere, mobile attentions ever on the alert" (DP, 214).

Foucault opposes this regime of surveillance and "power over life" to the spectacle of sovereignty and "right of death." He associates theories of sovereignty with "a historical type of society in which power was exercised mainly as a means of deduction, a subtraction mechanism." But deduction has come to play a smaller role in the exercise of power. Now, power is "bent on generating forces, making them grow, and ordering them," rather than impeding, destroying, or making them submit (HSI, 136). Networks of surveillance replace the spectacle of sovereignty and panoptic powers increase their force, and those of society, instead of confiscating them: "The productive increase of power can be assured only if, on the one hand, it can be exercised continuously in the very foundations of society, in the subtlest possible way, and if, on the other hand, it functions outside these sudden, violent, discontinuous forms that are bound up with the exercise of sovereignty" (DP, 208).

The old, sovereign power exerted itself directly upon bodies (potently inscribed itself in bodies, it was easy to see) and was exalted and strengthened by these visible manifestations. Because sovereignty is incapable of continual supervision, it sought "renewal of its effect in the spectacle of its individual manifestations" and was "recharged in the ritual display of its reality as 'super-power'" (DP, 57). But this power had its problems, not the least of which was that the spectacle of sovereign power might not only evoke renewed awe and submission but also provoke revolt and contest (DP, 73–9). Moreover, a singular, embodied sovereign could hardly be visible at all times and in all places.

In a regime of surveillance, "the scarcely sustainable visibility of the monarch is turned into the unavoidable visibility of the subjects" (DP, 189). The inversion of the visible and invisible assures the exercise of power in the lowest manifestations of the social body. Panopticism is the principle of a new 'political anatomy' whose object and end are not the relations of sovereignty but the relations of discipline (DP, 208).

> *Our society is one not of spectacle, but of surveillance;* under the surface of images, one invests bodies in depth; behind the great abstraction of exchange, there continues the meticulous, concrete training of useful forces; the circuits of communication are the supports of an accumulation and a centralization of knowledge; the play of signs defines the anchorages of power; it is not that the beautiful totality of the individual is amputated, repressed, altered by social order, it is rather that *the individual is carefully fabricated in it,* according to a whole technique of forces and bodies. (DP, 217, my emphasis)

In Foucault's carceral society, the vigilance of intersecting gazes replaces the pomp and marvel of sovereignty. "We are neither in the amphitheatre, nor on the stage, but in the panoptic machine, invested by its effects of power, which we bring to ourselves since we are part of its mechanism" (DP, 217). We make others and our selves subject-citizens, just as we are made by them.

The "automatic docility" of disciplinary regimes is "democratically controlled"; the exercise of power is supervised by society as a whole (DP, 207). The judges of normality are everywhere. It is upon them that "the universal reign of the normative is based" (DP, 304). But we are them, supervisors perpetually supervised.[18] Expectantly observed by others, we subject our bodies, gestures, behaviors, aptitudes, and achievements to their normalizing judgments; observing others, we would make them comply with the norms in which we find ourselves.

Foucault's carceral vision of society has had its share of critics.[19] Typically, their objections have centered on the following: the totalizing quality of Foucault's image of a disciplinary society; his erosion of the ground of critique; and the conception of agency generated by his representation of individual subjects constituted by disciplines. Foucault received the force of these criticisms in his own way, rarely taking them on their own terms, but nonetheless incorporating them into his thinking.[20] For all its insights into the character and functioning of modern powers, however, *Discipline and Punish* generates these criticisms in part because it continues to conceive power in largely negative terms. Though Foucault insists upon power's productivity and positivity, he continues to speak of domination. When we equate power and domination, however, we tend to represent subjects as targets rather than as agents of power. In *Discipline and Punish*, then, we find a vision of efficient machineries of power (DP, 164, 217), but little sense of how individual subjects, like "engines, springs, and wheels" (L, Intro:81) make them go. We are told that individuals carry governing powers, participate in and extend them, but we have little sense of how they do so as both actors and subjects.

Foucault's neglect of the specifically political aspect of disciplinary regimes—the domain of theories of sovereignty—is a principal source of these discrepancies. Oppositions between theories of sovereignty and the military dream of society, between spectacle and surveillance, displace crucial questions regarding "democratically controlled," if "automatic," docility. How are governing powers and norms elaborated? In *Discipline and Punish*, we are told that tactics and strategies are contingently deployed, but we have little feel for the cooperative activities that turn contingencies into perceived social necessities. We have little sense of how individuals and groups conform to or disrupt the functioning of disciplinary institutions. Yet Foucault presupposes resistance as well as its opposite, compliance.

Furthermore, where do norms come from? To pose this question is not to ask after the original (normative) ground of norms, whether sanctified or bloody, but instead to query their generation.[21] How is normal and abnormal specified and contingency mastered into inevitability? Why and how in any particular case does a norm assume one instantiation rather than another? Does the constitution of the political affect how principled norms are? Do we participate in the generation of norms (and if so, how), or are they simply imposed upon us (do they come from elsewhere and, if so, where)? In *Discipline and Punish*, these queries receive no answers because Foucault does not query the political and the significance of its predominant modern form, sovereignty.

Foucault discounts theories of sovereignty because he thinks they neglect the locality and productivity of modern powers. My reading, however, of Hobbes's sovereign corporeal soul and the governing powers its social rules generate suggests that Foucault is not exactly right about sovereign theories, or at least not about Hobbes. Although Hobbes is not an innovator of specific disciplinary techniques, his vision of an ideal commonwealth is parasitic upon such police powers and policy initiatives. In *Leviathan*, subject-citizens' freedom primarily depends not upon a "right of death" but upon local disciplines of governing powers and knowledges. Hobbes's ideal commonwealth finally cannot function without such "power over life" because without it the extensive "silence of the laws" he envisions would dissolve the body politic.

We need Foucault to reread Hobbes today, but we also need Hobbes to read Foucault politically today.[22] Foucault dismisses the importance of sovereignty (the "modern" instantiation of the political) and thereby neglects "the people" who authorize its governing powers. As a result, the middle Foucault both misses crucial elements of the specific productivity of modern powers and remains confined by Hobbes's corporeal imagination of power and the governmentality it cultivates.[23] The invisible governing powers at work in the modern body politic are generated by the *incorporeal* (neither entirely visible nor invisible, neither entirely corporeal nor noncorporeal) bodies of the people who authorize sovereignty. Reading Hobbes's political theory helps us conceive how we participate in the constitution of these powers, though, to be sure, it is the last thing that Hobbes would have us do.

Headless bodies

How do individual corporeal souls materialize? What, if any entity, constitutes a body politic's governing powers, its collective corporeal soul? Who, if anybody, authorizes sovereignty? According to Hobbes, "we" create a sovereign entity because we need a common power to arbitrate the unavoidable and sometimes deadly disputes that arise from our various makings and unmakings. Though we love to make and unmake ourselves and others, we introduce this restraint upon ourselves because we know our preservation and contentment depend upon it. Peace requires our subjection because human relations tend toward war when God is politically dead, all the more so until we accept that death. This is the upshot of Hobbes's lengthy disquisition on the differences between humans and ants or bees (L, 17:225–27). To secure commodious living we must institute an artificial order, for a natural one is not available to us. We constitute sovereignty because only such a common power can secure the performance of contracts, reasonable conduct, and predictable behavior. Sovereignty accomplishes this by making us subjects, by keeping us in awe.

The only way "to erect such a Common Power" is for each person "to confer all of their power and strength upon one Man, or Assembly of men, to bear their Person" (L, 17:227). When we authorize sovereignty in this way, we own and acknowledge ourselves to be the "authors" of this representative person's actions. It is as if every man were to say to every man "I authorize and give up my right of governing my self, to this Man, or to this assembly of men, on this condition, that thou give up thy right to him, and authorize all his actions, in like manner." We each thereby submit our will to a sovereign will, our judgment to a sovereign judgment. The result "is more than consent or concord, it is a real unity of them all in one and the same Person" (L, 17:227), the constitution of one sovereign body.[24]

Hannah Arendt judges Hobbes's founding of the modern body politic baneful because of his sovereign conception of the political. To persuade us of her judgment, she recovers a distinction between two sorts of social contract: "One was concluded between individual persons and supposedly gave birth to society; the other was concluded between a people and its ruler and supposedly resulted in legitimate government" (OR, 169). We have tended to neglect the decisive differences between these forms of social contract, Arendt says, in part because seventeenth-century theorists were interested primarily in finding a universal theory to encompass both political and social obligations. But these two forms of contract, Arendt claims, are "mutually exclusive." Both contracts are fictional, but they are determinative fictions of the political which cultivate quite different politics. The first, mutual contract, binds people together in a community. Mutual promise is based upon reciprocity, presupposes equality, and results in an alliance which "gathers together the isolated strength of the allied partners and binds them into a new power structure by virtue of 'free and sincere promise'" (OR, 170). In the second contract between a given society and its ruler, each member gives up his isolated strength and power in order to constitute a government. "Far from gaining a new power, and possibly more than he had before, he resigns his power such as it is, and far from binding himself through promises, he merely expresses his 'consent' to be ruled by the government, whose power consists of the sum total of forces which all individual persons have channeled into it and which are monopolized by the government for the alleged benefit of all subjects" (OR, 170).

In Arendt's view, each person gains as much power in the first contract as she or he loses in the second. "A body politic which is the result of covenant and 'combination' becomes the very source of power for each individual person who outside the constituted political realm remains impotent" (OR, 171). This is the case because "power comes into being only if and when men join themselves together for the purpose of action" (OR, 175). Mutual promise constitutes and sustains "civic bodies politic" that give us access to power and preclude a situation in which some are ruled while others rule (OR, 168). The "mutual subjection" of reciprocal promise, Arendt contends, renders rulership an "absurdity." By contrast, "the government which is the result of consent acquires a monopoly of power so that the governed are politically impotent" (OR, 171). Absolute rulership is the animating principle of this body politic, embodied in a sovereign nation construed in the image of a divine power that, like Hobbes's "Mortal God," overawes all (OR, 171). In the first contract, we are all powerful actors. In the second contract, we either are ruled or rule.

Are these two forms of contract mutually exclusive, as Arendt maintains? And why would anyone accept the second contract? How might we be induced to embrace antipolitical being? In short, how do we know, as Hobbes maintains we do, that we must become sovereign subjects? On my reading, Hobbes's prescient account of the popular authorization of sovereignty and its governing powers demonstrates that the two forms of social contract are not mutually exclusive. Indeed, Hobbes's combination of promising and consent to political impotence (what I call mutual promise without political bodies) is the key to his brilliant if finally fateful solution to the dubious foundations of modern governance. Mutual promise without political bodies authorizes rule by nobody or bureaucracy (CR, 137). The state—a network of administrative, regulatory schemes which constitute a social totality—is the political form of popular sovereignty.

Leviathan is generated by a mutual promise among its subject-citizens to confer their rights and powers upon a sovereign entity, the representative of their unified person, the state of the people. Hobbes calls this action among the people a covenant and not a contract, and he does so for a very good reason. Whereas a contract is a mutual transfer of right, a covenant is performed in expectation and trust that others will perform their part at some future time. When "both parts may contract now to perform hereafter this is called keeping of promise or faith" (L, 14:193). Mutual promise without political bodies expresses the political faith of popularly authorized sovereign states. Founding promises among sovereignty's subject-citizens do not create a contract (a mutual transfer of right) between them and the "one Man, or assembly of men" who represent their collective person and unity ("the people").

To construe the relations between subjects and their sovereign(ty) as a contract contradicts the meaning of authorization. Authorization requires representation as collective projection and personification. In this case, an "author" stands at at least one remove from his "act," for the sovereign unity of a representative person can be created only when we authorize and own its actions as our own, even when we have had no determinative say over and in them.[25] "A multitude of men are made One Person when they are by one man or one person represented so that it be done with the consent of everyone of the Multitude in particular"

(L, 16:220). Without such authorization sovereignty is impossible. However, the unity of the representer, not the represented, is decisive. Prior to the authorization of sovereignty, we are a multitude—not one but many, indeed a combative multiplicity. Therefore, collective personification is achieved only when we recognize and affirm this representative person as our person, the bearer of our collective body, a projected emanation of our selves as one people. It is only through the representative person that we are unified—become sovereign—and it is only by means of sovereign actions, as authorized and owned by us, that we come together in a united state in which we may recognize ourselves. As a consequence, to criticize sovereign actions and proclamations is to criticize oneself. Failing to recognize sovereignty as the bearer of the self is to lose oneself. Challenging sovereignty, then, not only puts us at war with the body politic but also at war with ourselves. In short, challenging the social necessities of sovereign causes and effects is self-defeating.

In the twenty-second chapter of *Leviathan*, "Of Systems Subject, Political, and Private," Hobbes addresses the "Muscles" of the body politic. There, as elsewhere, Hobbes allows only sovereignly authorized systems that, paradoxically, prove to be political bodies that appear not to be political bodies. The effective authorization and actions of sovereignty preclude alternative representations and incorporations of political powers. Sovereignly authorized political bodies are forms of association in which necessities that are socially produced appear to be natural. Our conformity to social rules of cause and effect make artifice appear natural and politics seem to disappear. Authoritative mutual promise (at least in Hobbes's sense of the term) deauthorizes citizens' nonsovereign political bodies and, as a consequence, consolidates governance and orders ordinary evil.

Any number of men joined in one interest or business constitute a system. Those systems are regular "where One Man, or Assembly of men, is constituted Representative of the whole number. All others are irregular." Only commonwealths are absolute and independent, that is, subject to none other than their own representative body. All other systems are dependent, that is, subordinate and subject to some sovereign power. Bodies politic are those public systems that are made by sovereign authorization. Private systems are constituted by subject-citizens among themselves. Only sovereignly authorized private systems are lawful; all others are unlawful. Unexpectedly, irregular, not regular, private systems are most likely to be lawful. Irregular systems consist of concourse among people and cohere without political representation:

they result from the conflux of the people to the likes of markets, shows, or any other "harmless end." Such popular concourse is lawful (and not evil) when disorganized so that citizens cohere apparently without political bodies. But concourse among the people is for "evil intentions" and unlawful whenever it appears to rival sovereignty—when citizens constitute alternative political bodies (L, 22:274–75). Sovereignty, even when authorized by mutual promise, can brook no challenge to its representative powers. Sovereignty requires the transubstantiation of a multitude into one person. The subjects' constitution of themselves as political bodies (unless sovereignly authorized) threatens the unity of representation and is an assault upon the common power that alone can curtail perpetual conflict and potential war.

Hobbes's account of authorization envisions mutual promise without political bodies. Sovereignty, and the unified representative person that embodies it, presupposes the disaggregation of multitudes. All their concourse must be irregular so that they proffer no visible representations that might contest the sovereign constitution of "common power" (the political). Irregular private systems are not without power, however, for the powers that constitute and are exercised within political bodies become invisible so that socially produced causes and effects appear beyond question. As we shall see, these invisible powers prove as crucial to the "muscle" of the "state" as do its visible powers. In Hobbes's corporeal imagination of power, however, only body is real, and we are authorized to say that power exists only when it matters like a *visible* body. Yet it is the invisibility of modern powers that secures their productivity. Hobbes's corporeal imagination of power, in effect, obscures the functioning of governing powers. Indeed, this is how Hobbes's political theory would sustain governance.

Social order and knowledge of good and evil necessarily depend upon our willing subjection. Becoming freely subject to the social processes that produce causes and effects, we elaborate and extend the social rules that secure order. Though human beings are makers of their selves and their world, they are also "sufferers from forces they did not produce and [can] little alter, . . . captives of a Fate,"[26] or so it appears. Hobbes's skeptical teaching secularizes the lessons of Job.[27] The invisible powers that make and unmake individuals also absolve them of ultimate responsibility, for we cannot help being what we are.[28] Job is overcome by the impression of an awesome and irresistible power that exceeds his comprehension, let alone his mastery. He finds peace and freedom through submission to his God.[29] Likewise, we may gain inner peace and a certain freedom if only we submit to the invisible powers that make our fate and remain skeptical of our ability to comprehend or alter them. The Immortal God is incomprehensible; so too are the Mortal God, Leviathan, and the invisible powers that constitute and generate its muscular strength. Hobbes's corporeal imagination obfuscates these powers and, in doing so, cultivates our responsibility.

If we accept Hobbes's teaching of what it means to be responsible—and if we become sovereign subjects by submitting to the social necessities of cause and effect which our subjection produces—we are promised peace in two respects. First, our commonwealth will be peaceful. The demands of public reason and the commands of civil law constitute a sovereign body politic. Our conformity to reason and law governs contests over divergent ways of seeing and making the world so that they become personally and publicly manageable. Second, we gain the inner peace that comes from a clear conscience. If we conform to the political conditions of sovereignty, we are not responsible for what we are or for what we do. A governed soul is pure and a conscience clear so long as their intentions are good. To the extent that we are implicated in harms that flow from conventional ways of making the world, it is the sovereign state's responsibility, not our own. Hobbes depoliticizes ethical questions to discipline resentment and contentiousness and to secure peace.

Yet Hobbes's skeptical teaching also promises freedom. Our conformity to public reason and civil law secures an order that allows a wide berth for a plurality of private makings. Where the laws are silent we are free. Peace and responsibility, order and freedom, demand only that we avoid political contestation of ethical questions. It is not only unwise to carry social disagreement to the point of violence, but nothing can justify embarking on a course of dissent and agitation that might lead a society into a civil war no one originally intended. In the end, Hobbes is less interested in *what* subjects believe than in *how* they hold and express their beliefs. Whatever our private judgment, "we will defer willingly and naturally to 'Publique Reason'" as subjects of Hobbes's skeptical conversion. Hobbes's science of sovereign politics seeks to cultivate this moral character.[30]

In the contemporary body politic, there is no original agent of power or primary "cause" of power relations. The inadequacy of conventional accounts of sovereignty and of repressive hypotheses about power informed Foucault's admonishment of contemporary analysts of power to "cut off the head of the king." In the same passage of *De Cive* with which I began my reading of Hobbes's figuration of the body politic, he offers an account of its "head": "A court of counselors is rather to be compared with the head, or one counselor, whose only counsel (if of any one alone) the chief ruler makes use of in matters of greatest moment: for the office of the head is to the counsel, as the soul's is to command" (DC, 6.19:188). The "counselors" represent the "mind" of the body politic; they are whatever offers direction to the "soul," the governing powers, the body's collective will. "Counselors" are the memory of a political body "by whom all things needful for it to know, are suggested unto it" (L, Intro:81). A body politic is without a "head" or "mind" when "command" is rendered without "counsel." The subject-citizens of a figurally headless body politic are thoughtless, which is to say, they exercise power without awareness or sufficient regard for others. As often as not, however, the thoughtless exercise of power is constituted by a political condition rather than by a will to dominate others. Mutual promise without political bodies orders ordinary evil. Such thoughtless evil is most often manifest in inadvertent and unseen harms that coincide with the benefits and pleasures of reasonable conduct, predictable behavior, and contractual performance.

A corporeal imagination of power like Hobbes's cultivates the appearance, then the actuality, of a headless body politic. Only visible power, like a body, is imagined to matter. As we have seen, however, the specific productivity of contemporary powers hinge upon their invisibility. These powers ("command") seem to proceed, because they are invisible, without human direction or agency ("counsel"). However, this appearance is attributable, at least in part, to our failure or incapacity to conceive, engage, and direct invisible powers. As a result, the appearance that command is without counsel, and power necessarily crude, non-deliberate, coercive, and unthinking—in short, that political bodies are headless—becomes a reality.

But where, in actuality, do the social norms that rule our political bodies orginate, and how does their power increase? On my account, normalizing social rules are generated through popular authorization of governing powers. These powers, and our exercise of them, are often invisible. As a result, the origination of norms and the elaboration of their power is difficult to discern. Mutual promise without political bodies renders the power that instantiates norms invisible and its excercise thoughtless, especially when we have a corporeal imagination of power. With its governing powers as difficult to conjure as a soul, the sovereign body politic assumes an ethereal quality and is figurally, when not actually, headless.

Hobbes wanted the body politic to appear headless. To be sure, my claim is counter-intuitive given our preconception of Hobbes as the theorist of absolute sovereignty and his professed preference for monarchy.[31] Yet in the impression, then actuality, of a headless body politic, we find Hobbes's solution to the dubious basis of modern governance and the problem of ordinary evil. The deauthorization of discourse regarding invisible powers and its result—sanctification of the constitution of the political—is Hobbes's response to the dubious basis of modern governance. We are authorized to name, and in time can only imagine, *visible* powers while invisible powers secure social rule(s). This detheologization of power in turn facilitates the depoliticization of ethical questions by making the popular "authors" of sovereignty invisible. As a consequence, the elaboration of governing powers and their effects are difficult to see and contest, let alone to assume responsibility for or to exercise freely. Depoliticization of ethical questions is Hobbes's response to the problem of ordinary evil.

In the face of invisible powers, a corporeal imagination renders the origination and elaboration of norms unrepresentable and unthinkable. This imagination of power stabilizes governance by securing subject-citizens' conformity and calculability. Through a process of collective projection and social rule, individual subject-citizens are made subjects by and to "the people." When this mutual promising occurs without political bodies, the norms that make claims upon and identify subject-citizens are shielded from contestation and transfiguration. Consequently, ethical questions are depoliticized. In this case, depoliticization has several meanings. First, ethical dilemmas are disconnected from the problem of constituting the political, specifically from the creation of individual and collective political bodies. Second, ethical questions are thereby shielded from specifically political contestation. Finally, ethical questions are individualized and made "private" (a matter of social rule), not "public" (a matter for political thinking and action).

To imagine how Hobbes would have the subject-citizens experience power, consider the frontispiece of *Leviathan*. What does it feel like to be one of those individual bodies, distinct and differentiated, yet imbricated in one body if only by virtue of the sword and scepter that represent, quite literally, its collective power? How does power appear to them? How do they think about it? How does it make them feel? How does it affect their actions? Sovereignty makes us subject-citizens by keeping us in awe. Like God, Leviathan—the body politic as a social totality—is inscrutable. We have learned Hobbes's lessons well if we do not presume to know either God or the sovereignty of Leviathan. We are induced to relinquish our imaginations to governing powers and knowledges and to regard the body politic as a social totality simultaneously incomprehensible and beyond doubt or questioning. Its powers appear at once monolithic, omnipotent and, paradoxically, undeniable and indescribable. We will see and feel the effects of its powers everywhere; we will even sense our own role in, and thus affirm, these powers, though finally we are unable to discern their generation and elaboration. The origin and agents of these powers will not be precisely identifiable, but their potency and pervasive effects will be indisputable. These impressions of power generated by the corporeal soul of the body politic will stagger us, and thus, for their own good, the "children of Pride" will be humbled.[32]

Ideally, Hobbes would have the body politic appear headless, its laws silent, its governing powers as invisible and difficult to conjure as a soul. Popular authorization makes the head of political bodies disappear, or seem not to matter, as the scarcely sustainable visibility of the body politic is turned into the unavoidable visibility of its subjects in everyday, ordinary ways. We authorize sovereignty's actions as our own when we consent to the necessities of social causes and effects purveyed by governing powers and knowledges, and, in accordance with social rules, when we introject a "sovereign head" (increasingly uniform will and judgment) within our corporeal souls.

Governing powers and knowledges produce calculable objects and become increasingly invisible as they constitute the visibility and facticity of their objects. Disciplines make bodies and engender souls; they are political scientific laboratories in which individuals become subjects by subjectifying themselves. The individual's corporeal soul, born in and through governing powers, forms and fashions the body/mind; its visibility establishes the facticity of the individual. As this body/mind becomes a power in its own right—carrying and exercising the effects of governing powers as corporeal souls—the powers that made the disciplinary individual are increasingly invisible. As a result, a "hybrid," a socially produced "natural" fact and calculable object, is "purified." The powers and means of its creation are incomprehensible because unrepresentable.

Within Hobbes's political imagination, only bodies themselves, corporeal and visible, are real. When the invisible powers that make a body matter become apparently noncorporeal—no longer evinced or recognized on the body—they appear unreal and their perception a "figment of absurd imaginations." Consequently, and like the soul Hobbes describes, governing powers increasingly become indiscernible, but, as Hobbes knows, they matter nonetheless. Hobbes's deauthorization of discourses regarding the incorporeal fosters this incomprehensibility; so too do oppositions between sovereignty and a military dream of society. If we are to comprehend how a carceral Leviathan is constituted, we need to discern how we participate in its founding.

The collective corporeal soul of the contemporary body politic is constituted by governing powers manifest in the norms, practices, and efficacy we bring to bear upon our own and others' conduct. These powers materialize social spaces and engender patterns of power which make them pliant to some persons and projects, recalcitrant toward others. Even when the laws are "silent," these patterns remain; they are reflected and fortified by the governing powers and knowledges we bear. In the contemporary body politic, the laws' silence has various meanings, but it never signifies the absence of power. The laws are silent (and we are "free") because governing powers and the patterns they extend are most often not repressive, but productive, enhancing our capacities and efficacy if we have the ability and willingness to flow with them. They are silent, also, in that their effects tend to be invisible, or at least the constraints they represent typically are not perceptible like walls or chains. Finally, these powers may be regarded as silent because they are not imposed by an authoritarian state or government acting as a unified agent. Instead, we incorporate and authorize these powers and perpetuate their patterns as we pursue our felicity.

Our ways of understanding and making the world leave traces on the surface of all to which the activities of our bodies/minds relate us, and in these often invisible traces patterns of power are manifest. Whether for good or for bad, each of us, individually and collectively, is the governing power of the body politic, albeit differently and assymetrically, contingent upon our relation to the norms embodied in civil codes and practices. The "head" of the body politic is constituted through traces upon and by our corporeal souls.

CHAPTER 3

Recovering Political Enthusiasm for Invisible Powers

Although everybody started his life by inserting himself into the human world through action and speech, nobody is the author or producer of his own life story. In other words, the stories, the results of action and speech, reveal an agent, but this agent is not an author or producer. Somebody began it and is its subject in the twofold sense of the word, namely, its actor and sufferer, but nobody is its author.

Hannah Arendt, *The Human Condition*

In the realm of human affairs, we know the author of the 'miracles.' It is men who perform them—men who have received the twofold gift of freedom and action can establish a reality of their own.

Hannah Arendt, *Between Past and Future*

We have not yet learned well enough how to think of responsibility and freedom without reference to an original, unified agent of power, whether the sovereign we conceive is an individual or collectivity. Sovereignty rules our politics and our selves. As Foucault says, we are still looking for the head of a headless body politic. In some respects, however, we are right to do so. After all, the "head" of the body politic has traditionally been the locus of questions regarding freedom and responsibility. For example, in the traditional political theories of sovereignty which Foucault criticizes, identifying the head is often part and parcel of limiting power and securing freedom. To know the head of a body politic is to know who is responsible for the lapses in governance that vitiate freedom or for the the excesses of power that threaten it.

Still, the search for a political body's head, at least as that task has been traditionally construed, obscures the challenges contemporary power relations pose to both freedom and responsibility. Once we recognize the extent to which governing powers are popularly authorized in "regular and irregular private systems," it makes little sense to conceive the preservation of freedom solely in terms of limiting the power of the state as institutional apparatus (whether repressive or productive). Likewise, it makes little sense to conceptualize responsibility as a matter of finding-out "who rules" once we have seen that every individual exercises governing powers and knowledges in his or her relations. To be sure, collective life- and liberty-threatening projects, galvanized by state institutions, must remain a central preoccupation. But as long as we focus upon these projects as something the state or other fictional personification presses upon us, we remain confined by a repressive, strictly negative model of power.

Reimagining the head of political bodies

A negative image of power obscures our instituting and perpetuating role in power relations, and it conceals how our pursuit of felicity flows into, depends upon, and reinforces project(ion)s of social rule. Ignorance of trespasses—our often unwitting yet willing participation in ordered evil—constitutes thoughtless subject-citizens. Relatedly, while sovereignty and its governing powers and knowledges facilitate liberty- and life-threatening projects, the fact that we authorize, carry, and continue these powers and knowledges means that conceiving responsibility for them must go beyond setting limits to state powers. We must engage the question of what it would mean to exercise power thoughtfully, in ways that both embolden and secure our own and others' freedom. What would being deliberate and free agents of power in a headless body politic entail? How can we transfigure our relationship to governing powers and knowledges that render us calculable and entangle us in harm to others? Responding to these questions requires us to reconceive the head of political bodies. More specifically, we must exceed the limits of the predominant conception of the political and its imagination of power.

Rethinking the meaning of the head in a headless body politic must begin with recognition of indeterminacy. The problem of the head itself must be transfigured: changed from a search for the subject of power as a sovereign agent of the body politic and into a question of how to affirmatively relate "command" and "counsel," power and thinking. Thus construed, the head of the body politic is indeterminate. What ways of thinking and forms of action foster the thoughtless exercise of power? Which minimize it? Affirmative relations between command and counsel, emerge when we freely and deliberately exercise the powers that make us what we are, the invisible powers both within and without us. Relations between power and thinking, body and mind, are interdependent, and the "soul" or self signifies their mediation.[1] Our soul is corporeal or incorporeal relative to our deliberate participation in the effects of the powers that make us what we are (which reveals who we are becoming). The relations between thinking and power which predominate distinguish the figural head of the body politic. Reconceiving the head of the body politic entails experimenting with the relationships among "body," "mind," and "soul," between corporeality and incorporeality, between visibility and invisibility. In other words, we must explore alternative political theologies as different ways of naming and enlisting invisible powers.

Alternative political theologies

Arendt fails to see that mutual promise may constitute (rather than inevitably oppose) the sovereign unity of the modern body politic. She does so, however, because of her effort to articulate an alternative conception of the political. Her recognition that sovereignty is neither inevitable nor wholly desirable remains instructive. Ideal-typic conceptions of the political represent competing understandings of political authority and power. More specifically, they represent alternative visions of how subject-citizens are imbricated in the body of "the people" they authorize. Pursuing these matters entails political theological speculation about each conception's imagination and engagement of "invisible powers." The last provision may sound odd, at best, to late modern ears. But if, as Max Weber maintained, each human association must have its god, then we must determine which deities we revere, even if "modern" gods are always already "crossed out."[2]

Monotheos is the political theological correlate of the people imagined as a mystical body and sovereign unity. *Entheos* corresponds to the people envisioned as organized multitudes. In the former, power and authority emanate from a single locus that, if not actually transcendent, nonetheless cannot be traced to identifiable authors in space and time. Though monotheos is a secular conception of the political, it functions like an absolute. When we are under its sway, invisible powers, when they are recognized at all, seem to come from above or elsewhere. Entheos challenges this sovereign conception of the political.[3] For those who are politically spirited, invisible powers are within and among us, enacted in the social body and authorized by the practices and relations of power which constitute political bodies. The "corporate witness" of political bodies enables us to discern relations of power and our role in the authority of political (con)texts. Once we recognize our authorizing role, we can engage invisible powers and become political actors in relation to them.

In the wake of the political death of God, the task of founding political power became a problem as it had not been before. Traditionally, theorists and founders have sought an origin of power that would bestow legitimacy on the powers that be. Thus the biblical account of creation was paradigmatic for those who sought an origin outside history that began history. Such an origin and order, whether divine or natural, could explain whence the efficacy of makings comes and why some succeed where others fail. The foundations of the modern body politic are inherently unstable, and claims to rule dubious, because no absolute, transcendent source is forthcoming. Political power makes and gains its potency from human artifice, not God or nature. How can peace be secured, then, given the dubious, contingent bases of all modern claims to rule? What "common power" can arbitrate contests among our competing, divergent makings?

Monotheos and entheos represent different conceptions of the founding sources and quality of "common power." For monotheos, a political body's constitution is a unifying theory of power; what it founds is conceived and instituted as God conceived and instituted the universe.[4] In this case, political power is analogous to a natural force and indistinguishable from what makes human artifice. According to the predominant biblical model, law is a command that requires our obedience. To the extent that we become subject(s) before laws and norms without recognizing our authorizing role in relation to them, they appear as commands demanding obedience. For monotheos, "the people" function as a secular absolute. When the people is represented as a sovereign unity and fictionally projected as a mystical body (rather than as organized multitudes of political bodies), our authorization of sovereignty, and our consent in particular to its governing powers, may become unthinkable for a corporeal imagination that does not recognize invisible powers. From this perspective, the norms and laws of collective life, though socially made, appear to be natural necessities. Arendt is right to claim that specifically political freedom and power are relinquished when we comply with the necessities of a sovereign body politic. But she is mistaken that we receive nothing in return for our embrace of anti-political being. In fact, we receive the efficacy of social rule: our makings succeed to the extent that we can and do conform to governing powers and the social necessities they produce. Social rule conceives power as a matter of will, more specifically, of willing what sovereignty would make us be.

By contrast, the power of entheos is generated through mutual promise in and by political bodies, that is, power appears as an effect of joint action. In this case, power is a matter of capacity and intimately bound to freedom as the potential to begin something new, as opposed to willing what already is. "I can," with others, found collective political bodies and, thereby, actively (freely) and deliberately (responsibly) participate in the political making of my own and others' individual bodies. Action forms power, both actualizing and redirecting it (OR, 176). For entheos, law is not a command but manifests a rapport between things, a relationship constituted through action (OR, 188–89). The enactment of principles can be contested by political bodies. Powerful principles do not come from above or elsewhere, but arise within and among us. As we shall see, these different foundations and representations of "common power" have consequences for our engagement of the often invisible governing powers that constitute our individual and collective bodies.

Like the founding of political power, the basis of political authority became a problem in the wake of the political death of God. Theorists and founders had sought an absolute source of law, whether divine or natural, that would bestow legality on posited, positive law. But God's Word had grown silent. Knowledge of good and evil became the product of human agreement. How can the legitimacy of law be assured without the sanction of religion? According to Tracy Strong, Hobbes's task is "to find an equivalent in the civil realm for Scripture and to guarantee the actuality of that authority in each member of the commonwealth." Scripture provided a paradigm case for the foundation of authority because in it Hobbes found "the written word of an author whose intentions could not be called into question" as long as the text was read and understood rationally. Hobbes's inspiration, Strong maintains, was the Lutheran understanding of the community of believers' relationship to Scripture as the written word of God. Hobbes sought to translate this early Protestant understanding into the basis of a political system resting on human equality and law. "The key lay in finding an equivalent in politics for Scripture, that is, a written document that, when taught, allowed each person severally access to the same authority without anyone ever being able to claim that he or she knew what the author intended." Hobbes's task was to "develop an authority that exists on and for this earth yet has no earthly author." According to Strong, *Leviathan* performs this task of writing an actual Scripture.[5]

Luther's notorious stance against the church at Wittenberg and later before the diet at Worms forcefully posed the problem of divergence between individual conscience and ecclesiastical authority. How could what an individual conscience found true be reconciled with the church's truth? Luther did not rely upon the extant authority of the church to decide the matter but sought to generate a new church consistent with the truth conscience found. The ultimate authority for any church, old or new, lay not in human power, however, but in the written word of God "made available" to humans in Scripture. By being written, Scripture was not subject to human authority but nonetheless "stood there and *required* understanding of each human subject" (Strong, 135). Holding forth conscience as the final arbiter of scriptural meaning, some thinkers concluded, would yield interpretive anarchy and, as a consequence, social and political disorder.

In response to this charge of fostering interpretive and social confusion, Luther (followed by Calvin) came upon an ingenious response. Strong puts it this way: "If human beings looked into their consciences honestly and deeply enough (we post-Kantians might say 'critically') when they read Scripture, they would find there an approach to the unrealizable truth of God" (136). The crucial matter is "what it means to read and find a text available." For the approach to God that the exchange between conscience and Scripture allows, Strong claims, is not a matter of interpretation. The text "requires" our understanding. If we approach it honestly, deeply, critically, we may be called to find something in our conscience that we have not seen before (137). The text produces this effect because it has no human author, or at least no discernible (visible) one. Scripture is revelation precisely because its author is hidden; it appears to come from elsewhere so that what we find in our conscience is apparently not of our own or others' making. Strong claims that the authority of a text whose author is hidden suggests to Hobbes a model for political authority. I think Strong is right. As the hiddenness of God sanctifies the word of Scripture, so too the invisibility of the popular authors of sovereignty sanctifies its political bodies.

Hobbes translates *nosce teipsum* ("know thyself") as "read thyself." This injunction begins his effort to constitute a sovereign authority for the body politic. "Reading oneself is Hobbes' model for knowledge—that is, having a text and finding that text in oneself, much as Luther held that the truth of the Scripture had to be found in oneself" (Strong, 143). But how do I find the text in myself and how do I know that you have found the same text within your self? How do we know that "we have thus found each other, that this text is the same authority and our common community" (Strong, 143–44)? Hobbes knows (and repeatedly reminds us) that the internal writing upon our hearts is difficult to read—passions and fancies are always getting in the way of rational reading of the text made available to us.[6] Just as the religious conscience needs written Scripture to find the way, so too political subjects need written laws. "Humans need external written laws, derived from a true reading of their hearts, in order to know what it is in their hearts to do" (Strong, 144).

How are these laws written and affirmed? How, according to (Strong's) Hobbes, does political authority work? "To have written (and thus shared) laws that would be read clearly by all, humans will first have to come together" (Strong, 144). More specifically, such significant speech begins with agreement on the correct definition of words. As Strong rightly emphasizes, in this formulation Hobbes mixes matters that we "moderns" typically believe are opposed (though, as Bruno Latour argues, we mix them all the time, even if we do not recognize it).[7]

> There is a definite sense that human agreement is a necessary and central part of the establishment of truth. In this sense we would say that [Hobbes] is a conventionalist, but he is also saying that human beings agree on *correct* definitions. In this sense he accepts the independent notion of truth and is an essentialist. He also indicates that the set of circumstances that permits arrival at correct definitions is itself God-given, and he thus appears as a theist of some kind. (Strong, 145)[8]

Strong notes the resonance between Hobbes' understanding and early Protestant views of how to read Scripture. In both cases, the truth of doctrine owes nothing to its antiquity; the truth rests on right rather than on "witnessing" or agreement in interpretation and opinion; and the availability and intentions of the author are of no significance for understanding the truth (148–49). In both cases, the author's indiscernibility authorizes the truth or right of doctrine. "For Protestants, the great advantage of the scriptural basis of authority is its apparent lack (or at least the unavailability) of an author. Hence it was authoritative precisely because it had no author" (Strong, 154). Likewise, Hobbes would have civil authority make itself available to humans without the quality of being authored.

We are not authors of the words we read or of the language we use, but we agree to them nonetheless. Wittgenstein helps clarify the claim: "True and false is what human beings say; and they agree in the language they use. This is not agreement in opinions but in form of life."[9] Like language, and as a product of language, "the public realm confronts us without *raising the question* of its authorization and authorship, its authority" (Strong, 155) because the sovereign body politic appears to be an authority without an apparent author. The body politic's sovereignty appears through an act of authorization made by each individual to the other, "from my ability to find myself in you, and you in me" (Strong, 157).

How do we find ourselves as one in the body of "the people"? Just as we submit to an authority to which we did not explicitly agree whenever we use language, so too it would seem that we cannot help but authorize this sovereign body. Popular authorization allegorized as covenant makes it "impossible for each individual ever to stop, of his or her own volition, authorization"; "the covenanting authorization is constant, cannot be recalled, and thus cannot be a problem" (Strong, 157).[10] Regardless, we are better for it since the definitions and truths to which we cannot help but subject our selves reflect what is written upon our hearts and enable us to know what it is in our hearts to do (Strong, 144). Sovereignty is the "Mortal God" (monotheos) through which we find our selves and the truths of our conscience. "The sovereign is our representative: our self represented to ourself. We are only free when we obey our self, and we are only able to do that if there is Leviathan" (Strong, 158). Sovereignty is a representative truth we take as authoritative and find written within ourselves and one another even though, indeed because, we (apparently) are not its author, and its author is not available to us. Hobbes's text, *Leviathan* is the Word, like the Protestant's Scripture, that enables us to read the truths written upon our hearts and soul which prove so difficult to read without the text's leadings.

It is in no small measure due to Hobbes's efforts that Strong can treat the Lutheran and Calvinist accounts of scriptural authority as the Protestant conception.[11] But from 1640, in fact, a good deal of controversy arose over the relationship between conscience and Scripture, the Spirit and the Word. To cast the contest as between papists and Protestants draws the field of the political too narrowly, and perhaps misses crucial aspects of Hobbes's concerns.[12] Hobbes's interest in distinguishing fancy or passion and reason has a correlate in debates *within* Protestantism or, more aptly, among "Puritans." The central question dividing orthodox Puritans from their enthusiast brethren was how to discern God's spirit. The orthodox response, following Luther and Calvin, was to cast scriptural word as the final arbiter. The enthusiasts' response, particularly the early Quakers, was to maintain a more fluid relationship between conscience and Scripture, Spirit and Word.

Orthodox and enthusiast Puritans shared much, particularly when compared to their "popish" opponents. Both invoked the authority of Scripture against religious and political authorities and shared a conviction that when they read Scripture something took place in their hearts and souls as well as in their heads. When Puritans read the Bible they felt the Holy Spirit at work within them, "illuminating what was written and enlightening their minds to understand it."[13] Reading Scripture made the Holy Spirit available to the reader, inscribing it upon their hearts and souls.

Nevertheless, discussion and controversy arose precisely around the issue of the work of the Holy Spirit within the believer. All agreed that the assistance of the Holy Spirit is necessary for the saving knowledge of Scripture: God's grace, not human work, saves. "But can the Spirit save, or even speak to, man apart from the Word of Scripture? or is the Spirit tied to Scripture? Is the Word to be interpreted by the Spirit? or should the Spirit's leadings, rather, be tested by the Word?" (Nuttall, 23). Generally, Puritans insisted upon the close conjunction of the Spirit and the Word. The Quakers were the first to disrupt this equilibrium. This disturbance was brought about in part by their devotion to Scripture and the seriousness with which they took it as a model for their own behavior. When early Quakers went through the streets naked or in sackcloth "as a sign," they were insisting that the same spirit that was in the prophets and in the writers of Scripture was in themselves (Nuttall, 26). To be sure, following Hobbes, it is easy to dismiss such beliefs and actions as madness.[14] But implicit in the Quaker's experience of the relationship between conscience and Scripture is an alternative understanding of political context and authority which cannot, or should not, be so readily dismissed. The political correlates of these different theological positions and religious practices affect whether and how we recognize, name, and engage invisible powers, whether our souls are corporeal or incorporeal.

From 1650 through the Restoration and the persecution of the Quakers for refusing to swear an oath to the Monarch/State, the question whether the Word is to be tried by the Spirit, or the Spirit by the Word, is a source of perpetual controversy (Nuttall, 28). The question turns upon whether the indwelling of the spirit is judged extraordinary or ordinary. In what measure Spirit or Word should be authoritative depends upon the prior question whether Spirit could exist in contemporaries as it had in the writers and actors of Scripture. In other words, are new revelations possible?

In the main, orthodox Puritans regarded the indwelling of the Spirit as extraordinary, while enthusiasts regarded it as ordinary because they felt it working within and among them. For orthodox Puritans, if the promptings of the Spirit conformed to Scripture, then one could feel some assurance of God's grace. For the Quakers, however, the "light within" channeled through "corporate witness," illuminating both text and action, was decisive (Nuttall, 45). "Friends . . . never stood for a bare individualist principle of the 'Inner Light': the Society . . . always existed 'to bear corporate witness to the principles and practices for which it stands'" (Nuttall, 46). The former view cultivated an individual conscience, the latter a collaborative one.

Difference of opinion between conservative and radical dissenters over the mode and manner of the Spirit's indwelling led to further differences in intellectual and practical spheres (Nuttall, 50). For those who regarded the indwelling of Spirit as ordinary, its presence often translated into immediate leadings and action. If all Puritans shared a certain skepticism toward university learning (prompted by the observed failings of clergy so educated) and extended an unprecedented tolerance toward lay preachers, orthodox and enthusiasts diverged when it came to disciplines of right reading, whether the relevant text was Scripture, oneself, or the body politic. To some extent, all Puritans believed that earnest dependence upon the Holy Spirit's assistance counted for more than education. But the Quakers took this premise to a logical (if perhaps extreme) conclusion. They did away altogether with a separate ministry, even recognizing women as legitimate preachers. Of course, some critics attacked them for contradicting Scripture—the leadings of their Spirit departed from the literal Word. George Fox and other Quaker leaders sought to justify their practice by reference to Scripture (a difficult task). Finally, however, they did not feel required by the political context to do so. In their eyes (at least initially), the principles founded in their practice and authorized by the "light within" them expressed the spirit, if not the letter, of the Word.

The controversy over the Spirit's indwelling—whether it was extraordinary and precluded new revelations or ordinary and thus prompted new actions—was a pivotal moment of contest between an individual and collaborative conscience. For the orthodox, individual conscience became primary, but its freedom required hierarchical orders to discipline reading and writing. Individual conscience submits to religious and political hierarchy and in the process becomes increasingly subjective, though it gains freedom by means of its subjection. From this perspective, not the actions, but the intentions of conscience are primary. For instance, Hobbes argues, if a sovereign commands disavowal of belief in Christ, such an act would belong to the sovereign, not to the person doing it (thus, no sin would have been committed, except by the sovereign). The Quaker's collective conscience—corporate witness enacted as a collaborative, interpretive activity—counseled against this orthodox distinction between doer and deed. Prior to their political subjection in return for religious toleration, the Quakers resisted the state in the name of their corporate conscience (not anarchy) and claimed the spirit (and authority) to constitute alternative political bodies and social orders.

In the end, the difference between orthodox and enthusiasts on the indwelling of the spirit comes down to the question of our role in the authority of what is written upon our hearts or souls, and whether or how we are enacters of the "invisible powers" that write it there. Strong's claim that, strictly speaking, we are not authors of the political contexts we read, whether our selves or the body politic, corresponds to the orthodox Puritan view of the relationship of the Spirit and the Word. Both evince corporeal imaginations of power. We are not authors of what we take to be authoritative, and the invisibility of its authors compels our affirmation of sovereignty. By contrast, the Quaker view of the relation between the Spirit and the Word seeks our role in the authority of these texts (which is *not* to say that the political contexts we read conform to our intentions or are mastered by our plans) and, thus, how we might become political, if not sovereign, actors in relation to them. From the perspective of an incorporeal imagination of power, we *are* actors in political contexts without authors and bodies politic without heads; the decisive matter is whether we are unwitting or thoughtful in relation to the invisible powers that constitute them.

Orthodox Puritans maintained that the Holy Spirit comes from above and only upon the converted and elect. The Quakers maintained that the Spirit is in everyman. Orthodox Puritans objected to the Quakers' claim because they thought it failed to grant sufficient importance to the reality of sin and the redemptive power found in God's grace alone. They suspected that the Quakers did not attribute enough importance to the singular appearance of Jesus as Christ, noting that the Quakers spoke allegorically and equivocally whenever they mentioned His name, often assuming Jesus' power and spirit as their own (Nuttall, 162). Moreover, the Quakers seemed to believe that they could do what the orthodox maintained only God could do, namely, recognize evil and forgive sins. For the orthodox, however, there was one founding moment, one finally redemptive revelation, one break between past and future, and they occurred elsewhere and in another time.

For the Quakers, however, revelation was a continual possibility. To act anew, to gain distance from ordinary concerns, and to transfigure everyday life were every man and woman's birthright. In fact, the integration of ecstasy and everyday life was the basis and goal of the Quakers' "practical mysticism."[15] Thought, word, and deed that open a gap between past and future are a perpetual prospect that, in George Fox's words, come with "the light that doth enlighten everyman that cometh into the World" (Nuttall, 161). The Quakers and other religious enthusiasts experienced a gap between past and future, a space for different thinking and new action. New thought and action that interrupt the continuity and process-character of history are like original revelations because they reveal something new—world and selves other than they have been made to be. Enthusiasts were profoundly conscious of change and discontinuity. They perceived that "they were living in an age altogether different from those which had gone before" (Nuttall, 104). They maintained that the kingdom of God was among them and that they, not God alone, had the power to forgive; indeed, if they were to receive God's forgiveness, they had to act.[16] Their experience of discontinuity fueled their sense of the need and possibility of "pressing on, through and beyond all outward and imprisoning forms" (Nuttall, 108). If, as Strong maintains, one loses one's self by failing to recognize and affirm sovereignty, this is exactly what the Quakers sought. They were seekers after something other than what governing powers made them to be.

The "light within" guided the early Quakers' seeking. In Part II I try to understand this light, and in Part III I explore its contemporary correlates and significance. But, I must acknowledge, to some degree this light must remain a mystery. For early Quakers the Holy Spirit was the source of this inner light and as such distinct from reason and conscience (though it might affect both). They emphasized the intuitive rather than the discursive side of reason, and believed the Holy Spirit enabled a spiritual perception analogous to the physical perception of the senses (Nuttall, 38). Thus, the inner light was thoroughly supernatural, unlike the light of conscience, nature, and reason. In Fox's thinking, orthodox Puritans' scriptural criterion for distinguishing spirit from fancy gave way to a Christocentric notion of light as the mediator between experience and intuitive reason (Nuttall, 39–40). What does the Holy Spirit as inner light reveal? It "shows a man evil."[17]

My emphasis on the importance of "invisible powers" to the productivity of individual and collective corporeal souls, their trespasses and ordered evil, casts contemporary power relations as spiritual matters, much as the early Quakers did. In the next section of this chapter I introduce what I explore in Part III: the importance of "spirit" in Arendt's and Foucault's resonant efforts to reveal the trespasses of ordinary life and the orders they constitute. Arendt and Foucault also reveal political thinking and action working upon the limits of our selves and our world; they hope to transgress these limits, to let the invisible, within and without us, unsettle the ordinariness of the visible. To be sure, Arendt and Foucault do not conceive the spirits they engage as divine. But like the Quakers' light within, their spirits do exceed any particular instantiation of individual conscience and reason. Arendt and Foucault find political possibility in what religious discourses meant by the powers they called spirit in the world and selves—and by spirit I mean the invisible within us which deals with the invisibles of the world (LM, 123). Political thinking and action unleash and enlist those aspects of experience that exceed governing forms of individual conscience and public reason. Spirited political thinking and action reveal, in the hope of overcoming, trespasses and acceding to different ways of being.

Contemporary spiritual matters

In each of his books, Foucault sought an experience of limits which might permit him, and us, to emerge transformed (RM, 34–36). What sort of experience do his last works afford? I will suggest that they may have an etho-poetic function, or enable us to question our own conduct, watch over and give shape to it, in order to constitute ourselves as ethical subjects (UP, 13). Our perceptions of experience assign meaning and value to individual conduct (UP, 4). Foucault's techniques of the self—critical ontology and arts of existence—are "spiritual" practices that seek to discern and transform the meaning, value, and effects of our conduct.[18]

Curiosity motivated Foucault's work on how individuals participate in their constitution as subjects, but curiosity of the sort "which enables one to get free of oneself" (UP, 8). Experiencing, and practicing freedom upon, the limits of the self are fundamentally ethical political impulses and enterprises. Both critical ontology and arts of existence have a role to play in this questioning. Each concerns one of the principal limits of our selves: the constitution of political bodies in both their individual and collective forms. On the one hand, critical ontology seeks to identify the contingency in what we take to be necessary to our selves; it problematizes how we are politically constituted as individual bodies. On the other hand, arts of existence comprise the collaborative practices we need if we are to recognize and transfigure those limits. We need others if we are to experience the limits of our own bodies/minds. We also need others to transform ourselves. Collaborative associations afford the conditions for self-transfiguration. Arts of existence are "those intentional and voluntary actions by which men not only set themselves rules of conduct, but also seek to transform themselves, to change themselves in their singular being, and to make their life into an oeuvre that carries certain aesthetic values and meets certain stylistic criteria" (UP, 10–11). Ascetic practice (*askēsis*) is the exercise of self in the activity of thought. Throughout his writings, Foucault sought to tell histories of his and our thinking in hopes of freeing thought from what it silently thinks and thus possibly enabling us to think differently (UP, 9). Thought working upon itself (critical ontology) may create the conditions for saying and doing differently (arts of existence).

Examining the conjunction of social rule and individual conduct is especially appropriate to the popularly authorized modern state because governance is carried out in the people's name by, through, and for their politically constituted bodies. To be sure, the opposite appears to be true; most everybody feels ruled by everybody else, or at least by somebody else. These impressions are characteristic of a political culture of resentment in which individuals are preoccupied with their own powerlessness and wounds rather than with the ways they exercise power and wound others.[19] In some respects, Foucault's middle works contributed to a politics of resentment, as he was interpreted in light of this predisposition. Interpreters hypostatized power as something that acts upon us, even as Foucault endeavored to articulate power as something of which we partake and in which we participate. The problematic of individual conduct represents a response to the limits of Foucault's middle works and enables him to more dramatically interrupt this cycle. His later writings concertedly engage how we can, or do, resist our constitution as subject-citizens. By focusing on individual conduct, Foucault endeavors to theorize the conditions and goals of this resistance and perhaps even to go beyond it to imagine and create new selves and practices of freedom.

How can subject-citizens become ethical political actors? The beginnings of Foucault's answer to this question can be discerned by attending to conceptual shifts between his middle and late writings. Foucault's last works conceptualize how subject-citizens participate in the political constitution of bodies/minds, thereby implicating them in forms of rule, not only of their selves, but also of others. By contrast, Foucault's middle works represented subjects as constituted in and through power-ladden schemes, which are socially produced but nonetheless exceed their individual control. This formulation may be right as far as it goes, but it obscures rather than illuminates the conundrums of political theodicy. Precisely what we need to discern is the active conjunction between individual agents and the governing powers that condition them to conceive how the freely subject produce social necessities.

The critical power of so-called moderns, Bruno Latour explains, lies in our deployment of a double language by which we are free to make and unmake our society even as we render its laws ineluctable, necessary, and absolute.[20] We observed a paradigmatic instance of this slippery process in Hobbes's mixture of conventionalism, essentialism, and political theism. Latour instructs us to imagine the intermediate space between society and nature, the human and nonhuman, where networks of power mix these binaries to produce everything as a hybrid. When we emphasize either side of these opposing terms, the processes that produce natural artifice and social facts become unthinkable. Extending Latour's suggestion, we might say that we shall never be able to conceive how necessities are socially produced unless we seek to trace the relationship between individual subject-citizens and the often invisible governing powers that constitute them. In political theological terms, thinking the invisible requires cultivating an incorporeal imagination of power and experimenting with the limits of our bodies/minds by recovering the transfigurative capacities of our "souls." On my reading, this is exactly what Foucault's late writings pursue.

The perspective of individual conduct reconfigures Foucault's previous problematics of knowledge/truth and power. Foucault had always claimed that power was not simply repressive but productive. Still, his middle works retained a fundamentally negative conception of power as imposed and inscribed, even as Foucault implied its incorporation. Sometimes he recurred to the language of domination even as he spoke of power's productivity and positivity. But in the late works, he explicitly distinguishes power and domination. Domination exists whenever a subject is so imposed upon as to be without freedom of movement or response (CSPF, 2–4). By contrast, situations of power consist of often assymetrical, but nonetheless mobile, contestable, relational effects. When we conceive power as *domination*, we tend to represent individuals as the targets of anonymous powers. By contrast, subjects of *power* authorize, carry, elaborate, and extend governing effects, if always within the constraints created by others' "free" exercise of power.

The later Foucault's explicit distinction between domination and power instigates a further differentiation between liberation and freedom. Like Arendt, Foucault maintains that liberation does not guarantee freedom (OR, 205; CSPF, 3). We must not only liberate ourselves from contingent necessities but also practice freedom. Politics requires the constitution of alternative orders in addition to disruptive action (OR, 223). Liberation depends upon and unleashes new relationships of power which, if liberation is to become freedom, must be deliberately directed by practices of liberty (CSPF, 4). On this understanding, freedom requires power and power is freedom. Arendt's and Foucault's common belief in the interdependence of freedom and power resonates with Montesquieu's understanding of *pouvoir*, according to which power is a matter of capacity. Relationships of power are always present in human interactions because human beings freely make their relationships, though others' free exercise of power means that we rarely do so wholly on our own terms (CSPF, 11). Freedom and power belong together because only "power arrests power." Freedom can be practiced only where we have the capacity to effectively act in the world (OR, 150–51). As Montesquieu maintained, we are free when we do not have to do what we should not and when we can do what we should.[21] For power to be free, not dominating, it must be deliberately efficacious.[22]

Both Foucault and Arendt disavow Habermas's and others' utopian imaginings of a society free of power (CSPF, 18). From the perspective of Foucault and Arendt, the vision of a society free of power is not simply unrealistic but mistaken in principle. Communicative ethicists might agree with the distinction between domination and power, while claiming that the difference is a semantic one: what Foucault and Arendt call power, they call communicative action. But this is not all there is to the difference. We cannot recognize states of domination in all their variety and near invisibility if we do not acknowledge also that the free exercise of power (or communicative action) has effects that constitute forms of rule which, at times, accumulate and solidify into states of domination. Between games of power and freedom on the one hand and states of domination on the other stand governmental technologies as ruling forms of rationality and power (CSPF, 18). Governing knowledges are not necessarily untrue or invalid because of their ties to ruling forms of power (CSPF, 16). Nonetheless, it is often by means of governing powers and knowledges that states of domination are maintained (CSPF, 19). Thus, the practice of freedom involves contesting the necessities of those techniques and the governing discourses that elaborate and extend them. Truth is not thereby renounced, but the dominion of one game of truth is challenged by recourse to another (CSPF, 15). The question becomes: What political ethos will enable games of truth and power to be practiced with minimal domination and maximal freedom (CSPF, 18)?

At times, however, Foucault seems to cede the critical ground gained by his distinctions between domination and power, liberation and freedom. For instance, Foucault assumes that free individuals try to control, determine, and limit the liberty (action and power) of others, and they deploy techniques of governance to do so (CSPF, 20). Furthermore, he claims, "governmentality" implies the relationship of "self to self" and captures the "totality of practices by which one can constitute, define, organize, instrumentalize the strategies which individuals in their liberty can have in regard to each other" (CSPF, 19). Foucault uses the concept of governmentality descriptively, whereas I have deployed the concept critically. I query the necessity of governance and the mentality that sustains it. The meaning Foucault ascribes to governmentality equates politics with governance, and the political with sovereignty, however paradoxical that may seem given his critique of sovereign theories of power. Moreover, and relatedly, Foucault's "technologies of the self" conceive ethics in terms of the self's relationship to itself, how it rules itself and, as a result, rules others.

By contrast, Arendt suggests a conception of the political which queries, contests, and transfigures the necessities of governance. She seeks to differentiate politics and ruling—terms that, following Hobbes, we may regard as roughly synonymous. For Arendt, and unlike Foucault, ruling is not equivalent to politics but rather evinces the sovereign mentality that would govern politics out of existence. Arendt's perspective helps us release Foucault's suggestive reflections upon domination and power, liberation and freedom, from their continued reliance upon a ruling framework and sovereign conception of the political.

According to Arendt's "genealogy," the equation of politics and governance sacrifices action to making, freedom to necessity. A will to sovereign mastery in the face of free actions' contingencies undergirds the presumption that rulership is inevitable. The human condition is characterized by the simultaneous presence of freedom and non-sovereignty: we are free to begin something new, but we are not able to control or even foretell its consequences (HC, 235). From a sovereign perspective, the unpredictability unleashed by the plurality of actors and the irreversibility of their actions are antithetical to freedom. Sovereign freedom conceives a political body, whether individual or collective, with complete dominion over itself. To secure such freedom, sovereignty seeks to unify—and as a consequence often obliterates—plurality, much as Hobbes's mathematical reasoning displaces sense by abstraction to make a multitude one body. "If it were true that sovereignty and freedom are the same, then indeed no man could be free, because sovereignty, the ideal of uncompromising self-sufficiency and mastership, is contradictory to the very condition of plurality. . . .[I]f this attempt to overcome the consequences of plurality were successful, the result would be not so much sovereign domination of one's self as arbitrary domination of all others" (HC, 234). From a sovereign perspective, mastery over oneself and others is the only way to bear the contingencies of action.

When action is sacrificed to making, two elements that coexist in free action are disjoined. Though individual initiative usually incites action, an event emerges or fails as a consequence of others' efforts. The collaborative conditions of action are a principal source of action's unpredictability and irreversibility. Governance masters the contingencies of action by making its subjects predictable. When making displaces action, however, beginning and achieving, knowing and doing, are bifurcated. This disjuncture is evinced in the distinction between the ruler (the one who begins, knows, and commands) and the ruled (the one who carries out, does, and obeys). But the inevitability of ruling depends upon the prior assumption that one is free only when sovereign. A disjuncture between will and capacity is folded into the center of sovereign politics, as beginning is separated from achieving and knowing from doing. Again, however, the presumption that ruling is inevitable and the disjunctures that follow from it depend upon the prior assumption that one is "free" only when "sovereign."

Arendt associates a sovereign perspective on political action with a philosophical ethos that seeks to liberate the self by resisting a political world and by mastering itself. From this perspective, ethics is a ruling relation primarily toward the self and secondarily toward others. When ethics is conceived as a matter of self-rule, in Arendt's view, the political has been equated with sovereignty, politics with governance. In that case, ethics concerns how we rule our selves and others; it seeks what is proper and appropriate in ruling. The inevitability of rulership comes from equating freedom with sovereignty which, in turn, undergirds the equation of politics and governance. These presumptions, Arendt maintains, result in a conception of ethics as a matter of relationship between me and myself. This conception of ethics resists (or ignores), rather than politically engages, the limits of selves. The result is the pursuit, if finally vain, of dominion over self, world, and others, on the one hand, and the inability to engage the actualities of the world, on the other.

In Arendt's view, the "ruling and being ruled" typical of making, and which likewise inform modern understandings of politics to the extent that we confuse it with governance and its powers, are antipolitical because they allow neither freedom nor political action (HC, 220–30). The ascriptive labels "public" or "private" are not decisive for whether our relations are political. Rather, our relations are political when we seek to fathom and acknowledge our effects on one another and open them to specifically political action. Politics is not so much a realm or sphere we enter as it is a form of relation we undertake. Political spaces do not simply reveal or provide a means of furthering our will to make ourselves and our world. Rather, in political spaces we encounter others who call our power effects to our attention, and we may do likewise. Ethics oriented toward political action, rather than ruling, looks to and depends upon others even as it works upon the self. We constitute political relations and create the possibility of political commonality when we think together about the ruling, necessity, and violence that dwell in all "making," whether they become manifest in individual acts, social behavior, or governance. When we associate politically, we thoughtfully redirect the invisible powers that make us what we are.

Foucault's definition of ethics as an arena of freedom and power would seem to affirm Arendt's political aspiration: he seeks an ethos that will allow games of power and truth to proceed with minimal domination and maximal freedom. Nevertheless, he recurs to the language of governance even as he acknowledges that its techniques are often the very means by which relations of power are transformed into states of domination. Foucault's imagination of the political offers insight into his ambiguity and ambivalence on this point. He proffers the concept of governmentality because, he claims, analyzing power from the perspective of political institutions leads one to a juridical conception of the political subject and a disregard of ethical questions. Governmentality allows one "to set off the freedom of the subject and the relationship to others, i.e., that which constitutes the very matter of ethics" (CSPF, 20).

Foucault's formulation is mistaken on two counts, however. First, Arendt enables us to see that politics and the political need not necessarily be equivalent to sovereignty and its juridical conception of the subject. Second, to equate the political with governance is not to approach the ethical but to elide it, at least in contexts of ordered evil. In such contexts, the ethical political question is not how to rule oneself and others—the aspiration to sovereign mastery and social rule—but how to regard social rules so as to create space for political thinking and action as practices of freedom. We can agree with Foucault (contrary to one reading of Arendt) that political action cannot altogether leave social rule behind. Nonetheless, for a nonsovereign conception of the political, ruling is not a solution, but ruling must never cease to be questioned, contested, and transfigured. To the extent that the political is imagined as sovereign monotheos (for which power is a matter of will and law a coded-command), we may fail to deliberately actualize the relationship between power and freedom. Free and responsible action requires an enthusiastic imagination of the political for which power is a matter of capacity and the law of moral codes a provocation to politics as an art of ethical relations.

Not without reason, Foucault avoids the question of the contemporary political conditions of critical attitudes toward what we are thinking, saying, and doing. Can such critique and effective self-transfiguration simply be an individual ascetic practice or aesthetic performance? Arendt's writings suggest not. Arendt intuits a connection between reflective capacities and political possibilities. On my understanding, Arendt suggests that thinking, or thoughtlessness, are conditioned by the configuration, or absence, of political spaces, by the availability and quality of specifically political power. Thinking needs a plurality of perspectives, and such plurality only takes effect in spaces convened by collaborative (not sovereign) "common power." What is more, political commonality and plurality are mutually dependent. Whatever assails the possibility of political commonality menaces a plurality of perspectives, and vice versa. This conviction explains Arendt's high regard for politics and the political, which stands in stark contrast to Foucault's suspicion of them. He, like most contemporary thinkers, confounds political commonality with sovereignty, politics with governance. This is Hobbes's legacy. But for Arendt, sovereign unity (whether individual or collective) is antithetical to specifically political relations, and ruling is an antipolitical manner of conduct which obviates ethical relations. The rule of sovereign unity is the product of "making." One could say that a unified, sovereign people is a massive, collective trespass.

From the perspective afforded by Arendt's writings, the care of self Foucault elaborates is not a manifestation of governmentality but a challenge to it. And the challenge is not mounted by individuality alone; Foucault himself suggests as much. For example, care for self is a way of caring for others even as that care brings benefits to the self (CSPF, 7). Following his classical sources, Foucault does often speak of such care in terms of *ruling* oneself and others, but specifically democratic practices of the self would seek to transfigure the ways one is ruled and rules others. This is the *political* practice of freedom. In my view, this reading is consistent with Foucault's spirit, if not always with his word. At one point, Foucault characterizes his work as a history which seeks to problematize governance as "a kind of permanent oppression in daily life . . . put into effect by the state or by other institutions and oppressive groups" (RM, 144). His work identifies, contributes, and responds to a "crisis in governance," to people's feelings of discomfort, difficulty, and impatience with the ways they are "led" (RM, 176–77). Foucault himself sought to practice freedom in relation to the ruling role governmentality afforded him, evinced by his conception of the relationship of theory and intellectuals to the powers and decisions of ordinary people. Although he seeks to work inside the body of society, he disavows the role of spokesman (RM, 159–60): "The masses have come of age, politically and morally. They are the ones who've got to choose individually and collectively. What counts is saying how a certain regime functions, in what it consists, so as to prevent an entire series of manipulations and mystifications. But the masses have to make the choice" (RM, 172).

When asked whether "care for self, thinking of itself, thinks of others?" Foucault replies, "Yes, absolutely" (CSPF, 8–9). Our practice of freedom not only affects our own relation to social rule but also how we are implicated in the governance of others. Historically, practices of the self have not been exclusively solitary; they are social practices that often result in an "intensification of social relations" and "a shared experience" from which each derives a benefit for himself (CS, 53). Problematization, not governance and normalization, intensify relations by presupposing and actualizing their "openness" (UP, 197).[23] "Open" relations constitute spaces of freedom where social relations are not necessarily predictable, certain, or already decided but a matter of deliberate choice. By contrast, relations of normalization are reified and grow stale and stagnant by virtue of our calculability in conformity with social rules. Care of self seeks a "conversion of power," a way of controlling and limiting it (CSPF, 7–8), which, in turn, entails a change in activity (CS, 65). Critical ontology enables us to identify the contingent necessities of our selves, thereby opening a space for arts of existence which transfigure—deliberately control and delimit—how we are ruled and rule others.

As I suggest in Part III, ethical self-constitution depends upon acceding to ways of being which enable us to create a deliberate form and particular style to our exercise of power. But where is such transfiguration pursued and what does it entail? What does Arendt mean when she speaks of the non-sovereign political? In the *Human Condition*, Arendt speaks of political spaces in terms of "the public realm" and "the common." I prefer to speak of politically constituted commonality. Politically constituted commonality is distinct from an ontologically common sense of the world, a public sphere oriented toward agreement (either as actuality or regulative ideal), and a sovereign unity or community. Politically constituted commonality is the conception of the political constituted by organized multitudes. Political enactment of the interdependence of commonality and plurality distinguishes politically constituted commonality from what it is not.

According to Arendt, contact between human beings facilitates the appearance of both commonality and plurality. Spaces where people speak and act politically together engender and sustain whatever perception of commonality we achieve (HC, 50, 52–53). Political commonality, in turn, facilitates recognition of our distinctness from other persons and the revelation of individual uniqueness or "natality" (HC, 49, 175–76, 178). Furthermore, politically constituted commonality creates boundaries that relate and separate myself and others (HC, 52). If political commonality is absent or unimaginable, then not only what we might share with others but also what distinguishes us from them—our distinctive bodies/minds and perspectives—become precarious (HC, 57–58, 199). Whatever assails the possibility of political commonality menaces plurality and vice versa. This is Arendt's view of our greatest threat, for "mass society not only destroys the public realm but the private as well, deprives men not only of their place in the world but of their private home" (HC, 59). Premonitions of this theoretical claim are evident in *The Origins of Totalitarianism*, where Arendt suggests connections between the destruction of political bodies and private homes (OT, 135–47, 351–52). Politically constituted commonality ends when the world "is seen only under one aspect and is permitted to present itself in only one perspective" (HC, 58, 39, 220). If political constitution is absent, or its processes invisible, both commonality and plurality are in danger.

What does Arendt mean by commonality and plurality? "For us, appearance—something that is being seen and heard by others as well as by ourselves—*constitutes reality*" (HC, 50, my emphasis). Others who see what we see and hear what we hear assure us of the reality of our world and ourselves. Here Arendt often has been taken to mean that there is an ontologically common world, but without the benefit of others' perspectives we do not have a certain, common sense of it. I think, however, that Arendt means "constitutes reality" in a stronger sense, namely, that what is common is "made," with all the violation and trespass it implies. A "common world" emerges through the fabrication of human hands and as a consequence of the affairs that go on among humans in relation to that human-made world (HC, 52). How can such a world be lost? More precisely, what does Arendt mean when she says that in mass society, characterized by the rule of the social, "the world between them has lost its power to gather them together, to relate and to separate them" (HC, 53)? Does Arendt mean that we once possessed an ontologically common sense of the world which now we have lost and for which she nostalgically mourns? Does she attribute the destruction of private homes and collective political bodies to ontological homelessness? Are Arendt's principal concerns anomie and loss of community? I do not think so, and I see some harm in reading her that way. Instead, I think Arendt means that the political constitution of a common world becomes invisible.[24] The fabricated world gathers us together, but it no longer separates us, that is, we do not discern the trespasses in the creation of boundaries and connections. Similarly, we are overcome by perception of the fabricated world's necessity and have no sense of the possibilities for free action within it. Politically constituted commonality responds to the trespasses inherent in the making of a common sense of the world. To lose a politically constituted world is to cease to answer, talk back, and measure up to the effects of our participant role in the making of a world (HC, 26). Here we approach the meaning of political action for Arendt.

Social rule constitutes "objective" common denominators for measuring and moderating relations among humans and the world they fabricate. By contrast, "the reality of the public realm" appears through "*innumerable* perspectives and aspects" with "no common measurement or denominator" (HC, 57). To bolster my reading of Arendt's "common world" as politically constituted, I emphasize innumerable perspectives in the absence of common measure. But Arendt, too, emphasizes a "reality rising out of the sum total of aspects presented by one object to a multitude of spectators" so that "they see *sameness* in utter diversity." Is there not a "worldly reality [that] truly and reliably appear[s]" to all (HC, 57)? The question is not a matter of metaphysical realism or antirealism but concerns whether even innumerable perspectives have the same sense of a common object. Arendt says that a "common nature" does not guarantee the perception of commonality. "If the sameness of the object can no longer be discerned, no common nature of men, least of all the unnatural conformism of mass society, can prevent the destruction of the common world" (HC, 58). Since the perception of commonality can be lost, it is not a common object but political constitution that creates this sense of reality. To see why this is the case we must first understand why Arendt thinks the indiscernibility of a common object "is usually preceded by the destruction of the many aspects in which it presents itself to human plurality" (HC, 58).

Because plurality as "the condition of human action" is the basis of a "common world," its absence signifies such a world's decline (HC, 50). Politically constituted commonality evinces the coexistence of multiple perspectives and meanings amid commonality. Both plurality and commonality are required if the perception of a "common world" and the political spaces that sustain it are to emerge, because multiple and diverse perspectives together create and hold that world. But what is plurality? whence does it come? What is its substantive content? "Plurality is the condition of human action because we are all the same, that is, human, in such a way that nobody is ever the same as anyone else who ever lived, lives, or will live."[25] Arendt uses plurality in one of two ways. Sometimes plurality appears to mean only "more than one," "that men, not Man, live on the earth and inhabit the world" (HC, 7). At other times, plurality seems to connote diversity as well, for example, in the different perspectives that together constitute a political space. A "common world" is the meeting ground of all. But we each have our different locations in the world, and we each see, hear, and act from those different locations (HC, 57). The significance of different locations must be more than their demonstration (through the existence of multiple places) that there are many rather than one. Different locations provide the substance of different perspectives on a common thing. In political spaces, we come together in speech and action, and our distinctness, our multiplicity *and* diversity, are confirmed by, and in contrast to, others' perspectives and those aspects of the world which they make appear (and disappear). In Arendt's view, the perception and actuality of commonality is impossible if plurality, and the innumerable perspectives it represents, is absent or inconceivable.

Arendt is notorious for advocating a hard and fast boundary between matters "public" and "private" (HC, 22–73, 192–220) in the interest of preserving the distinctness of political commonality from "biological sameness." Through political action, we leave behind, or silence for a glorious moment, the necessities of "biological life process" or what we are for freedom in the public world. But the absolute boundary Arendt would draw between public and private matters, between what and who we are, is eroded by her own insistence on the intrinsic import of plurality for the actuation of political commonality. Plurality is indispensable to the emergence of specifically political spaces, and the contour and character of our locations begin plurality's content. Though contrary to some of her most explicit views, Arendt's emphasis on plurality suggests that one's private location and body (what one is) weigh upon who one is revealed to be in political spaces.

Discerning what we appear to be, experiencing the limits of our bodies/minds, is therefore not irrelevant to, but a prerequisite of, political deliberation and action. Although political spaces constitute commonality, we each have our different locations in the world, and our views are a mixture of who we are as revealed in such spaces and the distinct locations that condition what we appear to be. Thus different locations afford differentiating perspectives on a common thing (HC, 57), and politically constituted commonality enables this plurality to appear. The means by which each body/mind is made and, in turn, affected by others' bodies/minds affords each body/mind some of its specific character and commences its differentiating perspective on the world. Histories of our bodies/minds may offer a critical purchase on Arendt's undifferentiated "mass society" and thereby facilitate the appearance of a plurality of perspectives.

Without thinking about and being responsive to such particularities, we lack the basis for a differentiating perspective, one among the many Arendt says are required to constitute political commonality (HC, 58–

65). Likewise, when political spaces are absent, the distinct perspectives our locations allow become indiscernible, and, again, both plurality and commonality are at risk and with them our political agency and the capacity to thoughtfully effect the conditions of our lives. Absent political commonality and the plurality of perspectives accompanying our different locations, we may lose our world, figuratively and literally (OT, 135–47, 269–302, 460–79; HC, 57–61, 208–9).

The distinctions between necessity and freedom, making and political action, are crucial to Arendt's political understanding and turn upon the degree of articulation in the latter term of each pair. Freedom and political action define spaces where we answer, talk back, and measure up to what has happened or what we have done, the effects of our location in the world (HC, 26). Necessity and making define relations that are leveling, forceful, and unresponsive. When necessity and making reign, as they typically do in the daily (nonpolitical) fabricating of our locations, we simply have effects upon others and receive their effects upon us; neither we nor they are called to answer for those effects. Power is exercised thoughtlessly. Combative rather than collaborative action prevails. Political spaces, however, do not simply reveal or provide a means of furthering our social rule and roles; rather, in them we encounter others who call how we bear its effects to our attention, and we may do likewise. We constitute political relations and create the possibility of political commonality when we think together about the ruling and necessity, compulsion and violation, inherent in all making, whether they become manifest in individual acts, social behavior, or governance. Indeed, if we do not respond to the trespasses of social rule, spaces of cooperative action are undermined and then destroyed by thoughtlessness. In political spaces, we have the opportunity to discern and answer for our effects and, at least potentially, to transfigure them by means of the political power generated when we act in concert.

Trespasses arise as we pursue our felicity; they are effects of our body/mind's ways of being in the world. Sometimes we retrace old wounds, at other times we trespass anew. Each individual is a multiplicity born of convention and artifice. By actuating spaces for ourselves, we contest others' understandings and makings, and we remold or destroy them altogether. As a result, and with our aid, the world accommodates some persons and projects while it resists others. Sedimented social patterns condition our bodies/minds and the identities they foster. We are neither responsible for, nor can we substantially change, *what* we are—how and what we have been made to be by history, institutions, and patterns of social rule preceding us for which no one person alone is responsible. In my view, however, we may become responsible for *who* we are—for how we carry and pass on the social effects configuring what we appear to be.

What we are represents all that appears to be given or beyond the reach of our agency, while who we are is revealed through our words and deeds. In the end, what we are cannot be known, and therefore the relationship between it and who we are is contingent, changing, and, finally, simply an analytic distinction.[26] Race and gender, for example, are usually regarded as aspects of what we are, but their meaning and significance changes depending on who we are, upon how we convey the social effects they generate. By transfiguring who we are, we may overcome (though not transcend) the trespasses embedded in our ways of living and the resentments they rouse.

PART II

A GENEALOGY OF THE MODERN SUBJECT-CITIZEN

The first part of my story is complete. I hope my sketch of the contemporary imagination of power has enabled us to feel anew our ethical and political predicaments as subject-citizens of a headless body politic. Now I wish to turn, in some detail, to controversies of the seventeenth and eighteenth centuries. Why? Of what relevance are the practices and persecution of religious enthusiasts in seventeenth-century England, and the founding of America in the eighteenth century, to the ethical and political crises of contemporary subject-citizens?[1]

In the political theological contests of the seventeenth and eighteenth centuries, we witness particularly graphic displays of the development and workings of the political forms and governing powers that tie the individual to the sovereign state as a social totality and, thereby, embed and implicate us in its rule. These forms and powers produce ordered evil; obscure even as they further, the functioning of social rule; and frustrate efforts to respond, freely and responsibly, to it. More specifically, for the early Quakers, enthusiasm for invisible powers inspired disruptions of sovereign social rule, until their conscience became relatively privatized and individualized. The Quakers' fate may help us understand why enthusiasm for invisible powers in American political culture more frequently serves than contests its national(ist) projects.[2]

The genealogy of the modern political subject I proffer may not only show us how this conversion of enthusiasm came to be, but also enable the recovery of suppressed alternatives that prove suggestive for facing contemporary ethical political dilemmas. In fact, I find resonances of the early Quakers' enthusiastic practices in the writings of Arendt and the later Foucault. Exploring the beginnings of these reverberations prepares us to think anew about living ethically and acting politically.

CHAPTER 4

The Politics of Conscience

Then the eyes of the spirit would become one with the eyes of the body, and god would be in us, not outside. God in us: entheos: enthusiasm; this is the essence of holy madness.

Norman O. Brown, *Apocalypse and/or Metamorphosis*

Any modern imprecation against Christianity—up to and including Nietzsche's—is an imprecation against forgiveness. Such "forgiveness," however, understood as connivance with degradation, moral softening, and refusal of power is perhaps only the image one has of decadent Christianity. On the other hand, the solemnity of forgiveness—as it functions in theological tradition and as it is rehabilitated in aesthetic experience, which identifies with abjection in order to traverse it, name it, expend it—is inherent in the economy of psychic rebirth . . . is a powerful fight against paranoia, which is hostile to forgiveness.

Julia Kristeva, *Black Sun*

Hobbes's widely shared judgment of religious enthusiasts institutes the predominant modern, sovereign conception of the political.[1] At stake in Hobbes's representations of the advocates of conscience is the theoretical and political question of whether or not a "multitude," holding a diversity of perspectives and opinions, can generate political power and act constructively (L, 8:140–41; L, 16:220–21).[2] Can individual and collective political bodies be constituted through collaborative rather than sovereign power? Hobbes's negative answer to this question constitutes a founding moment for his, and our, scientific politics. I read religious enthusiasts' collaborative practices of conscience to query the necessities of a sovereign body politic ruled by governing powers and knowledges. Hobbes and religious enthusiasts offer competing responses to the political death of God and the dubious foundations of modern governance that follow in its wake. Religious enthusiasts struggled to politicize conscience, and their efforts to constitute a politics of opinion are neglected resources for conceiving democratic politics.[3]

What is to be gained by telling this story of religious enthusiasm? Doesn't it necessarily have a certain fictional quality? A relationship exists between the experience I hope my story will induce and the experiences about which I tell. *Limit-experiences* enable a subject to become other than herself by dissociating a subjection given to the self. On my reading, many religious enthusiasts (the early Quakers in particular) were seekers after just such experiences. They sought to transfigure socially constituted selves and thereby to transform relations of power among subjects. Their experience of invisible powers not only within but also among them, inspired their political enthusiasm for the transfiguration of bodies/minds. One of Hobbes's principal objectives and accomplishments is to cast doubt upon the possibility of subject-citizens thinking, saying, and doing other than they are made to think, say, and do. He seeks to render such projects fictional, the ambition of absurd and seditious imaginations, and subjects of "eloquence without wisdom."

There is some truth to Hobbes's claim that transfigurative experiences are always fanciful or fictional. Such telling fictions, strictly speaking, may not be true, but they nonetheless may attain a certain reality by virtue of the experience they allow us to have. Limit-experiences may assume political significance, especially when they are linked to collective practices and ways of thinking (RM, 36–40). Given the spirited and spiritual milieu in which the story of this chapter unfolds, we might say that Foucault is an inspiration. The games of truth and fiction he plays enable us to see our modernity anew while at the same time experiencing its possible transformation.

The mad anarchy of Medea

John Aubrey tells us that before departing for Oxford, Hobbes presented his high school teacher with a gift of Euripides' *Medea* translated from Greek into Latin iambics.[4] The drama and the story which informed it must have made quite an impression on Hobbes, for Medea is a prominent figure in his accounts of the internal causes tending toward the dissolution of commonwealths. In *Elements of Law*, *De Cive*, and *Leviathan*, Hobbes criticizes the eloquence that, like Medea's witchcraft, leads the untutored to hope for political change and to pursue actions that bring disorder and ruin upon the commonwealth. Eloquence without wisdom, which the frenzied woman Medea symbolizes, defines sedition for Hobbes (EL, 2.8.13:175).

In *Medea*, Euripides creates a world much like Hobbes's state of nature where promises are meaningless and forgiveness impossible because people care and do only for themselves. All relationships are instrumental, as each person calculates his or her own good. Such ruthless, unchecked utilitarianism breeds disorder, but only after it has trampled every effort to act from principle or with mercy. The drama is framed by Medea's infamous deeds. A "barbarian" princess and sorceress, Medea murdered and dismembered her brother to aid Jason, with whom she had fallen in love. Scattering her brother's remains across the water, she turned her father's reverence for the dead and their rightful burial to her advantage, delaying his pursuit and securing her escape with Jason. In a later episode, which Hobbes recounts, Medea persuades King Pelias's daughters to cut up their father as a prelude to a magical rejuvenation; again, she hopes to advance Jason's interests. But the hoax that leaves the daughters with their father's blood on their hands backfires, for Jason does not benefit but is exiled with Medea. Jason's later efforts to break his dependence on Medea's witchcraft are to no avail. Her powers, once deployed for his benefit, are turned against him as she murders Creon, Creon's daughter, and Jason and Medea's own children.

Medea is a tragic figure because she does not disavow her deeds or evade accountability for them; she herself, not evil spirits, does the harm. Euripides, E. R. Dodds writes, "shows us men and women nakedly confronting the mystery of evil, no longer as an alien thing assailing their reason from without, but as part of their own being." Speaking specifically of *Medea*, Dodds presents her case as typical, "there is a civil war in every human heart."[5] Medea's deeds may be wicked, but their sources and objects are common and ordinary.

In *Elements of Law* and *De Cive*, Hobbes employs a story about Medea to convey the disorder and ruin that follow the ascendance of seditious, if eloquent, opinion over governing truths. Not all eloquence is subversive, however, for "eloquence is twofold." No doubt Hobbes would judge his writings eloquent linguistic artifices built out of the right apprehension of words. As such they are "an elegant and clear expression of the conceptions of the mind; and riseth partly from the contemplation of the things themselves, partly from an understanding of words taken in their own proper and definite signification." But eloquence also can be, like Medea's witchcraft, "a commotion of passions of the mind." Such speech may be vividly expressive, stirring passions such as hope, fear, anger, and pity, but it is derived from "a metaphorical use of words fitted to the passions" and is thus unwise. The first kind of eloquence forms its speech from true principles and by the art of logic. The latter simply expresses opinion; its art is rhetoric. The end of the first is truth while the latter's goal is victory (DC, 12.12:253). The distinction between opinion and knowledge sets off what is seditious from what is not. "Powerful eloquence, separated from the true knowledge of things," is characteristic of those "who solicit and stir up the people to innovations" and rebellion. In them, "folly and eloquence concur in the subversion of government, in the same manner (as the fable hath it) as to heretofore the daughters of Pelias . . . conspired with Medea against their father." The common people, "through their folly, like the daughters of Pelias, desiring to renew the ancient government," are drawn away by the "eloquence of ambitious men, as it were by the witchcraft of Medea," and are divided into factions and riven by divisions, which consume rather than reform the commonwealth by their flames (DC, 12.13:255).

In *Elements of Law* and *De Cive*, Hobbes counts as foremost among the beliefs fostering seditious arts and leading to the ruin of governments the notion "that the knowledge of good and evil belongs to each single man." Indeed, the state of nature is characterized by the reign of private opinion "where every man lives by equal right, and has not by mutual compacts submitted to the command of others" (DC, 12.1:244, 247, 249). If we are to manage the perpetual struggle our contentious opinions and makings forebode, we must submit our will and judgment to a sovereign entity we authorize. Hobbes's uneasy yet productive mixture of essentialism, conventionalism, and political theism cultivates a skepticism that is deep yet conducive to governance.[6]

Hobbes's skeptical teaching cultivates our recognition of the tension between civil law and conscience, and the wisdom of deferring to public reason when we feel this war within ourselves. From Hobbes's perspective, religious enthusiasts are troubled in mind (mad) and cause trouble (anarchy) because they grant too much credence to their conscience. Privately judging good and evil, they derogate public reason and undermine civil law. The failure to recognize the potent truth of governance attests to the ignorance and folly of those who employ Medea's craft. Governing powers are sanctified by popularly authorized extant laws that express the truth (knowledge of good and evil) produced by these powers. Those who use Medea's gifts, by contrast, have the audacity to arrogate truth-creating powers to themselves.[7] They do so not by the eloquence "which explains things as they are, but from that other, which by moving . . . minds, makes all things appear to be such as they in their minds, prepared before, had already conceived them." Seditious rhetoricians use language to suggest that we can become other than we are rather than to affirm what selves and world are made to be. They act as if minds can move and change bodies as in the "magical rejuvenation" the daughters of Pelias pursued. By this use of language they so bewitch their listeners that "they can make things to them who are ill-affected seem worse, to them who are well-affected seem evil," all the while passing off their opinion as if it were based on knowledge and expressive of truth (DC, 12.12:254).

The seditious, Hobbes maintains, are unwise or without knowledge in two respects. First, they are imprudent, for history teaches that they are unlikely to succeed: among the "movers and authors of sedition . . . for one man that hath thereby advanced himself to honour, twenty have come to reproachful end" (EL, 2.8.13:176). And they are foolhardy (which is why they usually fail), for in desiring change they contradict the truth and, moreover, undermine the sovereignty that determines and secures that truth. Indeed, their audacity embroils the seditious in a performative contradiction. The private language they use, whether to affirm or contest good and evil, denies and thereby destroys the rational and institutional basis for defining and knowing good and evil. Thus, lack of methodical knowledge is the second respect in which the seditious are unwise. When they read their souls they find written their own arbitrary opinion, not public reason (EL, 2.8.13:176). The "pretence of right" to rebellion originates in the failure to deposit one's judgment in all controversies in the hands of the sovereignty (EL, 2.8.5:171). The "eloquent unwise" fail to become subjects of public reason's sovereignty, and yet, Hobbes says, social order and knowledge of good and evil necessarily depend upon our becoming subject(s).

In *Leviathan*, Hobbes's discussion of Medea highlights one aspect of his earlier works, namely, the naive desire for change, the inevitable effect of which is the commonwealth's dissolution. Desire for change is naive from the perspective of Hobbes's skeptical disavowal of our ability to know and change our fate and the invisible powers that make it. Pelias's daughters are not only mistaken in their methods but foolish in their desire. Only the mad believe in the magical rejuvenation (or transfiguration) of bodies/minds. This is Hobbes's judgment of all spirited reformers of rules. Self-proclaimed definers of the Word and their followers "that go about by disobedience, to doe no more than reforme the Common-wealth, shall find they do thereby destroy it" (L, 30:380). The incorporeal imagination of the seditious would have its spirit try the word rather than being reformed by it. It would write its own political scripture rather than become subject before the sovereign political that is Hobbes's scripture.

"Anxiety for the future time, disposeth men to enquire into the causes of things" so that they may "order the present to their best advantage." We may follow "ambitious men" who claim to possess such truths or, even more audaciously, imagine that we possess such truths ourselves. Since all inquiry into the natural causes of things tends to lead to the conviction that there is "one God Eternall," some persons claim knowledge of God and thereby seek to justify their actions. But this avowal is only a sign of their ignorance of natural causes, for God cannot be known: "And they that make little, or no enquiry into the naturall causes of things, yet from the feare that proceeds from the ignorance it selfe, of what it is that hath the power to do them much good or harm, are enclined to suppose, and feign unto themselves, severall kinds of Powers Invisible; and to stand in awe of their own imaginations" (L, 11:167–68).

In Hobbes's view, discourses about invisible powers are epistemologically unwarranted claims to divine inspiration. The seditious feign inspiration by claiming knowledge of incorporeal substances and access to the vision and power they hold. Attributing such powers to themselves, they conjure enemies to be vanquished and withdraw their will and judgment from sovereignty: "Though the effect of folly, in them that are possessed of an opinion of being inspired, be not visible alwayes in one man, by any very extravagant action, that proceedeth from such Passion; yet when many of them conspire together, the Rage of the whole multitude is visible enough" (L, 8:140).

Seditious persons give the name of conscience to their own "secret facts and secret thoughts" (L, 7:132). They believe they are inspired by God, that what they see and know has been conveyed by invisible powers. They feel themselves possessed by good spirits while throughout the commonwealth they see the workings of evil spirits and powers. But where enthusiasts of the spirit see patterns to power and its abuse, Hobbes finds imaginations gone awry. What men and women call spirit is actually a projection of their own passions, for "Madnesse is nothing else, but too much appearing Passion" and "the Passions unguided" (L, 8:141–42). Persons feel and see spirits because they fail to reason the necessities of social cause and effect (L, 8:144). They speak of incorporeal substances when they lack the fortitude or ability to seek a cause through "natural" (for Hobbes, publicly constituted) reasoning. Having a false opinion concerning the force of their imaginations, seditious persons see patterns and pathologies of power. Seeking to act on this basis, they prove their madness. Challenging the governing truths of sovereignty, contesting its ends or seeking to incorporate political power for their own purposes, unauthorized multitudes destroy the basis of civil society and return everything to confusion. Their "performance" contradicts the basis of their selves and world.[8]

For some time, persons' imaginations were subject to the fanciful demonologies of their rulers (L, 45:657–81). Immaterial spirits, the products of other men's imaginations, were generated principally as instruments for ruling them (L, 11:168). Against this backdrop, Hobbes emerges as a radical liberator, casting out demons, demystifying superstitious images. Hobbes unveils the power behind the throne where faith and belief are placed, showing them to be tools for obtaining submission to mere human authority. Our belief and faith estrange us from our power "from whence we may inferre, that when wee believe any saying whatsoever it be, to be true . . . from the Authority, and good opinion wee have, of him that hath sayd it; then is the speaker, or person we believe in, or trust in, and whose words we take, the object of our Faith; and the Honour done in Believing, is done to him onely" (L, 7:133).

To honor is to bestow power, since "Reputation of power, is Power" (L, 10:152, 150). Believing in others' thoughts, we grant them our power. Hobbes proclaims the thoroughgoing conventionality of the things of this world and restores our power to us. Like early Protestants, he counsels against "a Submission of the Intellectual faculty to the Opinion of any other man." We must not renounce "our Senses and Experience; nor . . . our naturall Reason" (L, 32:409–10). Instead, we must think alone and for ourselves. Yet, if apparently by magic, when we think in accordance with public reason, we will enact the same thoughts. As a consequence, the obedience and concord that constitute sovereignty will prevail.

Individuals' attribution of imaginative and truth-generating capacities to themselves may appear to be a logical extension of this dual recognition of conventionality and human power. But when enthusiasts arrogate truth-creating powers to themselves, Hobbes believes, they deny the passions inherent in their makings. Invoking the authority of God, they seek to escape the humanness of their thinking, its conventionality and proximity to power. They peddle their opinions as if they were truths: "And last of all, men, vehemently in love with their own new opinions, (though never so absurd,) and obstinately bent to maintain them, gave those their opinions also that reverenced name of Conscience, as if they would have it seem unlawfull, to change or speak against them; and so pretend to know they are true, but that they think so" (L, 7:132).

Those who let their ungoverned conscience drive their politics are quite simply trying to make and unmake others and the world with an eye to their own felicity. "Conscience" signifies the private judgment of good and evil, and its free reign can lead to nothing but war unless it is chastened and disciplined by public reason. Hobbes exposes the hypocrisy of the conscientious as he does that of their former rulers.[9] Both obscure the fundamental distinction between knowledge (science) and opinion (conscience) by confusing the object with the image or the fancy of a thing (L, 1:86). They are so enthused by their spirit that they cannot read the Word. The cost to the commonwealth is great and much benefit will ensue from doing away with such spirited speculation. "If this superstitious fear of Spirits were taken away . . . and many other things depending thereon, by which, crafty ambitious persons abuse the simple people, men would be much more fitted than they are for civill Obedience" (L, 2:93). Ignoring Hobbes's warning, religious enthusiasts fail to become subject before sovereignty, the Mortal God in whose collective project(ion)s they should partake to find their selves and one another.

Knowing together

According to Hobbes, Medea is a frenzied woman who promises others magical rejuvenation in pursuit of her own evil designs. Hobbes's choice of Medea to signify the seditious persons and powers that threaten a commonwealth is not incidental. She would have been an evocative sign in the minds of seventeenth-century English people for whom spiritual powers were typically conceived as "female," infusing and energizing the body in polymorphous and morally ambiguous ways (VW, 45). As civil war loomed, all enemies of the propertied classes and religious establishment were portrayed symbolically as female. Challengers accepted this symbolization but endeavored to turn it to their rhetorical advantage. By imaginatively retelling their stories, I query the necessities and effects of a sovereign body politic ruled by popularly authorized governing powers and knowledges. The pervasiveness of feminine symbolism and the presence of real visionary women in the public arena attest to a social and epistemological crisis that turned upon the question of who may rightfully engage, enact, and direct invisible powers. In this controversy, we may find one beginning of our corporeal imagination of power.

Hobbes names conscience the private judgment of good and evil and regards the claims of ungoverned conscience as a seditious challenge to sovereignty, as well as an effort to make and unmake the world and others with an eye to our particular felicity. By contrast, some religious enthusiasts advanced a collaborative understanding of conscience as the spirit that animated associations where individuals transformed their interests and directed their power in response to others. The call for freedom of conscience had social and political manifestations, in addition to individualist and anarchic ones. Religious toleration is only one of the forms (albeit the victorious one) it assumed. Hobbes acknowledges as much when he first names conscience: "When two, or more men, know of one and the same fact, they are said to be CONSCIOUS of it one to another; which is as much as to know it together. And because such are fittest witnesses of the facts of one another, or of a third; it was, and ever will be reputed a very Evill act, for any man to speak against his *Conscience*; or to corrupt or force another so to do" (L, 7:131–32).

Two aspects of this definition of conscience are noteworthy. First, Hobbes implies a possibility he seems to deny elsewhere, namely, that persons may come to know something together. To be sure, Hobbes acknowledges and even counts on, shared understandings arising among persons with different bodies/minds as a result of the mediation of their opinions and makings by governing powers and knowledges. Such shared perspectives are not, however, the result of "corporate witness" but the product of the governing reasonable truths that apparently transcend individuals' and groups' contestable and contesting claims. They are sovereign, not collaborative, disciplines. What subject-citizens share is made as they become subject to governing powers and knowledges that appear to come from above and elsewhere. They regard their souls as found, not made, by a sovereign monotheos, their Mortal God.

By contrast, some religious enthusiasts pursue and generate political commonality through corporate witness, which enables them to redirect the previously invisible powers constituting individual and political bodies. Thus, they affirm the possibility that multitudes, holding a diversity of perspectives and opinions, can generate political power and act constructively. Moreover (and this is the second significance of Hobbes's first definition), "knowing together" is conscience conceived as a collaborative achievement. On this understanding, and contrary to Hobbes's definition, freedom of conscience signifies the political, not the private, judgment of good and evil. Conscience as corporate witness enables persons to recognize their participation in the authority of political contexts and to transfigure the trespasses in which this participation implicates them. In this case, the political is imaged as entheos, and its invisible powers, incorporated within and among us, are enacted in the social body and authorized in the practices and relations of power that constitute political bodies as organized multitudes. From this perspective, our bodies/minds are made and remade through collaborative activities, not found within, or above, us.

Our conception of souls as either corporeal or incorporeal decisively conditions the character and effects of our bodies/minds, as well as of the prevailing notion of the political. More specifically, the quality of soul shows our relation to the invisible powers coursing within and without our selves. In Hobbes's view, the soul, like any other nonimaginary part of the universe, is body and expresses our particular appetites and aversions. Hobbes hears dissenters claim that they are divinely inspired, but he believes their conscience, like their minds, necessarily manifests and advances their particular bodily felicity. For religious enthusiasts, meanwhile, the soul, as a vehicle of spiritual inspiration, opens a path to social transformation and, therefore has immaterial and invisible aspects. This is not to say, however, that they regard their souls as non-corporeal, for religious enthusiasts experience spiritual powers infusing and energizing their bodies. Like Hobbes, they believe their souls to be corporeal; unlike him, they conceive a dynamic, potentially conscientious interplay between body, soul, and mind. Religious enthusiasts experience *incorporeal* substances that are neither entirely material nor nonmaterial, neither entirely invisible nor visible. Religious enthusiasts' belief in the incorporeal potentialities of their souls emboldens their faith in corporate witness and the political entheos of organized multitudes. Likewise, Hobbes's corporeal imagination of power judges their faith a sign of madness and an anarchist challenge to public reason and sovereign monotheos.

Were all religious enthusiasts merely mad, fanatical, and intolerant; or did some have a prescient understanding of developing power relations? Did they apprehend the increasing importance of invisible powers at precisely the moment Hobbes sought to deauthorize discourses of the incorporeal, and might they, thereby, challenge Hobbes' representation of the popular authorization and incorporation of a governmentality? Religious enthusiasts often manifested their conscience as "knowing together" in speech about "powers invisible" that enabled them both to represent patterns of power they felt pressing upon them and to materialize their own apparently absent power.

Hobbes reads religious enthusiasts' discourse about invisible powers as epistemologically unwarranted claims to divine inspiration. This discourse might also be read as invoking invisible powers and the incorporeal potentialities of souls to represent and challenge the governing powers that constitute the Mortal God, the sovereign body politic, and its subject-citizens.[10] Religious enthusiasts invoke invisible powers to represent patterns of power they feel making and unmaking them. Hobbes labels them mad not for the substance of their views (though sometimes for that too) but for their feeling of oppression when they are perfectly free. If we are not physically opposed by the likes of walls and chains then we are free (L, 21:261–64). Hobbes notwithstanding, dissident voices in his time proclaimed the unfreedom they felt as they imagined powers' transformation. Even where the laws were silent, religious enthusiasts felt powers impinging upon them which made them feel unfree, though these powers and their effects were not always perceptible like walls or chains. Manifestations of others' makings and unmakings institute social necessities of cause and effect which press upon bodies/minds as invisible powers. Manifestations of power are not always visibly material, but they matter nonetheless. Hobbes's detheologization of power—his critique both of conscience as knowing with others and of speculation about invisible powers—rules out of order public discourse about the cumulative, not immediately visible, effects of power.

Generally, the "Medeas" of this period did not see themselves in the popular, traditional image of the female visionary "submerged beneath a tidal wave of occult energy" but "as seekers embarked on a quest for moral perfection" (VW, 89–90). Translating their sense of personal guilt into a vision of external evil and of a society corrupted by sin, prophetic women embraced the challenge of expelling that evil from the world. Though she sounds self-righteous, recognition of her own implication in the world's evil was often a turning point in her conversion (VW, 93–94, 148).

The Quakers in particular enacted a paradoxical mix of liminality and civility, demonstrating more collective energy and audacity than women visionaries of the civil war period yet prizing personal integrity and manifesting a degree of physical and moral restraint unprecedented in other sects (VW, 130, 132). All Quakers, but especially women, radically departed from conventions of gendered behavior. Indeed, in their role as prophets, they seemed to deny the reality of all outward cultural constraints. Yet the Quakers not only chastised others but also sought through their spiritual practices to dissolve assymetries of class, status, and gender among themselves. All human drives or appetites were viewed as superficial and transitory, traces of and upon a socially made self that they contrasted to conscience, what they called the "light" or "seed." From their perspective, "the hierarchical character of gender relations, indeed of all social relationships, . . . [were] *invisible prisons* whose walls could be demolished only by the painful annihilation of the outward self" (VW, 140, 133–34, my emphasis). The Quakers' concentration on the life of the soul was, however, neither a mad nor an anarchist disavowal of the conditioning effects of social rules, but an effort to respond to and transfigure them.

Whereas Hobbes presumes that our words and deeds can only express our body and its interests, religious enthusiasts conceive a dynamic, potentially transfigurative interplay between body, soul, and mind facilitated by individual and associational spiritual practices. Early Quakers' spirited practices of relentless self-negation aimed at more conscientious living. We might read the Quakers' practices of the self as a traditional, orthodox Christian impulse to renounce and transcend the body, but early Quakers did not denigrate the body so much as regard the dissolution of their socially made bodies/minds and dissociation of their given selves as paths to other ways of living. The Quakers' paradoxical relationship to the capacities of their bodies/minds as both invisible prisons and vehicles of freedom is nowhere more evident than in their attitudes toward silence and speech. Their silent meetings represent not a repudiation of speech but a preparation for speaking anew and differently. The dissociation of a subject(ion) was expressed through the loosening of bodily inhibitions in tears, groans, and shaking. The silence of the meeting allowed quaking to arise and, in turn, made a different kind of speaking possible, namely, words and deeds that disrupted and reordered social hierarchies and the rules that solidified them. If everyday, pre-ecstatic speech expressed what they were made to be, the silence and ecstasy of Quaker worship enabled them to speak and act otherwise (VW, 150–52).

Renunciation of self-will was the goal and condition of both silent worship and the dissolution of bodily habit that preceded the emergence of new speech and action.[11] "Having penetrated behind the false solidity of titles, personalities, mentalités, even their own biology, [Quakers] felt themselves to be gazing on reality, while the modern scholar sees only a void" (VW, 7–8). Can we at all bridge the gap between their experience and our perceptions? George Bataille provides one understanding of the aspirations and effects infusing mystical experience, the dissolution of self-will, the dissociation and "death" of a given subject. According to

Bataille, the mystic's detachment from material conditions "meets man's need to be independent of factors not chosen by himself but imposed from without."[12] The mystic seeks "non-attachment to ordinary life [and] indifference to its needs" (Bataille, 246). We might think of the mystic's "God" as "the lightning flash which exalts the creature above the concern to protect or increase his wealth in the dimension of time" (Bataille, 236). Engaging invisible powers in this way is to die so that one might live: "Dying can take on the active meaning of behavior that sets at nought the cautiousness inculcated by the fear of death" (Bataille, 233) and of defying social rules.

Quakers doubted whether self-transformation could be achieved through mere intellectual comprehension or reasoned affirmation of a particular doctrine (VW, 143–45). We can surmise two perfectly good reasons for their conviction. First, they regarded the leadings of their bodies/minds, prior to the transfigurative effects of their ecstatic spiritual practices, as symptomatic of social ills and their ruling role in them:

> The Quakers' peculiar style of worshipful expression—their quaking—was a social statement, a commentary on the body language of their contemporaries. For Quakers lived in a world in which many of the physical gestures of affection, association, deference, and punishment (kissing, eating, bowing, whipping, and the range of emotions that accompanied them) were more often associated with public ritual and convention than with authentic feeling and impulse. The early Quakers repudiated all such gestures of deference and oppression, and their displays of tears, symbolic dress and undress, partial paralysis, and involuntary quaking were clear statements that they had divorced themselves from all corrupt habits of social ritual, self-glorification, or control. (VW, 152)

Their socially made bodies/minds could not be a source of rejuvenation until they had renounced—quite literally shaken off—the social rule and roles that precipitated trespasses. Prior to such transfiguration, they could neither forgive, nor redirect the invisible powers that made, trespasses.

We can surmise another reason for the Quakers' disavowal of merely intellectual apprehension of the Word and for their embrace of bodily transfiguration: Our deeds, not our intentions or beliefs, finally matter most. In principle the Quakers' ethical precepts are not so distant from Hobbes's own; both advocate the teachings of the Gospel as the road to civility (L, 14:189–201). But for early Quakers, intellectual adherence to the teachings of the Gospel, or the presence of a clear conscience regardless of the deeds sovereignty demanded of them, was not enough. From the Quakers' perspective, the way principles are enacted makes all the difference. The ethical effects of our enactment of principle, not professed belief in codes per se, condition social relations.[13] The Quakers' enthusiastic worship was a limit-experience that enabled them to think, say, and do other than they were made to think, say, and do. Quaker visionaries claimed to have transcended their identities and the entire visible social order. We might say that they freely assumed multiple identifications and sought to constitute alternative orders.

The Quakers experienced invisible powers not only making their fate but also promising freedom. Invisible powers signify the ruling patterns that constitute individual and collective political bodies, and, equally important, invisible powers also signify the "light within" that enables subject-citizens to transfigure bodies/minds and their effects. If subject-citizens' "complaisance" causes the effects that reproduce the systems of power that in turn secure social order, then their efforts to direct the effects of their bodies/minds may begin the constitution of alternative orders. God's silent distance opens a breach where the "inner light" of bodies/minds may flow into experiences that contradict prevailing ways and precipitate challenges to reigning artifice.[14]

Hobbes chastised political and religious radicals for their anarchic tendencies. But associations of conscience were not only fora for disruptive action but also organs for constituting alternative order(s). The force and effects of social rules enabled Quakers' collaborative spiritual practices even as they were committed to the transfiguration of ruling. Simultaneously incorporating and interrogating the invisible powers of social rule, Quakers' representation and engagement of these powers funded their own agency. Integrating the fluid elements of an ecstatic movement with social identities that were stable and also surprisingly traditional, "Quakers anchored themselves to the specific social position into which they were born and raised while allowing themselves to be possessed by forces that rendered that position temporarily null and void" (VW, 239).

The Quakers' integration of ecstasy and everyday life illuminates the difference between a monotheistic and enthusiastic political ethos. Unlike the subject-citizens of a sovereign body politic, the Quakers recognized their participation in the authority of political contexts. Recognizing invisible powers within and among them, they conceived and enacted their agency in relation to social rule. To live an ordinary life in a politically spirited way is to testify and reckon and, where possible, disrupt and reorder the exclusions and trespasses that inevitably underlie ordinary lives. Detaching themselves from the compulsive, thoughtless demands of everyday life, early Quakers gained critical purchase upon their socially made selves and the collaborative power to transfigure them by at once replicating traditional discourses and roles and deploying them in creative ways:

> In a world of cascading wigs, extreme décolletage, high-heeled shoes, and massively applied cosmetics, Quaker women preached in public with loose or covered hair and wearing clothes stripped of buttons, lace, or any sort of trimming. Standing alone or accompanied by other Friends, they chastised neighbors, judges, clergyman, and monarchs, face to face, in churches, graveyards, private houses, and before the doors of Parliament. As worshipers they had melted, wept, and quaked in an atmosphere of ecstatic, sympathetic bonding. In public they shouted, insulted, and provoked, seeking to trigger in their audiences a process of self-scrutiny and inward repentance, proving the authenticity of their message by their own upright bearing as they were punched, bludgeoned, and whipped by enraged ministers and magistrates. (VW, 166)

For early Friends, power was everywhere and nowhere; no individual or group "owned" it. Rather, one was "'in' the power only insofar as one had transcended individual identity or class loyalty" (VW, 295). The freedom this power promised was freedom in relation to (not freedom from) a socially made subjection and the social rules that bind subject, state, and society.

The Quakers' fusion of spiritual intensity and moral integrity inspired their claim to have attained the perfection of Eden, to have found a way to exist outside given law and politics. In a sense they had done so, for the relatively free exercise of power of the Interregnum gave them space to attempt new modes of worship and behavior (VW, 246). In time, however, their apocalyptic hopes were disappointed. The Quakers attracted more adherents than any other seventeenth-century sect. They also provoked more violent hostility and persistent persecution than any other group (VW, 247–48). While they claimed to be the conscience of their society, Quakers were repeatedly prosecuted for destroying the right ordering of society (VW, 249–50). Like Medea, Quaker women in particular seemed to embody disorder.

> The Quaker woman visionary displayed the attributes of the solid citizen, the fluid behavior of the religious ecstatic, and the masculine behavior of

> the aggressive biblical prophet. In a society characterized by heightened concern about the means of distinguishing divine truth from diabolical illusion, the trustworthy citizen from the usurper of authority, her public persona surely impressed many observers as profoundly threatening. (VW, 252)

But where and what were the dangers?

Entheos confronts monotheos

At stake in the practices and persecution of the Quakers, and dramatically symbolized by the controversy over the swearing of oaths, is a contest over the constitution of the political.[15] When we cast this as a contest between religious and political authority, between God and state, we avoid squarely facing the ethical political predicaments embedded in it. We also reassure ourselves of the justice, or at least inevitability, of the Quakers' defeat: do not religious freedom and a tolerant, secular state depend upon it? Instead, I suggest, the Quakers' refusal to swear oaths dramatized a confrontation between the power of a sovereign state (monotheos) and the collaborative conscience of organized multitudes (entheos).

The Quakers were far from alone in challenging oaths before and after the Restoration, but they were distinguished by the extremity and persistence of their collective opposition, which did not cease until the advent of toleration in 1689. For more than thirty years, the Quakers persevered in their testimony to "swear not at all." As in all their practices, the Quakers felt bound by biblical injunction (in this case, the Sermon on the Mount). The authority of the claim, however, depended less (or not only) upon its being found in Scripture (for Old Testament texts could be, and were, cited to the contrary by the Quakers' critics) and more upon the truths they felt through their prophetic practice and collaborative conscience. I read the early Quakers' response to God's earthly silence (or God's presence only in what is silent to the world) as political. Their collaborative conscience, enacted by the consensual exchange among their different perspectives, granted their judgments authority, if of a discernible, human sort. Their participation in the authority of their words and deeds was apparent, even if they did not accept their social identities as given. Ultimately, the Quakers project a politics of opinion rather than knowledge, which is not to say that they disavowed seeking the truth. But amid ontotheological silence, the willing, thoughtless subjection governing truths command evade the ethical predicaments of political living. The early Quakers' practices of waiting and weighing placed greater emphasis on losing the self in pursuit of forgiveness than on finding themselves in ignorance of trespass.

The Quakers' decision to suffer rather than submit and violate their conscience opened them to a variety of inconveniences and ill-effects. They faced the most dire consequences in the case of political oaths, when they came into direct, public conflict with the state. The first wave of state persecution of Quakers came in 1655–56, but it reached greater intensity during and after the Restoration in 1660. The fact that Quakers were persecuted for disloyalty to both commonwealth and king suggests that their refusal to submit to the sovereign authority of the state, not the substance of their views, was the fundamental issue. Indeed, the Quakers were willing to subscribe to everything the political oaths required of them in terms of loyalty to the state; they refused only to do so through the act of swearing. Why was this not enough for the state? What does an oath accomplish that made the government persist in its demand that the Quakers swear one, and what made the government perceive such a threat in their refusal that it forbade them to meet? The fundamental issue may concern where first (at least public) allegiance resides, in God or the state. But given the Quakers' understanding of invisible powers as within and among them, and their collective conception of conscience, matters may be neither as obvious nor as easily resolved as they first appear. In this case, the conflict is not between the state and an individual whose conscience claims direct access to God. What we see is a confrontation between "Quaker conscience," the ethical political convictions of an organized multitude, as it were, and the authority of sovereignty.

The Quakers accepted prosecution and punishment if they violated while contesting civil law, and they expected to be held accountable if they broke their promises. Why, when faced with a threat to their corporate existence, did the Quakers not publicly submit and settle for being loyal to the king (which they claimed to be already) and free to privately believe as they would? To be sure, theological matters, especially political ones, are notoriously speculative. Nonetheless, in my view, the Quakers' refusal to swear an oath opposed the location of invisible powers and the representation of authority. They seemed to object specifically to the sort of judgment they were being asked to make (or to forego making) and the manner in which they were being asked to make it. The state's demand for recognition in the form of a sworn oath established it as the ultimate source of the invisible powers and laws that constitute the body politic. For their part, the Quakers located these powers within and among themselves. Ultimately at issue is the ground of the promises that hold us.

The Quakers' testimony not to swear amounted to a refusal to turn a performative deed into a constative law. Swearing turns a performative deed into a constative law by relinquishing the power to withdraw, or amend, affirmation of what we authorize.[16] Because Quakers regarded themselves as participants in the authority of the invisible powers that made them and of the laws that made claims upon them, they would not subject their judgment to sovereignty. What was the basis and effect of the Quakers' refusal to swear as sovereignty commanded? Quakers objected not to affirming civil law and social rules, but to doing so formally, routinely, thoughtlessly. "What is Truth in the Oath we can promise," but they would not swear to it. Swearing would surrender—or lead them to forget—their capacity to interrogate, disrupt, and reorder the social rules they authorized by their words and deeds. They would not swear because submission to a sovereign authority would constitute the subjection of their collaborative conscience.

If this reading seems too speculative, perhaps it will appear more convincing in light of the resolution of the conflict. Persecution of the Quakers did not abate for decades, focusing first on public trials of "great Friends." When those trials failed to have the desired effect on the mass of adherents to the Quaker faith, state authorities stepped up their campaign to destroy spaces and resources for the Quaker meetings. The basis of state actions was the Quaker Act of 1662 and the Conventicle Act of 1664. These Hobbesian measures claimed that the Quakers "obstruct the proceeding of justice by their obstinate refusal to take the Oath lawfully tendered unto them in the ordinary course of law." Even while the majority of Quakers persisted in their refusal to swear, the internal response that would secure toleration and an end to (public) persecution was already emerging in the 1660s. Edward Burrough called for Friends to "walk in meekness and humility" and to seek to be inoffensive in all matters relating to their neighbors. In 1672 the "Epistle from Friends" of the General Meeting held in London concurred with Burrough's direction, in effect affirming George Fox's slogan: "Study to be quiet."[17] By 1689, the year of the Toleration Act, this new relation to sovereign authority and social rule had become the official position of the Society of Friends.

The Friends' wise, even eloquent, command would have pleased

Hobbes. The message was clear: Be harmless; avoid giving offense to authorities and fellow subject-citizens; stay out of public affairs. But was it wise counsel, or a thoughtless submission to social rule? The Quakers, like many before and after them, sacrificed their engagement in worldly politics to purchase their religious freedom. The impulse toward silence, which once had precipitated ecstatic worship that prepared the way for disruption and reordering of social rule, became "a policy of quietest disengagement from law and government." Perhaps this is a small and necessary price to pay for religious freedom and an end to persecution.

The scientific basis of individual conscience

Hobbes would teach us to be skeptical of our ability to comprehend or alter invisible powers. Hobbes's skeptical teaching cultivates willing dependence of the free individual upon the sensibility that sustains governance. The subjective freedom of individual conscience needs the objectivity of public reason; indeed, this dependence and subjection is the source of its freedom. Our willing conformity to public reason and social rule promises social efficacy, while the subjective, nonpolitical character of conscience leaves us free to believe as we will. Likewise, the political rationality of sovereignty garners power by its methodical, rule-governed difference and distance from subjects.[18]

Governed conscience ties us to the state by incorporating us into its social totality, shaping our individuality and conscience into forms consistent with patterns of social rule. Public reason articulates governing truths through which we, and others, find our selves in one sovereign political body. In this way, governing powers and knowledges make individuals subjects, subjecting us to others by control and dependence, and binding us to our social identities by conscience as individual self-knowledge (SP, 212). The manner in which we are tied to our identities by individual conscience subjects us to others and them to us; the ways we become subject-citizens constitute relations of control and dependence among us. Subscribing to governing truths and willing what governing powers have made us, we establish both a conscience to be known and relations of power to be sustained. Our participation in the domestication and governance of our own and others' conscience incorporates us into a sovereign totality, not in opposition to our individuality, but as an expression of it. The fate of the Quakers suggests how this is the case and comes to be. In light of their fate, we witness new problems of responsibility and freedom.[19]

In the face of continuous persecution, the Quakers perceived that their spiritual well-being and material survival depended upon their organizing anew. In one way or another, they had to respond to social demands and state commands to perform contracts, behave predictably, and conduct themselves reasonably. Friends adopted a formal peace testimony, pledging their willingness to behave as good and loyal citizens. Ultimately, their compliance brought an end to persecution. It was one in a series of measures that seem to tell the familiar story of the rationalization of a loose, egalitarian, charismatic religious movement into a tightly knit, bureaucratized, hierarchical church. The routinization of charisma does not completely capture these changes, however, for Friends never altogether renounced the experience and principles that founded their association. Instead, they blended the ideal of orderly thinking and behavior with spiritual ecstasy and enlightenment (VW, 273–80). Consistent with Hobbes's counsel, they did not repudiate ecstatic prophecy but privatized it. As a consequence, they were increasingly inclined to submit in awe to invisible powers as if they represented the sublimity of nature. Like Job, they became subject before an irresistible and incomprehensible sovereign entity. Their spirited participation in entheos is transmuted into awe for a monotheos whose invisible powers they increasingly, if inadvertently, authorize.[20]

If Friends did not lose their enthusiasm, their new system of organization did alter their relationship to social rule and, thus, to the object of their enthusiasm. New strictures on authorship and preaching altered their individual and collective relation to political contexts, whether Scripture, their selves, or the body politic (VW, 283–86, 308–11, 351–402). Hobbes's skeptical teaching would affirm the new disciplines of reading and writing that changed how Quakers held their beliefs and where they expressed them. But what were the effects of these new methods on Quaker selves, their bodies/minds?

Beneath Quakers' new strict outward behavior and the sober style for which they became famous emerged an increasingly complex and volatile inner life. Bodily metaphors no longer served as signs of transfiguration and overcoming but had meaning only in relation to conditions of suffering and damnation. Such self-debasement is different from self-negation, and the difference matters for the experience of bodies/minds.[21] Early Quakers' public, ecstatic worship led them, beyond what their selves and world were made to be, toward ethical political action that enacted more conscientious bodies/minds. By the close of the seventeenth century, however, a process of "spiritual implosion" had begun as the practical and the mystical became increasingly bifurcated in Quaker experience. The most pious of eighteenth century Friends "were quietists, defining the light as emanating from a being utterly outside the self" (VW, 356). The possibility of transfiguring bodies/minds appears foreclosed as the weight of what they are increases until all they can do is "go heavily on," becoming subject to the sublimity of their maker's nature. The spirited potential of their souls is forsaken; powers were once within because among them; now powers are within because above them, until once incorporeal souls become corporeal. They converted from an enthusiastic to a monotheistic political ethos, one in which the invisible powers that made their bodies, souls, and minds appeared to come from above and beyond them. Selves and bodies once felt to be both invisible prisons and vehicles of transfiguration are now depicted as burdensome or insignificant (VW, 354–56). Their bodies/minds became fateful, *visible* prisons. Perhaps, as Hobbes would claim, they had become responsible subject-citizens, but they certainly felt less free.

The Quakers' political story is prototypically "modern." After decades of collective resistance, they finally cede their powers of political constitution—their capacities for disruptive action and establishing alternative orders—in return for religious toleration and private freedom. Celebrants of citizen action tend to read such stories as a total loss—when persons give up their constituent power and forgo political action, they lose their power. Subject-citizens who cease to act politically, however, gain social efficacy by means of their compliance with social rule. Quakers were obliged to sacrifice enthusiastic engagement in politics to secure religious toleration, but in addition they achieved a solid, if sometimes rigid, group identity, as well as security within their community and beyond it.

Limit-experiences like religious ecstasy are heady and disorienting: they reveal the contingency of what selves and world are made to be, and they throw into question all guides for action and the necessity of their effects. Increasingly, most Quakers had difficulty living this contingency, especially in the face of external hostility and persecution.[22] For a time their collaborative practice of conscience enabled them to resist and respond ethically and politically to the force of social rules, to disrupt them and seek alternatives. Eventually, internal anxiety and external insecurity apparently became too much to bear and, like so many others, they answered the contingency of the aims and effects of action in a world where God is silent by settling for the certainty afforded by extant social rules. They thereby became effective agents of those rules. As it turns out, the Quakers not only felt less free, they also were tempted to become irresponsible—because willing and increasingly thoughtless—subjects.

Paradoxically, while Quaker complaisance expanded their social efficacy, it also rendered them increasingly unfree in relation to their selves. "The Quakers' developing subjectivity not only involved an increased attentiveness toward personal motivation and emotion but a self-censoring process that rendered aspects of bodily experience as forbidden territory." Early Friends achieved physical ecstasy and "self-transcendence" by refiguring their social bodies/minds. Once Friends refocused on their corporeal souls and based their claim to authority on the reasonable fulfillment rather than the disruption and reordering of social roles, "their bodies' potential range of expression inevitably became tied to notions of appropriate behavior" (VW, 406). An experience of spiritual isolation and illness where they once felt healing corresponds to their new negativity about physical sensation. Increasingly, they regard their bodies as fateful objects demanding denigration (for their unpredictability or creatureliness) or compliance (with their gendered "nature"). Their bodies/minds are no longer vehicles of transfiguration. Their collaborative interpretive practices are overcome by an increasingly individual and subjective conscience. And their once collaborative enthusiasm becomes private.

CHAPTER 5

Hobbes's America

> The famous sovereignty of political bodies has always been an illusion, which, moreover, can be maintained only by the instruments of violence, that is, with essentially nonpolitical means. Under human conditions, which are determined by the fact that not man but men live on the earth, freedom and sovereignty are so little identical that they cannot ever exist simultaneously. Where men wish to be sovereign, as individuals or as organized groups, they must submit to the oppression of the will, be this the individual will with which I force myself, or the 'general will' of an organized group. If men wish to be free, it is precisely sovereignty they must renounce.
>
> Hannah Arendt, *Between Past and Future*

Arendt is among the many who say that Hobbes is not America's theorist. His account of the authorization of sovereignty may involve mutual promise, but it is promise without political bodies and thereby generates the "mythical fiction" of a uniform people. In America, however, Arendt finds mutual promise actuated in civic bodies politic—not the "imagined community" of a sovereign nation, but an "organized multitude whose power was exerted in accordance with laws and limited by them" (OR, 166).[1] America, Arendt claims, never assumed the disguise of a nation, and sovereignty never played a role in its founding constitution (OR, 153, 195).

Yet Arendt's own account of the legacy of the American constitutional founding suggests that this judgment may be premature, even mistaken. A sovereign fiction lurks in the authorizing "We, The People" of the Constitution, and the political development it set in motion can be read (Arendt herself reads it so) as a story of the deauthorization, disorganization, and disappearance of the organs of action and order—the political bodies—that animated America's revolutionary beginnings. The founding generations' constitutional acts did not provide categories of thought for the remembrance of revolutionary spirit or organs of action for its practice (OR, 220–21).[2] In the new republic, it turned out, "there was no space reserved for the exercise of precisely those qualities which had been instrumental in building it" (OR, 232). Founding mutual promises are sundered from political bodies when the political spirit of civil associations becomes invisible. As a consequence, individuals cannot see their everyday participation in the constitution of their individual and collective political bodies; invisible powers appear to be above them, rather than within because among them. To the degree that the generation and exercise of power become indiscernible, America becomes a sovereign nation. Contrary to Arendt's hope, Hobbes may prove to be the most prescient political theorist of America.[3]

The authorization of sovereignty in *Leviathan* distinguishes it from Hobbes's other political writings and should unsettle any predilection to read Leviathan's governing powers as repressive and only centrally generated.[4] Subject-citizens do not simply and grudgingly submit to civil laws, having relinquished their natural rights to a sovereign who stands above them. The people authorize the action and identify with the power of sovereignty, affirming it (albeit never altogether laying claim to it) as their own. In the case of monarchy, Hobbes's account of authorization may stretch the meaning of consent to the breaking point; the divine origins of the monarch's power became untraceable so that his or her subjects increasingly had difficulty finding themselves in the monarch's person. But Hobbes's account of authorization is a prescient representation of the workings of the sovereignty of "the people" in modern liberal states. Subject-citizens who are not officeholders relinquish their powers of political institution and authorize the actions of their representatives as their own. In turn, the latter lay claim to the will of "the people" gleaned from the latest public opinion poll or tally of constituents. By means of such fictional personification and projection, "the people" come into being.

The mythical, mystical people

"We, The People" is an invention, a fiction. According to Edmund Morgan's *Inventing the People*, we all know that the whole people cannot themselves rule because (to name only the most commonsensical obstacle) there are too many of them.[5] But to call popular sovereignty a fiction, Morgan says, is not to deny its determinative effects or principled importance. The tension between fact and the fiction of popular sovereignty generates the idea's power. The fictional quality of the people's rule sustains rather than threatens the values associated with it (Morgan, 15). "In the strange commingling of political make-believe and reality the governing few no less than the governed many may find themselves limited—we may even say reformed—by the fiction on which their authority depends" (Morgan, 14).

The fiction of popular sovereignty poses, and responds to, a twofold danger. First, because the people as a whole can act only fictionally, the danger arises that governmental bodies will find and abide no limits to their power. Early versions of the new fiction placed authority and subjection in the same hands, thereby potentially depriving ordinary people (who were actually subjects) of effective control over a government that claimed to speak for them (Morgan, 83). Thus, the fiction of popular sovereignty, and of "the people" who are its source, must be articulated so as to provide a limit to potentially boundless governmental power. If the fiction is to be maintained and the willing suspension of disbelief in it sustained, then perceived reality must not depart too much from fiction. At the same time, however, dangers accompany the fiction's literalization. Morgan concurs with this governmental perspective: "A fiction taken too literally could destroy the government it was intended to support. A government that surrendered to direct popular action would cease to govern. The fiction must approach the fact but never reach it" (91). How is this precarious neverland between fiction and fact enacted and supported? How are "the people" invented and made fictionally real but never actually so?

In Morgan's view, political fictions give some measure of control over the entity to which they seem to subject us absolutely (18). This was certainly the case in political regimes legitimated by divine right. Invoking the king's divinity was a way of limiting the monarch's actions, just as it kept his subjects in their place by supplying rhetorical means for chastising aspirants to his power (for example, court and counselors). Over time this strategy effected a paradoxical reversal. When the House of Commons insisted that the monarch's power was inalienable and not to be shared, they were discovering a way of sharing it themselves (Morgan, 35). The result, after much strife, struggle, and the beheading of a king, was a transfer of "divine sanction" from the king to his people and their representatives. "The divine right had never been more than a fiction, and as used by the Commons it led toward the fiction that replaced it, the sovereignty of the people" (Morgan, 36). If many found the monarch's rule increasingly onerous, and his or her divinity dubious, he or she did possess the distinct advantage of requiring little imagination to appear as a political reality and fictional fact. In short, the monarch was a visible presence. The same cannot be said of "the people." They were neither immediately visible, nor would they ever become so. They must be imagined.

> Before we ascribe sovereignty to the people, we have to imagine that there is such a thing, something we personify as though it were a single body, capable of thinking, of acting, of making decisions and carrying them out, something quite apart from government, and able to alter or remove a government at will, a collective entity more powerful and less fallible than a king or than any individual within it or than any group of individuals it singles out to govern it. To sustain a fiction so palpably contrary to fact is not easy. (Morgan, 153)

"The people" is a fictional personification. How can this fiction become real, without at the same time being taken literally? After all, partisans of representative government invented the sovereignty of the people to claim it for themselves (Morgan, 49–50). The purpose of this political fiction remained the same as the preceding one, namely, to persuade the many to submit to government by the few. At the same time, in its cause against the king, the Parliament needed popular support to make the new fiction actual. But "mere people, however many in number, were not *the* people, and the sovereignty of the people must not be confused with the unauthorized actions of individuals or of crowds or even of organized groups [like the early Quakers] outside Parliament" (Morgan, 60). Herein lies the subversive idea at the root of popular sovereignty: Many of the people have the troublesome habit of taking the fiction literally—as authorizing a greater degree of popular participation in government or, in some cases, as calling for the dissolution of government as we have known it.[6] This was the Levellers' mistake, as Morgan understands it. Although their challenges to the relationship between popular sovereignty and actual people ultimately proved instructive, "they took the new fictions too literally, endowing the people with capacities for action that so ideal a body—ideal in the philosophical sense—can never possess" (Morgan, 68).

If popular sovereignty were to provide an effective foundation for government (become dubious after the political demise of God and His earthly representative the monarch) it had to remain fictional. The people to whom the Parliament "attributed supreme power were themselves fictional and could most usefully remain so, a *mystical body*, existing as a people only in the actions of the Parliament that claimed to act for them" (Morgan, 49, my emphasis). The Levellers mistakenly confused a hypothetical mutual promise with an actual "Agreement of the People."[7] But the fact that the sovereignty of the people "rested upon supposed acts of the people, both present and past, that were almost as difficult to examine as acts of God" (Morgan, 58) proved not a deficiency but an advantage. The invisibility of the people and the indiscernibility of their authoritative acts secured rather than threatened government. This salutary effect is achieved when ruling fictions constitute the corporeal souls of the individual bodies/minds that symbolically authorize and partake of the people's sovereignty. The fiction of popular sovereignty at once increasingly obscures the people's rule, and figuratively speaking, decapitates their political bodies.[8]

For representative government to work and the conflicts inherent to the fiction of popular sovereignty to remain muted, different communities must be "willing and able most of the time, and on most issues, to perceive their local interests as being involved in, if not identical with, the interests of the larger society" (Morgan, 51). In other words, they must imagine themselves as a national community. Morgan's self-professed Whiggish outlook prevents him from fully recognizing the mystery (and invisible powers) at the heart of this invention and imagined community. He sometimes misrecognizes political struggle or shrouds the viability of suppressed alternatives whose defeat resulted in the people coming to feel themselves "one nation." Nationalist sentiment makes the fiction of popular sovereignty work (Morgan, 237). For instance, Morgan presumes that all early "Americans" thought in terms of a continent (as he and we now most always do) long before the continent was conquered (Morgan, 246). Like the Federalists, he valorizes representatives who disdained the local and revered the then yet to be invented and to this day always somewhat fictional "national interest" (Morgan, 248). Morgan notes that the English and American people might not have located sovereignty in a national people, and yet it seems that they could not help but do so.

> There would have been no logical barrier to thinking of the people of every village as a sovereign body, but that is not what happened. The people whose sovereignty was proclaimed were the whole people of the country or colony, far too numerous a group to deliberate or act as a body. It was their representatives who claimed for them the authority that only

> a representative body could exercise. The sovereignty of the people was not said to reside in the particular constituencies that chose representatives, it resided in the people at large and reached the representatives without the people at large doing anything to confer it (49).

Although Morgan acknowledges the interested parties who found imagining a sovereign nation preferable to locating power in actual constituencies, his misrecognition of the alternative to it belies an unconscious affinity with the contestable presumptions of those interests. Morgan overlooks what Arendt emphasizes, namely, that organized multitudes represent a competing conception of the political, an alternative to one sovereign body. Indeed, organized multitudes are antithetical to sovereignty, which is why the people of every village could not imagine themselves as sovereign but would have had to imagine themselves other than sovereign. Sovereign bodies are necessarily abstract and ascendant; no local body can appear as sovereign. Colonists may have said little about sovereignty, not (as Morgan claims) because they recognized the king as its locus (Morgan, 147), but because their political practices opposed the conception of politics and power definitive of sovereignty. "What was lacking in the Old World," Arendt writes, "were the townships of the colonies, and, seen with the eyes of a European observer, 'the American revolution broke out, and the doctrine of the sovereignty of the people came out of the townships and took possession of the state'" (OR, 166). Arendt offers an alternative reading. The colonists' political bodies were not conceived as "governments strictly speaking; they did not imply rule and the division of the people into rulers and ruled." These were really "'political societies,' and their great importance for the future lay in the formation of a political realm that enjoyed power and was entitled to claim rights without possessing or claiming sovereignty" (OR, 168). Arendt overestimates the *visibility* of political bodies in the American future, but she does reveal what Morgan does not see, namely, that sovereignty is not the only possible conception of the political. In our time, as we observe the growing inefficacy of the sovereign, national state, a reconsideration of the inevitability of a sovereign conception of the political may have salutary effects. I have argued that we are, and exist within, political bodies. The crucial matter is whether we discern their political constitution and the freedoms and responsibilities that accompany our exercise of their governing powers and knowledges. A sovereign conception of the political conceals both.

Like Hobbes, Morgan assumes that if the people themselves are to materialize and protect themselves, they must always do so fictionally—their sovereign authorization must be a mutual promise without political bodies. The entire people are too diverse and large a body to deliberate and act together. Indeed, Morgan concurs with Hobbes, the people have no corporeal existence prior to their fictional authorization: The people without a government are a confused multitude without order or connection (120). But these commonsensical conclusions already presuppose the political constitution they advance. True, viewed from the perspective of an entire continent, the actual deliberation and action of individual citizens seems highly inefficacious, implausible, even detrimental to the quest. True, if one wants to imagine a nation, individual citizens and the political bodies to which they are attached pose obstacles to a nationalist imagination. But these judgments presume the logic and goals they have yet to achieve. This "common sense" represents as necessary and inevitable what was the product of political struggle. Is it best that "the American people" were invented? Is it best that the people became one nation, an imagined community? Is it best that empire became our way of life?[9] To be sure, these achievements seem irreversible. But this irreversibility does not justify our projecting backward their necessity, or overlooking their costs, both for ourselves and others.

Techniques that tame popular power in the course of celebrating it prevent the literalization of the fiction of popular sovereignty. Ruling fictions recognize popular power while fashioning it in ways that support extant social and political order. As Morgan argues, the ideology of the yeoman farmer, the political rituals of election campaigns, and the instructions to representatives were specific techniques of domestication which exalted popular power in order to direct and control it (152). By these and other means, the people's active powers were tamed and contained by a governing fiction. The success of domestication poses dangers of its own, however, especially the possibility that governmental bodies claiming the right to speak for the people will find and abide no limits to their power. How could the fiction of popular sovereignty, and "the people" who are its source, be articulated so as to provide a limit to potentially boundless governmental powers? In Morgan's view, the mystical body of the people (49), which is analogous to the symbolic, eternal, divine body of the king, provided the solution to this problem. "The American people" invented by the U.S. Constitution is perhaps its most illuminating example.

"The people" have two bodies animated by different powers. The mystical body of the people corresponds to the constituent power "to begin, end, or alter government" while a literal, representative body possesses the actual power to legislate (Morgan, 81). The viability of popular sovereignty depends upon mechanisms and metaphors that assure that perceived reality does not depart too far from fiction. The U.S. Constitution enacts the people's mystical body; it engenders and is authored by their constituent power. The American's invention resonated with Leveller principles (though it did not suffer from the latter's literal-mindedness) "in giving the putative people a commanding voice outside the government they created and embodying their rights as subjects in the commands they thereby gave their government" (Morgan, 87).

Surpassing literalism and transubstantiating the people's body was, however, neither automatic nor easily won in the American case. To a far greater degree than in the English context, the political history of the colonies fostered a concept of direct, accountable representation. The constitution of political bodies and the generation of governing powers were visible through representatives conceived as agents of the people who chose them. The American challenge, if "the people" were to be invented and a national community imagined, was to resolve the sovereignty of the people with these predominantly local notions of representation (Morgan, 245). The onetime colonists were reluctant to entrust governmental powers to anybody not subject to the veto of their locally elected representatives (Morgan, 265). As the unifying goals of revolutionary action receded, local attachments and mistrust of distant, relatively unaccountable powers proved a barrier to national identity and projects. The loyalty of citizens and representatives alike to local and state institutions, and their preoccupation with the interests of the "fields and woods of their own neighborhoods" (Morgan, 248), eviscerated national powers. The boldness of the Continental Congress, which had done so much to facilitate revolutionary victory, began to fade. How grave were the dangers posed by this situation remains a matter of contention (Morgan, 267), but it may be true that "a people must cease to exist if the persons in whose minds it has its being, cease to consider themselves as belonging to it" (Morgan, 237). States' and citizens' defiance of congressional actions became commonplace (Morgan, 265) and suggests the waning of the national imagination of the American people within individual and collective political bodies even before it had been fully invented.

Morgan recounts a familiar story of the American founding: Madison, Hamilton, and Jay invented a sovereign "American people" to overcome the authoritative claims of local and state institutions (Morgan, 267).

The Federalists' government assured a breadth of vision, informed by a distinctly nationalist imagination, which wedded "the people" and their representatives to its grand, expansive projects.[10] According to this common account, the U.S. Constitution not only created a national, collective identity and set in place governmental structures to organize and generate the powers needed to sustain it, but it also protected the fiction of the people's sovereignty while securing their individual rights. The idea of an expansive republic is crucial to this accomplishment that purportedly rendered "tyrannies of the majority" less likely, in part because majorities could not be so easily formed (Morgan, 269).[11] Disruptive, concerted action, once possible at the state and local level, would prove more difficult for citizens and their locally minded representatives to effect on a national stage. At the same time, while nationally subversive action was effectively blocked, a credible claim could be made that the Constitution represented the "will of the people" (Morgan, 270). The government would at least appear to provide some kind of representation of the people, and in the realm of political fictions appearances are everything. The fiction would not become fact, but neither could fact be said to depart too far from fiction. Direct, popular elections symbolically authorized government. Government, in turn, would act directly upon the people, facilitating a far more intimate relationship between individuals and a national community than was possible under the highly mediated structures of power of the Articles of Confederation.

Individual subject-citizens find themselves in "the people," by willing what governing powers and knowledges make them to be; they are induced to comply not only by threats actual and imagined but also by benefits and pleasures promised. As individuals find "the people" within their corporeal souls, the claim that the people rule becomes as credible as any fictional fact. With the ratification of the Constitution and the continual actualization of the structure of governance it imagined, the crucial fiction of "the American people" finds realization (Morgan, 285) in a collective body whose power is as actual as it is invisible.

The Constitution instituted a governing fiction of popular sovereignty which formed rulers and ruled alike (Morgan, 14). Like the political fiction that preceded it, the sovereignty of the people enacted by the Constitution gives a measure of control over the entity to which it seems to subject us absolutely (Morgan, 18). Who or what body exercises this control over often invisible governing powers remains, however, something of a mystery. Who or what is the "head" of this body politic? Where and what is its body? Morgan tells a tale of simultaneous reform and victory for both the people and their rulers as a consequence of constitutional ratification. But the political struggle that resulted in our constitutional regime can also be read as a process by which an alternative conception of the political was defeated and the memory (according to Hobbes's figuration, the head) of its political bodies suppressed. The founding of the constitutional regime witnessed the disappearance of organized multitudes once enacted in and empowered by visible political bodies; in time, a sovereign, national state constituted by mutual promise sundered from political bodies ascended and assumed their place.

The ratification and, more importantly, the subsequent establishment and development of the constitutional regime accomplished a redefinition of politics which delegitimated and dissuaded citizen interest and involvement in political matters. As one student of the early republic recently put it, the institutional design and rhetorical structure of the Constitution attempted, quite successfully, to minimize the involvement, the influence, and the interest that ordinary people would take in government.[12] Citizens' lack of interest is self-deceptive, however, for the disappearance of political bodies, the invisibility of their powers, and our difficulty discerning our authorizing role in governance do not mean that the people do not rule, though we do tend to do so thoughtlessly.

The constitutional solution Morgan presents as necessary and inevitable was actually contingent and an object of intense political struggle. Recovering this contest and contingency reveals assumptions that continue to constrict our political imaginations, including Arendt's assumption that mutual promise and consent to political impotence are inevitably opposed. The common sense of Morgan's assumptions and conclusions dissolves when illuminated by political struggle. Morgan himself acknowledges widespread popular interest and involvement in politics leading up to and succeeding the revolution. Citizen bodies for direct action not only challenged existing government but also supplemented it. In Morgan's view, it is "only a small step from elected conventions aimed at supplementing government to the elected conventions exercising the people's constituent power to define and limit government" (258). But were self-organizing political bodies and the constitutional conventions that authorized the U.S. Constitution conterminous, as Morgan imagines?[13] The process of ratification and the political contests succeeding it suggest not.

All participants in the political struggle over the ratification of the U.S. Constitution agreed that the form of power it favored was a powerful, centralized government. Disagreement turned on whether or not this centralization was desirable. The Federalists adopted an international perspective on state-building and, from that perspective, the weakness of (national) government seemed to be the source of all the political and social problems they confronted. The principal threats to the new nation were cast as external (economic and military), but to the extent that internal dissension and differences undermined the national power to deal with these threats, they too were characterized not only as seditious but also as treasonous.[14] "Without Leviathan, the argument went, the war of all against all would continue to be waged at home as well as in the international arena" (Hemberger, 47, 42–47).

The extant political cultures of the former colonies fostered wariness about an increase in national powers. There was much to suggest (and the Antifederalists explicitly argued) that the national government would be as distant and unaccountable as had the English king and parliament. To overcome this distrust of centralized power, the Federalists externalized the threat to individual liberties, urged citizens to identify their interests with those of the national government, and asked them to trust that government with virtually unlimited powers. By endowing the national government with power, as the Federalists' logic would have it, "citizens would institutionalize their own power so that it could be used more effectively. Thus the more power government was given, the more power the people would have" (Hemberger, 49, 43, 48, 114). It remains to be seen, however, just what sort of power the people would "have." Would the people be participants in the uses of their power or mere watchers of how their powers were being used?[15] In fact, the efficacy of governing powers is to be found in the people perceiving themselves to be mere spectators of powers they actually exercise.

The Antifederalists were wary that the proposed constitutional regime would make citizens spectators of power. By way of contrast to the Federalist's "top-down" perspective on state-building driven by the requirements of the international system, the Antifederalists envisioned a constitution "built upon local institutions, practices, and understandings." From their perspective, the articulation, proliferation, and maintenance of such political bodies would determine whether government ultimately would rest upon force or persuasion, or what we might call nonconsensual or consensual disciplines. The Antifederalists believed that people should have ways of organizing their power outside of government, not just mythically or fictionally, but actually. The legitimacy of the constitutional regime, they averred, would depend upon citizens' capacity for resistance keeping pace with the development of national governing powers. But the Federalists could not countenance such a perspective, for "their first premise was that, to become a credible force on the international scene, the United States had to create a government that was indisputably in control of the nation" (Hemberger, 72, 54, 61). This control could be achieved only by undermining citizens' attachments to local institutions and by sundering mutual promise from visible political bodies.

The constitution of an imaginary community generated national powers by reconceiving the citizenry, at once nationalizing and individualizing "the people." "Nationalism entailed individualism because the construction of an American national identity involved undermining attachments to more local communities. In giving the national government direct access to individual citizens, the Constitution envisioned a situation in which each citizen confronted "the people" (and their government) alone (Hemberger, 74–75). From Morgan's perspective, this is one of the salutary effects of political fictions, for they give some measure of control over that to which they seem to subject us absolutely (Morgan, 18). Contrary to the facts of American political cultures at the time, however, "the Constitution posits the existence of a people who have no pre-existing institutional embodiment and therefore no recognizable voice" (Hemberger, 75). As the Antifederalists well knew, this fiction of a disorganized multitude bore no relationship to the facts of extant political bodies or cultures.

In effect, the Constitution represented the willful supersession of previously constituted political bodies by an allegedly direct relationship between the national government and the people. Constitutional conventions were not conterminous with the self-organizing action of citizens, as Morgan maintains, but sought to circumvent and finally undermine them.[16] Whereas previous (state) constitutions attributed a corporate existence to the people independent of government, the new constitutional regime disaggregated the people. Fictionalizing ordinary people's political power was the condition of "the people's" sovereignty (Hemberger, 77–78, 82, 112).

The nationalist community's hold upon the collective imagination was neither as easily nor as readily achieved as Morgan suggests. The self-organizing bodies of citizens prevalent in both pre- and post-revolutionary America stood at odds with the constitutional antipolitical culture.[17] During the revolution, various forms of improvisational politics gained currency and legitimacy. They exemplified the civic bodies politic Arendt invokes. These forms enabled people to represent themselves corporeally (if not sovereignly) while remaining "outside" of government.

The Whiskey Rebellion and other events like it demonstrate the degree to which these self-organizing forms possessed and retained cultural legitimacy. The effect of "nationalizing the people," according to the Federalists' understanding, was to endow the national government with the exclusive right to speak for them. The people, however, had other ideas and acted accordingly as they continued to organize extralegally after constitutional ratification. Just how fictional the framers' intended popular sovereignty to be is indicated by some Federalists' claim that these traditional political practices represented (quite literally) a threat to the national government's authority (Hemberger, 86, 89, 94). As Hobbes teaches, if a nation is to be sovereign, it can abide no rivals to its representative prowess and powers. The Whiskey Rebellion suggests that, at least initially, the constitutional regime was far from incontestably sovereign. To be sure, the Whiskey Rebellion is often represented as a degeneration into lawlessness and anarchy—the sort of local form of tyranny that motivated the establishment of national governing powers. But such rebellions may also be read as appeals to political tradition. We misunderstand the Whiskey Rebellion if we believe that the threat it posed to the regime was based on a rival armed force. That threat was never credible or in earnest pursued. In fact, the survival of the constitutional regime was threatened by conflicting understandings of how popular will would be expressed and represented, and thus we witness another confrontation between monotheos and entheos.

It was far from obvious to local participants in the rebellion, and even to some observers, whether "the people" were best represented by the rebels or the national government. For its part the federal government could not tolerate the simultaneous existence of alternative political orders, because its powers and projects depended upon its being in sole control of the nation. "When Federalist Congressmen condemned 'the disorganizing spirit" of organized resistance, it became clear that they objected to parties because of their capacity to unify the people as well as their capacity to divide them" (Hemberger, 103–6, 109). The collaborative action of organized multitudes poses a threat to sovereign government as much for its capacity to constitute alternative orders as for its powers of disruption. Organized multitudes make visible, and thus contestable, the political constitution of individual and collective bodies. In short, organized multitudes reveal the myth of sovereignty. As Arendt says in the epigraph to this chapter, only willful pressure upon individual and collective bodies makes them appear uniform (BPF, 164–65). Hemberger summarizes the political consequences of struggles over representation of "the people":

> Having acknowledged that the people are a fiction and that the regime is essentially one of representations, the government found itself confronting alternative embodiments claiming to speak in the people's voice. The Whiskey Rebellion posed the question, 'If the people can only be known through representation, through which representations shall they be known?' Washington's condemnation of self-created societies proposes an account of how an authentic reproduction can be recognized. Seen in this light, the President embodied the militia not to put down an insurrection, but to demonstrate that the people would, quite literally, line up behind the national government. Apparently an original could be produced, if the authenticity of the copy was effectively challenged. But this people would be seen and not heard. Their voice was not sovereign; the Sovereign was their voice. (112)

As we come to recognize our selves in "the people" and incorporate their image into our corporeal souls, our individual and collective bodies appear increasingly sovereign, which is to say, one in their uniformity.

The political struggles of postrevolutionary America evince a contest between competing images of "the people." In the Antifederalists, we find some inkling of political enthusiasm and precedent for Arendt's vision of a people born in mutual promise enacted in and by visibly political bodies. The personification of entheos is mapped by the power of individuals' action embodied in political associations. Their collective projection is of organized multitudes, without an absolute center or head, but not without order. In the victorious Federalists, we find a people, much as Hobbes envisioned them, constituted through mutual promise but increasingly without political bodies. Their collective personification is always fictional, their politically constituted bodies mystical and invisible. Their collective projection is of a sovereign unity, an imagined community before which each individual becomes a subject. The political theology of the U.S. constitutional regime shows Hobbes to be the most prescient theorist of America.

Social rule and sovereign enthusiasm

A popularly authorized state constituted by mutual promising in the absence or invisibility of political bodies does not mean that the people do not materialize; it means that they do so without a "head," which is to say, thoughtlessly. The statement seems paradoxical. How can the disappearance of political *bodies* yield *mind*lessness? The relative corporeality or incorporeality of our individual and collective souls—how spirited our role in the constitution of bodies/minds—decides the matter. Figuratively speaking, the soul articulates the relationship of mind and body, and signifies the degree to which mind is in body and body in mind. Subjection by a corporeal soul precludes reflection upon these incorporations by obscuring subject-citizens' participant role in the political constitution of bodies, both individual and collective. The incorporeal potential of our bodies/minds is forsaken when what we are made to be colonizes who we are so that we appear to be mere spectators of powers we actually exercise. When we endeavor to discern the political constitution of our individual bodies in political associations (collective bodies), we seek to fathom the interpenetration of body and mind. On the one hand, we must seek to recognize the body in our mind, how the political constitution of our bodies/minds affects our perspectives on the world and how, in pursuit of our felicity, we trespass against others. Social rules trace the body in our mind. On the other hand, we actualize the mind in our body when we reveal how our participation in the constitution of our bodies/minds, especially when thoughtful rather than thoughtless, can transfigure both individual and collective bodies. A body/mind infused with an incorporeal soul can reveal who we are as distinct from what reigning social rules make us.

The constitution of the political concerns how the people materialize, how individual and collective bodies come to matter. The challenge and promise of popular sovereignty, as we have seen, turns on whether and how the purportedly ultimate and unlimited power of the people can be reformed and restrained. The U.S. Constitution accomplishes this feat (much as Hobbes advocates) by means of a distinctive articulation of popular authorization as mutual promise without political bodies, which, among other things, prevents the literalization of the fiction of the people's political powers. In Alexander Hamilton's reflections on the constitutional regime, we find the substantiation of this solution, for Hamilton transforms the power of the people to mean the very substance of power, not simply its authorization. "In Hamilton's expansive view, a constitution represented a way of organizing and generating power for the pursuit of great national objectives. The Constitution was to be a means of assuring a continuous generation of power." According to Hamilton, the power of the people was sovereign or unlimited by reference to the material power of the entire collectivity, "the aggregate of its social resources that consent now made potentially available to the state."[18]

Popular authorization does not merely sanction or sanctify governing powers but creates the possibility of an "uninterrupted transfer of substance from the 'fountain'" of power. By means of the collective projection of a mythical, mystical people, and in accordance with their social rule(s), we "consent in particular" to governing knowledges and powers. More specifically, actual persons concede access to their powers (in the form of resources such as money, skills, and bodily strength) which the governors—representatives of "the people"—collect, regularize, and channel (through taxation, conscription, and other ruling techniques). The collective corporeal soul—the state as a social totality—begins with the materialization of the activity of the people through the making of their individual corporeal souls. "What [the people's] consent signifies is their willingness to make over, in whole or in part, their powers and products to be used by the state."[19] A sovereign people materialize, individually and collectively, as they remake themselves in conformity with social rule.

From some perspectives, speaking of the people's materialization misrepresents the most distinctive aspects of modern democratic regimes. Seyla Benhabib submits that we must desubstantialize the model of a thinking and acting super-subject to grasp "those *anonymous yet intelligible* collective rules, procedures, and practices" that form a liberal democratic way of life.[20] Likewise, Claude Lefort claims that treating the state as an organ of society misses the symbolic dimensions of power in modern democracies. "The legitimacy of power is based on the people; but the image of popular sovereignty is linked to the image of an empty place, impossible to occupy." In other words, "the people" materialize only symbolically, which is to say literally not at all. From this perspective, though governed subject-citizens do relinquish their powers of political constitution to governing officeholders, when the latter lay claim to the will of "the people" everyone involved recognizes the fictional character of the invocation. "Democracy combines these two apparently contradictory principles: on the one hand, power emanates from the people; on the other, it is the power of nobody."[21] Democracy, Lefort says, thrives on this contradiction as long as the place of power remains only symbolically empty, not actually so, and the people are not embodied in a head or organ. The symbolic logic of democracy is threatened in the first case by thoroughgoing privatization and corruption of public activity which may dissolve *civil* society as such; and in the second case by a corporealization of society in accordance with a totalitarian logic (Lefort, 279–80).

According to Lefort's typology, bureaucracy, democracy, and totalitarianism are distinctively modern political forms that can only be understood in relation to one another. Bureaucracy and totalitarianism respond to the paradoxes of the symbolic logic of democracy by endeavoring to substantiate societies that in the wake of democratic revolution and the political death of God are intrinsically indeterminate and unstable. "The democratic revolution, for so long subterranean, burst out when the body of the king was destroyed, when the body politic was decapitated and when, at the same time, the corporeality of the social was dissolved" (Lefort, 303). When society and the individual are disincorporated, neither is any longer absolutely subject to a domesticated collective space previously cosubstantial with the body of the king (Lefort, 303, 290). Instead, distinctly economic, legal, educational, and scientific relations emerge with their own particular dynamics. As a consequence, the spheres of power, law, and knowledge are disentangled until the identity of a single body politic disappears (Lefort, 303).

More generally, Lefort says, civil society becomes disengaged from the state so that social power apparently does not cohere in one body. On a symbolic register, "the modern democratic revolution is best recognized in this mutation: *there is no power linked to a body*" (Lefort, 303, my emphasis). Power is an empty place provisionally occupied by mortals who make no claim, as the monarch did, to be God's representative of the whole social body. As a result, the political is disembodied; democracy is symbolized by a collectivity with neither head nor body. Likewise, the social is fundamentally open, unfixed, and contestable.[22] "Democracy inaugurates the experience of an ungraspable, uncontrollable society in which the people will be said to be sovereign, of course, but whose identity will constantly be open to question, whose identity will remain latent" (Lefort, 303–4). Modern democracy is that regime in which the "body politic" tends to vanish (Lefort, 302)—or so it appears.

We may nonetheless experience "a certain vertigo" in the face of contingency. Experiences of the ungraspable and, we might add, invisible character of social power precipitate various discourses that endeavor to grasp society. Indeed, there is another, countervailing aspect to the symbolic mutation inaugurated by the democratic revolution.

> What emerges with democracy is the image of society as such, society as purely human but, at the same time, society as *sui generis*, whose own

> nature requires objective knowledge. It is the image of society which is homogeneous in principle, capable of being subsumed to the overview of power and knowledge, arising through the dissolution of the monarchical forces of legitimacy and the destruction of the architecture of bodies. It is the image of the omniscient, omnipotent state, of a state both anonymous and, as Tocqueville puts it, tutelary (Lefort, 304).

The indeterminate "people" is susceptible to being determined. At the level of fantasy, the state may actualize an image of the People-as-One and of one sovereign opinion (Lefort, 304).

Democracy's promise of free social relations coexists with inherent paradoxes and dangers that may precipitate even graver dangers. The people are sovereign when the place of power remains symbolically empty and no class or party claims that "the people" are themselves. Yet rule by nobody constantly threatens to cancel the symbolic functions of power when collective representations cohere at the level of the real and contingent (Lefort, 305) and individuals and groups invoke the people's name in pursuit of their own particular interests. The empty place of power becomes not only symbolically empty but actually so. Social conflict becomes sharper and increasingly contemptuous as every part vies to represent the whole, potentially leading to the death of civility and bringing society to the edge of collapse (Lefort, 305).

Totalitarianism seeks to transcend the dangerous (because paradoxical) symbolic logic of democracy ("the people rule"; "nobody rules") by constituting an apparatus that welds power and society together so that the People appear as One in an organ that embodies society as transparent, homogeneous, all-knowing, and in control of itself. In other words, totalitarianism revitalizes the image of the body politic which "vanishes" in democracy. The party or some other organ constitutes its head (Lefort, 305–6, 299). Unlike the fundamentally differentiated image of the body in monarchical society, however, the totalitarian body politic seeks to corporealize without difference. According to the medieval formula, the collective political body was underpinned by the body of Christ and invested by a division between the visible and invisible so that the monarch's representative body was both above and below itself. "That does not seem to be the position of the Egocrat or of his substitutes, the bureaucratic leaders. The Egocrat coincides with himself, as society is supposed to coincide with itself. An impossible swallowing up of the body in the head begins to take place, as does an impossible swallowing up of the head in the body" (Lefort, 306). Consequently, we witness the violent campaign against difference and division in the closed, uniform, imaginary space of totalitarianism.

Democracy, it appears, avoids totalitarian corporealizations as long as it remains headless. But Lefort's theorization of political forms cautions against too readily drawing this reassuring conclusion. "State bureaucracy" embodies aspects of totalitarian logic and mutation. Tocqueville is perhaps the most perspicacious theorist of this "democratic" tendency, and traces of his understanding are evident in Lefort:

> In a society in which homogeneity is increasing as a result of the dissolution of the old 'natural' hierarchies [which differentially incorporated the individual into the body of society], which is more and more concerned with the problem of its organization, which no longer has recourse to a transcendent guarantee of its order, which no longer finds in the language of religion a justification for its inequalities: in such a society, the state alone appears to all and represents itself to itself as the sole instituting principle, as the great actor that possesses the means of social transformation and knowledge of all things (Lefort, 280).

Hobbes projected this modern development. In the wake of the political death of God, what Lefort calls "the point of view of the state" claims legitimacy as a center of power and knowledge because of its alleged sovereign distance from, and impartiality in relation to, those who are administered. The modern state "qua centre of decision, regulation and control, tends increasingly to subordinate the detail of social life to itself" (Lefort, 280). The democratic revolution gives birth to a political form that threatens to reincorporate a disincorporated society, thus violating the separation of power, knowledge, and law, and the disengagement of society and state, which Lefort identifies as definitive of democracy's symbolic logic of power. Could not what Lefort says of totalitarianism be said of "democratic" state bureaucracy as well, namely, that it aspires to create a society "which *seems* to institute itself without divisions, which *seems* to have mastery over its own organization, a society in which each part is related to every other and imbued by one and the same project" (Lefort, 284, my emphasis)? In this case, however, the overarching project is not the "building of socialism" but the accumulation and expansion of capital. To many, I expect, this sounds like so much hyperbole. And, in fact, it may be, unless we attend to the popular authorization of the state conceived as a social totality. Our "consent in particular" to the governing knowledges and powers of regulatory, administrative systems materialize democratic rule and constitute bureaucracy as rule by nobody. The invisibility of political bodies does not necessarily chasten the totalizing tendencies of social rule but facilitates, expands, and deepens them. Our compliance with social rules constitutes Leviathan's sovereign necessities by and through "free" subject(ion)s.

According to Lefort's theory of democracy, popular sovereignty symbolically distinguishes political and social power. Because the people never literally rule, their rule is symbolically political, not an actual social power. Likewise, because the people are not literally incorporated into the state but signify an empty place, the state is not coeval with actual social powers. A corporeal, totalitarian logic, however, violates this symbolic distinction by declaring or conceiving a social power that represents "society itself *qua* conscious, acting power" (Lefort, 284). As a result the dividing line between state and society becomes invisible, as does the dividing line between political power and administrative power (Lefort, 284). Thus, in a reversal of the democratic symbolic logic, power ceases to designate an empty space and materializes in an organ or head (Lefort, 285).

But the people can materialize without a head, it would seem, through a corporeal (totalizing, if not totalitarian) logic at work in apparently democratic regimes. Indeed, it may be that such a "revolutionary transformation of civil society" captures the dynamics of power in late twentieth-century America where civil society increasingly presents itself as a structure of control and discipline rather than as a paradigm of freedom and spontaneity. The collectivity is coporealized but not, strictly speaking, as the result of the reemergence of a "head" atop the body politic or in a social body that is actually one. Rather, a totalizing power increasingly unifies state and civil society where the latter represents "structures of power which self-consciously exercise disciplinary functions that erase the differences between state and society, public and private."[23] The collective projection of a fictional "people" and its social rule facilitate the "democratically controlled" automatic docility of civil society. By means of collective projection the fictional personification of "the people" emerges before and within individual subject-citizens as "thousands of eyes posted everywhere, mobile attentions ever on the alert" (DP, 214). The people's "faceless gaze" evokes awe and reverence for the body politic and its social rules.

In the wake of democratic revolution and the political death of God, Lefort says, "there is no power linked to a body." I read popularly authorized states differently. The apparent absence of political bodies facilitates their invisible materialization; the invisibility of political bodies, especially from the perspective of a corporeal imagination of power, tends to make us spectators of powers we actually exercise. Only when we trace the political constitution of individual and collective bodies will we begin to render visible the invisible social powers that make bodies politic.

Lefort is right that the people do not materialize as a unified, coherent social body. But he is wrong to conclude that this means that the people do not constitute a cohesive (if often internally incoherent) body politic. Domestic divisions do not prohibit grand national and international projects, as any subject or object of these United States' powers would no doubt confirm.[24] Social differences and division persist, as do competition and contest among our diverse ways of understanding and making the world. Yet the remaking of individual corporeal souls renders this incoherent social body governable. Indeed, difference and its orderings are a source of the collective body's strength. On the one hand, the powers of the modern state expand as it manages difference and division, even when it apparently loses or relinquishes its power.[25] On the other hand, membership in an invisible, highly differentiated social body enables individual subject-citizens to imagine—at least when their conscience demurs—that they play no part in a collective body politic because (in Lefort's words) it has vanished. Nonetheless, the people, individually and collectively, supply the social totality with the resources for "grand national projects."

Individual and collective corporeal souls represent the link between power and the body in democratic regimes. It is too simple to conceive "state bureaucracy" as the head or organ that governs the social body: the "head" of the body politic is actualized, so to speak, in each individual corporeal soul. That is to say, "the people" materialize within each individual corporeal soul as we (our individual bodies) comply with the "commands" of governing knowledges and powers (the collective corporeal soul). As a consequence, at the level of fantasy, the People increasingly appear as One and of one sovereign opinion in which we find our selves. *Either* "the people" commands our consensual conformity to its social rules and materializes in our imaginations as a unified personification before which others represent foreign bodies, *or* we may grow resentful of its (the people's) demands and conceive politics as resistance to the commands of a "common power" in which (at least in our imaginations) we do not participate. In both cases, the body politic is imagined and articulated as a sovereign unity (monotheos) rather than as organized multitudes (entheos). In either case, each of us remains inexorably, if often invisibly, imbricated in a social totality upon which we depend for our felicity. The lucky among us receive benefits and pleasures from the state's liberty- and life-threatening projects, even as that social totality often would use us for purposes other than our own.

Representing the state as an institutional apparatus rather than a social totality obscures subject-citizens' participant role in the exercise, elaboration, and extension of governing powers and knowledges. As we saw above, Lefort finds some guidance in Tocqueville's theorization of a tutelary state. But Lefort's exclusive association of bureaucracy with the "point of view of the state" misses Tocqueville's attention to the role of individual and collective political bodies (or lack thereof) in the constitution of a specifically democratic form of despotism. By contrast, Arendt's conception of bureaucracy as rule by nobody reminds us of our political constitution. Democracy's despotic potential is unleashed when mutual promises are made in the absence of political bodies, which is to say, when individual and collective corporeal souls lose or renounce their transfigurative potential and become supervisors perpetually, if thoughtlessly, supervised. Expectantly observed by others, we subject our bodies, gestures, behaviors, aptitudes, and achievements to their anticipated judgments; observing others, we would make them comply with the social image in which we find ourselves. By contrast, mutual promising by and within political bodies renders invisible powers visible, thereby counteracting subject-citizens' inclination to rely thoughtlessly on governing powers and knowledges that not only embolden centralized, consolidated powers but also incorporate us into a social totality and implicate us in its rule. Collective political bodies (associations) facilitate recognition of the political constitution of individual bodies and thereby may disperse into organized multitudes the fictional personification and collective projection of a sovereign "people."

Hobbes understood that "the people" could evoke awe and reverence for the collective body politic and its social rules if popular authorization proceeds by means of mutual promise without political bodies. The rule of public opinion without associational forms, as Tocqueville noted, results in a waning of independence of mind and free discussion. "The great and imposing image of the people" assumes the place of political bodies.[26] If political bodies are invisible, the origination and elaboration of social rules are not apparent. The constitution of the political, as Lefort says, concerns a certain representation of power for "it is the essence of power to present and make visible a model of social organization" (282). In this respect, power is the agency of legitimacy and identity (Lefort, 305). But the specific productivity of "democratic" powers inheres in their tendency to hide the exercise of power which makes (certain among other possible) forms of social organization visible. As a consequence, what is socially made appears necessary, what is conventional seems essential.

The making of corporeal souls by means of individual subject-citizens' consent to governing powers and knowledges is crucial to this process by which an internally indeterminate and incoherent social body "acts" as a cohesive collective body politic. To speak in Hobbesian terms, the unity of the representer (the image of "the people" and the social totality that bears its name), not the unity of the represented (the individual and collective political bodies that supply the resources which infuse a potent body politic), is decisive for the constitution of sovereignty. The people can materialize without a "head" (at least as it traditionally has been construed) and can generate a cohesive collective body without subject-citizens being able to discern the origination and elaboration of either its corporeal powers or their own. Indeed, the disjuncture between cohesion and coherence facilitates the depoliticization of ethical questions: subject-citizens regard themselves as free and not responsible for the actions of that collective body, even as the name of "the people" authorizes its actions and their social powers provide it with resources for national and international projects. This depoliticization is facilitated by the detheologization of power. Mutual promise without political bodies means that it is difficult to discern how the people materialize; at most, they seem a mythical, mystical body. In a sense they are, though they are no less potent for that. When we do not recognize the political constitution of our own and others' individual bodies—the relationship between our exercise of social rule(s) and the materialization of a social totality—the powers that make a model of social organization visible themselves become invisible. Before a sovereign monotheos, secular laws carry the weight of divine commands.

Founding and everyday promises

Founding promises sundered from promising's everyday forms and political bodies constitute a sovereign state and a unified people who are potent, even if (indeed because) they are mythical and mystical. Because Arendt presumes that promising and sovereignty are mutually exclusive, she does not fully recognize how constitutional piety may foster ethical irresponsibility and threaten political freedom. While Arendt regrets the constitutional founders' failure to incorporate organs of revolutionary spirit into the new republic, she regards Americans' constitution-worship as a sign of their great good fortune and genius (OR, 198). The legitimate authority of the Constitution, which, Arendt says, Americans rightfully revere, resides in its inherent capacity to be augmented and amended (OR, 202). How we regard the Constitution is what matters. Arendt crafts a story of the American founding to teach us to make it our own.

In Arendt's view, the United States cannot be characterized as a sovereign nation because the sources of power and authority remain distinct (OR, 179–82). In America, the people are the seat of power, and the Constitution is the source of law (OR, 157). Given the colonists' predilection for organizing themselves as political bodies (at least initially), the foundation of power did not present a problem in America, but the foundation of authority did (OR, 178). Laws owed their factual existence to the power of the people and their representatives, but if laws were to secure "a perpetual union" and prove authoritative, they had to be derived from a higher source (OR, 182). To this day, many Americans, sharing what Arendt regards as the founders' theoretical confusion, identify the source of this authoritative power in God or Nature. Arendt, however, locates authority in the act of founding itself (OR, 192–96). Is it, though, the actual founding, or the capacity for political action that the founding of political bodies represents, that matters most? How we answer this question decides what comes to matter politically.

The authority conveyed by the founding of a body politic, while entirely different from an absolute, nonetheless assumes its function (OR, 199). The beginning of a body politic procures its perpetuity, and, in the case of the United States, the written Constitution memorializes this beginning. Constitution-worship is a form of *religare* expressed in willing and being bound back to a particular beginning. In Arendt's estimation, this political piety assured the stability of the new republic (OR, 198–99). The act of foundation develops its own equilibrium and permanence. In this context, authority is "a kind of necessary 'augmentation' by virtue of which all innovations and changes remain tied back to the foundation which, at the same time, they augment and increase" (OR, 202). Thus, the founding itself is the source of authority. However, because the authority of the beginning is dependent upon those who come after for its continuation, the beginning of the body politic is also the heirs' own. "Our commitment to augmentation and amendment may derive from our reverence for a beginning that is in the past; but our practices of augmentation and amendment make that beginning our own, not merely our legacy but our own construction and performative."[27] The stipulations of this practice seem minimal, namely, "common subscription to the shared authoritative linguistic practice of promising."[28] But, as the early Quakers demonstrated, there is more than one way to make a promise.

In chapter 4, I argued that the Quakers' testimony against swearing oaths was a refusal to turn a performative deed into a constative law. In this respect, they foreshadow Arendt's objection to the moment in the Declaration of Independence which invokes "self-evident truths" to grant an antipolitical certainty to the promises "we hold" (OR, 192–93). In Arendt's view, this folding of the constative into the performative introduces an absolute into the founding of the political—truths that compel as irresistibly as despotic power because they are taken to be beyond argumentative demonstration or political persuasion. Can the constative in fact be renounced or avoided, either from a political or philosophical perspective? From a political perspective, the refusal of the constative denies the stability necessary to the appearance of the political. The loss of the political "is a loss that cannot fail to happen" because "promising can effectively *lay down the law* of freedom only by immediately violating the same law; it is a free act that at once makes less than fully free all acts that follow its law and example."[29] Likewise, from a philosophical perspective, the constative is unavoidable. A constative element is present within every performative utterance, for that presence produces the performative's effect, even if (in fact, because) the relationship between the constative and performative is undecidable.[30] "God," as Jacques Derrida names this place of the last instance in every promise, authors and authorizes a promise's authority, guarantees its power, and secures its innovation. From these perspectives, the Quakers and Arendt make an impossible demand; because of that demand, and contrary to their intentions, they deny or obscure the constative moment in their own performative deeds.

Necessarily, every performative utterance needs and hides within it a constative element, and it may be that Arendt recognized this necessity when she spoke of the "measure of complete arbitrariness" that accompanies every beginning (OR, 206).[31] But how are we to envision and engage this necessity? Arendt seeks to commit us to the interrogation of the constative, of what we are inclined to take as inevitable and unalterable. Recognizing and sustaining the performative aspect of promising enables us to resist its constative elements and thus to distinguish secular law from divine command. Recognizing founding promises as performative deeds prevents the founding from relying upon, or turning into, an absolute, a law of laws *above* man. The performative aspect of promising keeps the beginning present, as Bonnie Honig has argued, not as an unquestionable source of authority, but as the source of authority for our own questioning. Reading the Constitution entails interpreting the written document that memorializes the American founding. Augmenting its meaning is a process of translation that brings the beginning into our present. "Translation augments, *necessarily*. It does not merely copy, or reproduce; it is a new linguistic event, it produces new 'textual bodies'."[32] Augmentation and amendment make the beginning our own construction and performative. But do they necessarily do so? Or when they necessarily do so, are they really our own new beginnings? What prevents them from being mere repetitions? What might they repeat even as they perform anew?

By way of an answer to these questions I suggest another reading of the Quakers' and Arendt's refusal to turn performative deeds into constative laws. The Quakers do not deny God's existence, and Arendt does not deny the elemental arbitrariness of every beginning. Neither denies the necessity of the constative. Like Derrida, they agree (at least in practice) that every promise invokes a last instance for which it cannot account in its own terms but which it nonetheless needs. What they contest is the embodiment of God or, politically speaking, the location of invisible powers and the representation of authority.[33] The resistability of the constative may distinguish secular law from divine command, but the distinction is not as easily sustained in practice as it appears in theory.[34] Augmentation does not necessarily preclude mere repetition. What matters is how "God," or the invisible powers that every promise makes, is envisioned and engaged. The political is founded through this imagination of power. A monotheistic political ethos binds us to the beginning, in this case, to the American way of life. By contrast, an enthusiastic political ethos binds us to what the human capacity for beginning promises, perhaps even to imaginings beyond America.

Augmenting and amending the U.S. Constitution commits us to its beginning even as we make it our own construction and performative. To what do we bind ourselves when we authorize, even as we resist, the necessities of this particular constitutional beginning? Of course, the answer is contestable and therefore undecidable. Yet the founding would not be a founding if it made everything possible. On my reading, the

U.S. Constitution enacted mutual promise without political bodies: it located the political and its invisible powers in a governing state that monopolizes the political and which acts in the name of "We, The People" to constitute a sovereign social totality. When we augment and amend the Constitution we affirm this beginning and become subjects of sovereignty (and are positioned as sovereign subjects) even as we resist it.

By combining permanence and augmentation the U.S. Constitution may truly foster a politics that questions and innovates the terms of its life. As we have seen, however, a sovereign body politic requires a cohesive social body, not necessarily a coherent one. For example, Hobbes's ideal commonwealth, popularly authorized by means of mutual promise without political bodies, does not prohibit free making and individuality. Indeed, Leviathan's governing powers grow in response to the needs and desires of the freely subject. But, like the U.S. Constitution, Leviathan's maintenance does preclude the contestation of its sovereign conception of the political. It does this in part by rendering unimaginable transgressive "revolutionary action" that challenges the necessities of sovereign governance.

As Machiavelli teaches, the durability of republics depends upon their power to expand. Does expansion through augmentation of the foundations of the republic require violent conquest and colonial expansion? Strictly speaking, perhaps not, or at least not any longer. The social rules enabled by the popularly authorized Constitution increase its subject-citizens' efficacy without visible conquest. But social rule does not necessarily promote our ethicality—our responsiveness to the trespasses that found the republic—or the freedom it promises. A properly constituted republic increases our world-building capacities, but not all world-building is political, or at least not ethically political. When we are indifferent to our conduct's continuation and expansion of social rules, we not only exclude others, we also intensify the social necessities that circumscribe our own action. Social rules are the means by which individuals remake themselves in conformity with the collective projection of "the people" within their corporeal souls. A body politic's prevailing views and practices reflect and reinforce congealed patterns of social rule. Governing powers—exhibited in the norms, practices, and efficacy we bring to bear upon our own and others' conduct—institute often invisible social patterns. These powers are not wielded exclusively by government, but are borne and extended by subject-citizens pursuing their felicity. We do not possess these powers, however; we carry and exercise them. Even shared goals that bind us to others reveal and mobilize our differential effects partly fashioned by disparate histories. Our bodies/minds, our identities and pursuits, resonate with, extend, resist, and are stifled by force fields traversing the body politic. Subject-citizens continually display conflicting, asymmetrical effects begot by our differential relation to norms, the varied social efficacy that accrues with those norms, and the diverse psychological and material consequences issuing from our locations in the body politic.

The people of a sovereign body politic materialize powerfully, but when the mutual promising that accomplishes this incarnation is sundered from political bodies, they also tend to do so thoughtlessly. The contemporary crisis of the subject-citizen is not addressed simply by increasing our active efficacy, in part because the forms of power which precipitate this crisis are distinguished by their tendency to render us excessively efficacious. Overcoming the contemporary crisis of the subject-citizen requires conceiving *thoughtful* efficacy, which is to say, reconceiving the head of a headless political bodies, the relationship between "command" and "counsel," between our power and thinking, bodies and minds.

PART III

LIVING ETHICALLY, ACTING POLITICALLY

In Part I, I traced political theoretical connections among ordered evil, the headlessness of the contemporary body politic, and the thoughtlessness of its subject-citizens. My aim was to narrate the generation of this political condition and to reveal the ethical political predicaments we face today as a consequence of our political constitution. What does it mean to live ethically when every effort to understand and make a world entails trespass? What does living responsibly and freely entail when, for instance, securing a home for oneself implicates one in social processes that make others homeless? In Part II, I offered a genealogy of the subject-citizen and suggested that predominant responses to these ethical predicaments obscure or evade conundrums of political theodicy even as they claim to foster free and responsible living. If we are to conceive how the freely subject produce social necessities, we need to be able to think about invisible powers, as well as to discern our active role in their extension and elaboration. Predominant forms of rationality and ethics, however, tend either to neglect invisible powers or to understate their normalizing, unethical effects. In contexts of ordered evil, harm and wrongdoing are often inadvertent, unseen, and contrary to our good intentions; they are nonetheless the effect of our actions, often the very actions that mark us as reasonable and predictable. In this third part, I explore what it might mean and entail to live ethically under conditions of ordered evil, where trespass and thoughtlessness, not sin and malevolence, matter most.

CHAPTER 6

Seeking the Limits of Our Selves

There are two kinds of madness, one resulting from human ailments, the other from a divine disturbance of our conventions of conduct.

Phaedrus 265a

Think of God's mercy, my brothers, and worship him, I beg you, in a way that is worthy of thinking beings, by offering your living bodies as a holy sacrifice, truly pleasing to God. Do not model yourself on the behavior of the world around you, but let your behavior change, modeled by your new mind.

Rom. 12:2

Foucault imagines subjects who at once are produced by regimes of power/knowledge and who can resist their subjection. Judith Butler, among others, has asked whether Foucault's formulation of the body as a "cultural construction" that nonetheless resists its construction presupposes both a power external to the body and a body external to power.[1] According to Butler, Foucault "appears to assume a materiality to the body prior to its signification."[2] Butler finds the metaphor of power's inscription on bodily surface especially symptomatic: The "very mechanism of 'inscription' implies power that is necessarily external to the body itself" (603), as well as a "body which is external to its construction, invariant in some of its structures, and which, in fact, represents a dynamic locus of resistance to culture per se" (602). In Butler's view, such presumptions pose a problem for Foucault since genealogy should trace the discursive constitution of bodies that appear to be ontologically given. If, as Butler says elsewhere, power operates successfully "by constituting an object domain, a field of intelligibility, as a taken-for-granted ontology," Foucault would appear to obfuscate power relations while claiming to illuminate them.[3]

Butler performs her critique of Foucault in different forms and contexts. Her reading of power as inscription upon bodily surface is most important for my purposes, however, because it touches upon the relative corporeality and incorporeality of the soul in the contemporary imagination of power, or how spirited our role is in the constitution of our selves and others. Considering these matters will accent the later Foucault's reconfiguration of the crisis of the subject-citizen.

Like Kafka in *The Penal Colony*, Butler says, Foucault seems to conceive a body culturally constructed by "history" that, like a writing instrument, "produces cultural significations" upon a body "figured as a ready surface or blank page available for inscription" (Butler, 603). On Butler's reading of *Discipline and Punish*, the law that constitutes the body is not literally internalized (as in Nietzsche) "but incorporated *on* bodies: there the law is manifest as a sign of the essence of their selves, the meaning of their soul, their conscience, the law of their desire" (Butler, 605). The soul that imprisons the body appears to be deep within, but in fact the appearance of depth is a surface effect (Butler, 605). Foucault shows us that "the soul is a surface signification that contests and displaces the inner/outer distinction itself, a figure of interior psychic space inscribed on the body as a social signification that perpetually conceals itself as such" (Butler, 606). But Foucault undermines the critical edge of this insight, Butler thinks, when he identifies power tracing surfaces as the "single drama" of history (Butler, 603). As a consequence, both the process of inscription and the body inscribed assume a universality genealogy should contest (Butler, 607). In Butler's terms, when we project a body "outside" the law we are in danger of failing to see how the law maintains this "outside" within itself. When Butler senses Foucault falling prey to a liberatory ideal (for example, the romance of a prediscursive multiplicity of bodily forces), she emphasizes "the law's uncanny capacity to produce only those rebellions that it can guarantee will—out of fidelity—defeat themselves and those subjects who, utterly subjected, have no choice but to reiterate the law of their own genesis." If subversion is possible, Butler counters, "it will be subversion from within the terms of the law, through the possibilities that emerge when the law turns against itself and spawns unexpected permutations of itself."[4]

I too find a problem in the middle Foucault.[5] But I think Butler misconstrues the problem and thereby neglects a difficulty concerning human agency she shares with Foucault. It is not their problem alone. Once we acknowledge the discursive dependence of the subject, it is far from clear how a subject of social rule can be a political actor. But Butler's critique simply reinstates the question Foucault confronted as a result of what *Discipline and Punish* had accomplished: if the subject is constituted by power/knowledge, how is resistance possible and what is its goal? My critique of the middle Foucault proceeds on a different register from Butler's. In my view the passive corporeality of the soul of *Discipline and Punish* marks the limit of that work. The metaphor of power as inscription is problematic not because its emphasis upon surfaces conceives power as external to the body and not because Foucault seems to presuppose a body that exceeds any particular discursive regime. The problem is what and who traces the surface of bodies/minds. Foucault's ethical turn introduces the problem of individual conduct to address this question and the political problems embedded within it.

The middle Foucault obscures, even as he reveals, how subject-citizens exercise the governing powers that constitute them. Foucault's limit is not a personal failing, but it illuminates an imagination of power and political condition. Until Foucault introduces the problem of individual conduct ("soul"), alongside those of knowledge ("mind") and power ("body") which had always preoccupied him, he represents subjects as passive targets of governing powers and knowledges, not as agents who participate in their own and others' constitution. But subjects come to be as they leave and receive traces on the surface of all to which their bodies/minds relate them. These traces and tracings implicate them in ordered evil, in the trespasses that found social order and their selves. Foucault's turn to ethics seeks to conceptualize this agency—how our actions affect others' actions—and to address the new problems of responsibility and freedom it poses. The later Foucault recovers the soul's incorporeal potential by theorizing our capacity to exercise power freely and deliberately within the necessity and upon the limits of what our bodies/minds have been made to be.

One could argue that Butler remains preoccupied with codes while Foucault turns to the ethical relations which enact codes. One could say that Butler's reliance upon "the law" to theorize performativity continues to evade the problems of agency Foucault confronts in his last works. But I prefer to see analogous movement in Butler's turn from the language of construction to materialization (in *Bodies That Matter*) and Foucault's later concern with ethics and practices of the self. Both theorize how bodies come to matter and with what effects upon our selves and others.[6] Both seek "to refigure the necessary 'outside' as a future horizon, one in which the violence of exclusion is perpetually in the process of being overcome." Foucault's ethos, like Butler's, seeks to "begin, without ending, without mastering, to own—and yet never fully to own—the exclusions by which we proceed."[7] In contexts of ordered evil, politics requires ethical arts of freely exercising power in relation to socially produced necessities.

Problems of responsibility and freedom

Foucault helps us imagine subjects as creatures of discourse. Doing so, however, problematizes conventional understandings of responsibility and freedom. How, if at all, can we be responsible for our effects upon others when those effects themselves are the effect of what we have been made to be? How, if at all, can individuals be free who are subjects of normalizing powers? Foucault's last writings evince increasing interest in how our ties to our own identity (conscience as self-knowledge) create relations of control and dependence among us (the rule of social norms). How we become subjects—what binds us to our selves and submits us to others (and vice versa)—are integral to the governing powers and functions of the modern state and implicate us in its rule. Individuals are integrated into this social totality as our individuality assumes forms that reinforce, elaborate, and extend patterns of social rule. Disciplinary powers' spectacles of surveillance are both individualizing and totalizing: as we incorporate our selves into a social totality, we supply the material resources for the modern state's governing force and projects from which, in turn, we may garner our own benefits and pleasures.[8] As we saw in the last section, enthusiasm, which once challenged social rules, may come to serve their sovereignty.

The ethical crisis of subject-citizens of a headless body politic is cultivated by a political ethos of governmentality and fostered by a corporeal imagination of power. More specifically, headlessness in all its senses—from the absence of a unified, original agent of power relations to the crises of agency which are both the product and producer of the thoughtless exercise of power—are generated in the contact between our ways of thinking, our notions of ethical conduct, and the actualities of power. As a consequence of a disjuncture between our rationalities and ethics, on the one hand, and contemporary power relations, on the other, our thinking and ethics do not do justice to the problem of evil as it has been transposed by contemporary power relations. The contemporary body politic is headless not only because it is without a single, original agent of power but also because its reigning governmentality tends to render "command" without "counsel"; we appear to be without affect in the constitution of our selves and others, until, in time, we become without deliberate affect. That is to say, governmentality cultivates subjection to social rules in ways that often foster thoughtlessness about governing powers' effects and about how we participate in the constitution of political bodies both individual and collective. We are thoughtless subjects when we exercise power without either self-reflection or regard for others. In contexts of ordered evil, performing contracts, behaving predictably, and conducting oneself reasonably do not guarantee responsibility and freedom; indeed, they may produce the opposite.

We have difficulty forming ourselves into free and deliberate subjects of our actions when the truth of our selves—what we are, what we do, what we can accomplish—becomes problematic (CS, 68, 85). In contemporary contexts, being what we are made to be—for example, enacting our race, gender, or sexuality in expected manners—may implicate us in the rule of others in ways which we neither see nor intend.[9] "Acting like a man," following your inclination to associate only with colleagues and neighbors with whom you readily feel comfortable, making presumptions about others' intimate relations, these and other "free" actions reinforce forms of social rule which may exclude and harm others. It is neither obvious nor certain that being what we are—especially those aspects of what we are that we are "made" to be—yields ethical conduct. Indeed, ethical political action may require us to contest and transfigure what we are made to be so as to reveal who we are becoming.

But as seventeenth century Quakers found, changing who you are is not easy, and it has become no easier. Simply increasing our agency will not address the contemporary crisis of the subject, because often we are excessively efficacious, implicated in distant, if often invisible, harms. Yet, even if willing what we are made to be implicates us in such harm, it is not at all clear what, if anything, we can do about it or why, even if we could, we would want to. The subject-citizen experiences disjunctures among will, capacity, and desire; these are sources of its ethical crisis. To the extent that we will what we are made to be, we possess a kind of power which renders us responsible for the world, our selves, and others. But power as will is not necessarily power as capacity. We are free subjects to the extent that we will social necessities, but their necessary character seems to obviate our capacity to think, say, or do differently. If free subjects produce social necessities, how can they do otherwise, and why would they want to? On the one hand, we would desire to limit and direct our power effects to the extent that they implicate us in harm to others. On the other hand, this limitation and control would require an increase in the free and deliberate exercise of power both in relation to our selves and others. Living ethically and acting politically require in one respect a delimiting of power, yet in another respect its expansion.[10] In short, we must better understand how we become subjects (UP, 5). How and why do we come to will what we are, and how might we do otherwise?[11]

For the later Foucault, the way in which individuals affect one another's action provides a working definition of power relations. Governance is no longer conceived in determined situations and modalities but as something groups and individuals do to one another which need not necessarily occur. As a result, discipline is revaluated and a pragmatic distinction introduced between its nonconsensual and consensual modes (FR, 378–79) or what we might call its sovereign and collaborative forms. No practice is free of discipline, of power and its effects. But relations of power differ in the practices of freedom which they enact and enable.

The pragmatic difference between consensual and nonconsensual disciplines, between collaborative and sovereign selves and powers, is illuminated by the example of military discipline. In *Discipline and Punish*, military training and tactics are paradigmatic disciplinary techniques that create docile, productive bodies (DP, 135–69). There is much truth to this story. At the same time, in the absence of a distinction between consensual and nonconsensual disciplines, between collaborative and sovereign powers, a phenomenon like the new model army of Hobbes's time becomes incomprehensible. One need not overstate the radical elements of the new model army to recognize a struggle over the meaning and degrees of consensuality in political contests over its organization and goals. The subsequent professionalization of the new model army signifies the prevalence of nonconsensual, sovereign disciplines.[12] Nothing antithetical to the practice of freedom necessarily inheres in disciplinary techniques and spaces, however. Perhaps Foucault believed this when he wrote *Discipline and Punish*, but he makes the point explicit subsequently.

The practice of freedom, not techniques or spaces of discipline, conditions power relations. For example, a space might be structured panoptically—so that no one could enter or leave without being seen by everyone—"but it could only be oppressive if people were prepared to use their presence in order to watch over others" (FL, 266). In other words, the free subject's renunciation of the practice of freedom is a condition of the popularly authorized, "automatic docility" I have discussed in previous chapters. Foucault speculates about the consensual and nonconsensual disciplines, the "emotional fabric and relational virtualities," that permeate and challenge military institutions today, even as disciplinary institutions govern the practices of freedom they incite.

> The institution is caught in a contradiction: affective intensities traverse it which at one and the same time keep it going and shake it up. Look at the army, where love of men is ceaselessly provoked and shamed. Institutional codes can't validate these relations with multiple intensities, variable colors, imperceptible movements and challenging forms. These relations short-circuit it and introduce love where there's supposed to be only law, rule or habit. (FL, 205).[13]

In Foucault's later writings, the problem of power concerns not only what is done to us (institutional codes), but also what we do to our selves and others (rule-bound habits and relational virtualities). Power relations encompass the effect of our actions upon others' actions. Practices of freedom bring power to bear upon our selves so that we deliberately exercise the power we necessarily bring to bear upon others (UP, 80). Foucault's attention to individual conduct reconfigures the problem of truth/knowledge. Legal and moral codes make demands upon us; yet how we enact principle not only conditions our power effects but also the meaning and significance of principle. How knowledges are incorporated and codes enacted, and the effects upon oneself and others, become the principal concern of ethics. Who we are affects what we are (for example, the meaning and significance of our race or gender), but who we are also exemplifies principle and conditions its meaning.

A subject experiences a crisis whenever she has difficulty forming herself into the ethical subject of her actions. Such a crisis occurs when the consequences of professed adherence to normative codes is neither obvious nor sufficient to guarantee ethical conduct (UP, 36). Under such conditions, our style of activity, rather than our simple conformity to a code, becomes decisive (CS, 173). From this perspective, a normative principle is defined less by its law and more by the forms of relating and manner(s) of conduct it inspires. To say that a principle is defined less by moral law (command) and more by ethical relation (rapport) is to say that principles materialize in the effects they enact.[14] Ordinary evil precipitates an ethical crisis of the subject because the effects of our actions, not good intentions, matter most when predominant forms of evil are nonintentional.

Foucault turned to Hellenic practices of the self because he found their ethical political situations formally analogous to our own.[15] Consider the changes in conditions of "the political game" to which the "cultivation of the self" as a stylistics of existence constituted an original response (CS, 71). Traditionally, scholars have narrated the displacement of city-states by imperial regimes as a story of the simultaneous decline of political activity and withdrawal into the self. Foucault recognizes some truth in this story. But he prefers to emphasize a problematization and redefinition of political activity in response to changing conditions of power. Like the subject-citizens of *Discipline and Punish* and *The History of Sexuality*, citizens of Hellenic states increasingly encountered multiple, decentered, complex spaces of power in which everyday life and the stylistics of the individual bond (as opposed to "techniques of government") assumed greater importance (CS, 82, 148). In part this trend was due to the increasing positivity and productivity of power which relied more on self-imposed than direct administration. These changes in the conditions of power informed growing interest in personal ethics, the morality of everyday conduct, private life, and pleasure. Problems of responsibility and power incited this interest. "The new rules of the political game made it more difficult to define the relations between what one was, what one could do, and what one was expected to accomplish" so that the "formation of oneself as an ethical subject of one's own actions became problematic" (CS, 84). The exercise of power took place in a complex field of relations where the individual occupied an important transition point. His status (what he was made to be) placed him there, but that prescribed identity did not determine rules to follow and limits to observe (who he was becoming) (CS, 88).

As the weight of what one is accumulates, the problematization of free and responsible individuality may also grow.

> We may suppose that starting from the moment when new conditions of political life modified the relations between status, functions, powers, and duties, two opposite phenomena occurred. . . .On the one hand, there is an accentuation of everything that allows the individual to define his identity in accordance with his status and with the elements that manifest it in a most visible way. . . . But at the opposite extreme one finds the attitude that consists, on the contrary, in defining what one is purely in relation to oneself . . . in the sovereignty that one exercises over oneself. (CS, 85)

Foucault reads texts that emphasize either one of these strategies—the intensification of status or withdrawal into a sovereign self (CS, 86).[16]

What interests him most, however, are practices of the self which take action between these strategies. The most significant line of division is not a choice between participation or abstention from politics, but the concern "to define the principle of a relation to self that will make it possible to set the forms and conditions in which political action, participation in the offices of power, the exercise of a function, will be possible or not possible, acceptable or necessary" (CS, 86). Politics is a "life" and "practice" to which one devotes oneself by free and deliberate choice (CS, 87). One exercises power within a complex network in which one occupies a key position as both ruler and ruled. Signs of status mark what one is and place one in a position to exercise power, but they do not prescribe political action. What we are conditions but does not (or at least need not) determine who we are. "The foundation, the link between oneself and political activity, that which establishes the individual as a political actor, is not—or not merely—his status; it is, in the general context defined by his birth and standing, a personal act" (CS, 87). In my view, the early Quakers' relationship to social rule exemplifies this principled, personal stance.

In Hellenic practices of the self, Foucault identifies "the search for a new way of conceiving the relationship that one ought to have with one's status, one's function, one's activities, and one's obligations" (CS, 84). We might characterize this as a problematization of the relationship between what and who we are. The meaning and value of responsibility and freedom are no longer assumed, but become the source of intensified reflection and attention.

> In a political space where the political structure of the city and the laws with which it is endowed have unquestionably lost some of their importance . . . where the decisive elements reside more and more in men, in their decisions, in the manner in which they bring their authority to bear, in the wisdom they manifest in the interplay of equilibria and transactions, it appears that the art of governing oneself becomes a crucial political factor (CS, 89).

Universal codes are insufficient—because indeterminant—to prescribe ethical conduct, which precipitates questioning and practice upon the self. A principle may be universal in form, but it is singular in its manifestation (CS, 93). An aesthetics of existence addresses how ethical principles are enacted; more specifically, "the *manner* in which one ought to form oneself as an ethical subject in the entire sphere of social, political, and civic activities" (CS, 94, my emphasis).

In the Hellenic context, the crisis of the subject instigated a reelaboration of an ethics of self-mastery. Ruling men sought to form themselves into ethical subjects of their actions through a devotion to the self which enabled submission to rules and gave purpose to existence (CS, 95). Foucault found the Hellenic ethos at times disgusting and, regardless, irrecoverable. But contemporary subject-citizens may find counsel for their own problems of responsibility and freedom in practices of the self which stylize existence in response to crises of subjectivation. Aesthetics of existence seek to give a "deliberate form" and "particular style" to the exercise of power (CS, 163). Such thoughtful self-transfiguration becomes ethical political action when it begins the responsible and free exercise of power in relation to socially produced necessities.

How might we enact this possibility? What are the obstacles to doing so? The subtleties of trespass and ordered evil make answering either question difficult. A consideration of Arendt's reflections upon Adolph Eichmann may clarify matters. Eichmann's case is extreme. But the extremity he illustrates may magnify (so that we can see) what is otherwise invisible. Organized evil on the massive scale of the Nazi regime in part functioned as a result of countless individual failures to interrogate which forms of "participation in the offices of power" and the "exercise of a function" were "possible or impossible, acceptable or necessary" (CS, 87).[17] Precisely because Eichmann's deeds were not trespasses, they graphically convey the consequences of thoughtlessness about the conditions and effects of one's exercise of power. What his case makes visible may help us see what has heretofore been invisible in our own exercise of power.

Eichmann, Arendt says, was "an average, 'normal' person, neither feeble-minded nor indoctrinated nor cynical." Nonetheless, he proved "perfectly incapable of telling right from wrong" (E, 26). But this inability was not due to an absence of conscience. "For the sad and very uncomfortable truth of the matter probably was that it was not his fanaticism but his very conscience that prompted Eichmann to adopt [an] uncompromising attitude" toward his part in carrying out the Final Solution (E, 146). In this respect Eichmann was not unlike others who put great stock in being law-abiding subject-citizens, though he was situated to be more efficacious than most. Arendt explains:

> And just as the law in all civilized countries assumes that the voice of conscience tells everybody "Thou shalt not kill," even though man's natural desires and inclinations may at times be murderous, so the law in

> Hitler's land demanded that the voice of conscience tell everybody: 'Thou shalt kill,' although organizers of the massacres knew full well that murder is against the normal desires and inclinations of most people. Evil in the Third Reich had lost the quality by which most people recognize it—the quality of temptation. Many Germans and many Nazis, probably an overwhelming majority of them, must have been tempted *not* to murder, *not* to rob, *not* to let their neighbors go off to their doom (for that the Jews were transported to their doom they knew, of course, even though many of them may not have known the gruesome details), and not to become accomplices in all these crimes by benefiting from them. But, God knows, they had learned how to resist temptation. (E, 150)

Paradoxically, Eichmann's inability to think for himself was related to his inability to think with others. Eichmann lacked a collaborative conscience, manifest in his "almost total inability ever to look at anything from the other fellow's point of view" (E, 47–48). Absent this collaborative capacity, Eichmann was incapable of communication and immune to the "presence of others and hence [to] reality as such" (E, 49). The fact that Eichmann was convinced that he thought and acted otherwise only compounds Arendt's disconcerting insight.

> [Eichmann] and his men and the Jews were all "pulling together," and whenever there were any difficulties the Jewish functionaries would come running to him "to unburden their hearts," to tell him "all their grief and sorrow," and to ask for his help. The Jews "desired" to emigrate, and he, Eichmann, was there to help them, because it so happened that at the same time the Nazi authorities had expressed a desire to see their Reich *judenrein*. The two desires coincided, and he, Eichmann, could "do justice to both parties." (E, 48)

Eichmann's "analysis" of the situation attests to a correlation between the inability to think from the perspective of another and obliviousness to the conditions of power—the relations supporting his own "responsibilities" and circumscribing others' "desires" and "choices." We should not be surprised, however, that Eichmann found the voice of his conscience so reassuring. As we saw in chapters 4 and 5, the governing form of modern individual conscience tends to confirm our social identity and roles, binding us to a social totality in which we are ruled and, in turn, rule others. Ordered evil accentuates the limitations of both individual conscience and reasonable public judgment. Response to our trespasses may require us to exceed these limits and accede to others.

Thinking the invisible, silent, outside

Socrates, unlike Eichmann (to say the least), acclimated himself to the dizzying to and fro movement between thinking and everyday living where each is continually interrupting the other (LM, 166). Socrates unified thinking and action, "being equally at home in both spheres and able to move from one sphere to the other with the greatest apparent ease, very much as we ourselves constantly move back and forth between experiences in the world of appearances and the need for reflecting upon them" (LM, 167). The example of Socrates suggests why it is appropriate to call Eichmann thoughtless. At certain moments, all of us are immune to thinking. "Standardized codes of expression and conduct have the socially recognized function of protecting us against reality, that is, against the claim on our thinking attention that all events and facts make by virtue of their existence." Social rules always demand a degree of thoughtlessness. If we were responsive all the time to the claims existence makes upon our thinking "we would soon be exhausted." Eichmann "differed from the rest of us only in that he clearly knew of no such claim at all" (LM, 4). By contrast, Socrates is exemplary of the demands daily living place on thought.

Arendt's "Socrates" believes that "talking and thinking about piety, justice, courage, and the rest [are] likely to make men more pious, more just, more courageous, despite the fact that neither definitions nor 'values' [are] given to them to direct their future conduct" (LM, 171). Indeed, thinking dissolves all rules of ordinary conduct (LM, 192). If, practically speaking, "thinking means that each time you are confronted with some difficulty in your life you have to make up your mind anew" (LM, 177), what does the activity promise in the way of the avoidance of harm or wrongdoing? Why does Socrates claim that it is always better to be wronged than to do wrong? In Arendt's view, the experience of thinking provides Socrates with this insight.

According to Arendt's most explicit account (the limits of which I push), the activity of thinking fulfills the two-in-one of consciousness where to think means to "know with and by myself." When we are with others, Arendt says, we appear to them and to ourselves as one. Only when we "stop and think" is difference inserted into this oneness, the "*duality* of myself with myself that makes thinking a true activity, in which I am both the one who asks and the one who answers" (LM, 185). The thinking dialogue between me and myself is significant not only for my experience of myself but also for others, because it suggests that the "difference and otherness which are such outstanding characteristics of the world of appearances" are also intrinsic to the subject (though only to the extent that he or she thinks). "The ego—the I-am-I—experiences difference in identity precisely when it is not related to the things that appear but only related to itself" (LM, 187). In *Eichmann*, Arendt suggests a relationship between his thoughtlessness and "why he must hang." Now we see why. Eichmann's inability to think is the root of his disregard for the plurality of the human condition (E, 279). According to this account, the experience of difference in identity, actualized when we think, opens us to the experience of plurality even when we are alone. "The Socratic two-in-one heals the solitariness of thought; its inherent duality points to the infinite plurality which is the law of the earth" (LM, 187). Eichmann's thoughtlessness destroys the plurality both within and without him.

The duality of self inherent in thinking not only opens us to plurality but also commits us to its preservation.[18] Thinking's enactment of the self's duality makes us aware of the plurality of the world and, thus, of the relationship between remaining on good terms with ourselves and refraining from harming others. Encountering the other within oneself, and caring for it, exposes and binds us to others in the world.

> To Socrates, the duality of the two-in-one meant no more than that if you want to think, you must see to it that the two who carry on the dialogue be in good shape, that the partners be *friends*. The partner who comes to life when you are alert and alone is the only one from whom you can never get away—except by ceasing to think. It is better to suffer wrong than to do wrong, because you can remain the friend of the sufferer. (LM, 187–88)

We have given the name of conscience, Arendt says, to the one who awaits Socrates at home.[19] "Before its tribunal, to adopt Kantian language, we have to appear and give account of ourselves" (LM, 190). Only if we are in agreement—and thereby on friendly terms—with ourselves can we feel some security when we go home. Conscience does not tell us what to do, but it may fill us full of obstacles before the temptation of evil. "What causes a man to fear [conscience] is the anticipation of the witness who awaits him *if* and when he goes home" (LM, 190). Arendt's emphasis suggests that some may choose not to go home, which is to say they never stop and think. "A person who does not know the silent intercourse (in which we examine what we say and what we do) will not mind contradicting himself, and this means that he will never be either able or willing to account for what he says and does; nor will he mind committing any crime, since he can count on it being forgotten the next moment" (LM, 191). Heedless of the other within her own identity, the thoughtless person has no reason to be receptive to the perspectives of the plurality of others who inhabit the world.

Still, Arendt considers thinking of only indirect political significance. Thinking prepares the way for judgment that, like its particular objects, is housed in the world as thinking is not (LM, 92). To have political affect, Arendt says, thinking must become attuned to *sensus communis*. Thinking withdraws from the world as it appears close at hand. According to Arendt, judgment is the by-product of thinking's liberating effect, and it is realized in our ability to tell right from wrong, beautiful from ugly (LM, 191–93). Our judgment is manifest in the communicability of our taste which is both discerning and accessible to others.

Echoing Socrates' practice and Kant's teaching, Arendtian thinking leads us toward others and, at least potentially, makes us responsive to them. Human beings are "interdependent not merely in their needs and cares but in their highest faculty, the human mind, which will not function outside of human society" (LK, 10). One cannot learn how to think without publicity, "without the testing that arises from contact with other people's thinking" (LK, 42). Arendt criticizes Plato for separating knowing and doing, thinking and acting and she appears to find a solution to these antinomies in Kant's conception of judgment which mediates theory and practice (LK, 36), the general and the particular (LK, 76).

In Kant, Arendt finds a theorist of an "enlarged mentality" who recognizes that "critical thinking is possible only where the standpoints of all others are open to inspection" (LK, 43). We test our thoughts by communicating them to others: I must expose myself to others' opinions and weave them into my judgments and, as Kant wrote, "afford them the opportunity of overturning all of my most cherished beliefs" (LK, 42). As we enlarge our perspective to take others into account, we may find our opinions changed. According to this view, thinking may be a solitary activity, but the force of imagination makes others present. Imagination makes the presence of other perspectives matter by abstracting from our "subjective private conditions" (LK, 43). In other words, judgment leaves our particular body behind. As a result, Arendt says, we acquire an impartial perspective, or at least a more general, enlarged outlook in relation to relevant particulars (LK, 42–44).

Both Kant and Arendt believe that only the spectator is capable of impartiality and generality (LK, 54, 58). The onlooker's disinterestedness establishes the meaning of an event (LK, 54–58) because she disavows the actor's partiality but also for the same common sense reason that genius is subordinate to taste: what cannot be communicated cannot be appreciated. Communicability is the criterion of truth in art and action. Taste is the faculty that guides communicability.

> Taste or judgment is not the privilege of genius. The conditions *sine qua non* for the existence of beautiful objects is communicability; the judgment of the spectator creates the space without which no objects could appear at all. The public realm is constituted by the critics and the spectators, not by the actors or the makers. And this critic and spectator sits in every actor and fabricator; without this critical, judging faculty the doer or the maker would be so isolated from the spectator that he would not even be perceived. (LK, 63)

Indeed, "insanity" consists in having lost this common sense that enables us to judge as spectators or to make ourselves heard as political actors (LK, 64). This judgment affords one perspective on why the Quakers seemed "mad" to so many of their contemporaries.[20]

How can so discerning a faculty as judgment be based upon taste—the most private and noncommunicative of our senses? Arendt's answer relies upon the representative powers of imagination. Imagination creates an image for critical reflection by representing what is absent; thus, we do not perceive an external object only as a phantasm of our inner sense (LK, 65). (Hobbes accused enthusiasts like the Quakers of falling prey to the latter.) "One then speaks of judgment and no longer of taste because, though it still affects one like a matter of taste, one now has, by means of representation, established the proper distance, the remoteness or uninvolvedness or disinterestedness, that is requisite for approbation and disapprobation, for evaluating something at its proper worth" (LK, 67). The represented object arouses one's pleasure or displeasure, one's approbation or disapprobation, but reflective, communicative judgment must bear in mind others' perspectives.

Common sense demands that taste be considerate of others, at least if it is to be communicable. *Sensus communis* is the extra sense that fits us into community, the greater body with more generalizable tastes than particular, individual bodies.[21] Keeping in mind others' perspectives and allowing their perspectives to affect our own make communication of taste and judgment possible. To the maxims "Think for yourself" and "Remain in agreement with yourself," judgment adds: "Put yourself in thought in the place of everyone else" (LK, 71). Every judgment appeals to the *sensus communis* in others, and the validity of one's judgments can be established only by "courting" and "wooing" others' agreement (LK, 72). "Private conditions condition us; imagination and reflection enable us to *liberate* ourselves from them and to attain that relative impartiality that is the specific virtue of judgment" (LK, 73, my emphasis). Obviously, the less idiosyncratic one's taste and judgment, the better they can be communicated to others.

Under Arendt's guidance, Kantian communicability becomes a regulative idea inspiring both spectator and actor to alter him or herself as communication requires. "It is by virtue of this idea of mankind [a compact of communicability], present in every single man, that men are human, and they can be called civilized or humane to the extent that this idea becomes the principle not only of their judgments but also of their actions" (LK, 75). One judges always as a member of a community and guided by one's *sensus communis*. "But in the last analysis, one is a member of a world community by the sheer fact of being human" (LK, 75). Thus, one's actions and judgments take their bearing from this general compact of communicability among mankind. Arendt's account seems nicely summarized by the regulative idea of a communicative ethics: we should act and judge actions in light of reasons to which all affected could agree.[22] In Arendt's words, the categorical imperative for action would read: "Always act on the maxim through which this original compact [of communicability] can be actualized into a general law" (LK, 75).

It seems, however, that our judgments may reveal more about what we have been made to be than about who we could become. Once again the example of Eichmann proves illuminating, revealing the boundaries of both individual conscience and reasonable public judgment. *The Life of the Mind* suggests that because Eichmann never came home to himself—because he did not think—he lacked a conscience and, thus, proved a willing, if witless, participant in evil. Internal obstacles might have stood between Eichmann and evil had he only felt compelled to think and remain on friendly terms with his interlocutor. Yet this account seems at odds with Arendt's earlier claim that it was precisely Eichmann's conscience that enabled him to become a willing accomplice in the Final Solution. In *Eichmann in Jerusalem*, she emphasizes his inability to look at matters from others' points of view as definitive of his thoughtlessness. From this perspective, it was not Eichmann's failure to come home to himself but his inability to think about the implications for others of his figurative and literal home that made him a willing participant in ordered evil. Eichmann *did* go home to himself, and there he found friendly agreement with a conscience that prized being reasonable and law-abiding: Who was he, Eichmann, to question what is reasonable (E, 114)? His individual conscience attached him to a social identity that ruled him while prescribing his rule of others. Eichmann was oblivious to the conditions of power which secured his social identity (self) and livelihood (home). In short, Eichmann was thoughtless not because he failed to remain in agreement with himself but because he was unable to get free of himself. Eichmann never experienced the limits of his self.

Yet Eichmann believed himself to be a principled, conscientious subject-citizen. In a sense, he was right. I do not mean to suggest that Eichmann was actually thoughtful. But we miss the ethical political challenge he poses if we ignore the fact that he regarded himself as thoughtful and conscientious. (Again, Eichmann's case is instructive because it enables us to see what may be difficult to recognize in relatively more subtle forms of ordered evil.) Eichmann claimed personally to feel no ill-will towards Jews. Yet it is hard to imagine that he could have done anything more than he did to destroy them. What would have enabled Eichmann to think and act otherwise?

We could read Arendt's *Lectures on Kant's Political Philosophy* as an answer to this question. Judgment's requirement to put myself in thought in the place of everyone else is added to thinking's effort to remain on friendly terms with myself. Thus, Arendt's *Lectures* would seem to recognize the insufficiency of individual conscience and favor a collaborative conscience and communicative ethic. Imaginative reflection, guided by *sensus communis*, "liberates" us from the private conditions that block the impartiality and generality judgment requires and exemplifies.

Liberation alone, however, as both Arendt and Foucault teach us, is no guarantee of freedom. Freedom entails not only liberation from domination but also the deliberate exercise of power. And in contexts of ordered evil, thinking, not judgment, may prove of more direct political significance for freedom and responsibility than Arendt initially suggests. In this distinction between judgment and thinking, the character of the imagination representing others' perspectives is at issue. Thinking questions the *sensus communis* that informs our judgments, for thinking envisions the effects of what appears faraway upon what appears close at hand. Thinking's imagination is incorporeal, judgment's corporeal (LCP, 177–78). Thinking's incorporeal imagination enables us to experience the limits of our present bodies/minds, thereby revealing their transfigurative potential.

In Arendt's most explicit account, thinking forgets the body, and likewise judgment abstracts from a particular body and its private, unreflective tastes. Though Hobbes claims that we are subject by and to our body, and Arendt represents the thinking mind leaving the body behind, both enact a corporeal imagination of power. That is to say, both conceive a body impervious to deliberate transfiguration (though for Hobbes our words and deeds always express our body, while for Arendt the body itself is silent). In this respect, Arendt, like Hobbes, obscures the political constitution of bodies/minds, not only the powers and knowledges that make and unmake subjects who judge and think, but also our participation in our self- and political-constitution. Judging in accordance with *sensus communis* affords another example of how becoming subject-citizens may conceal our participant role in the authority of political contexts.

Imagination makes what is absent present. Judgment's corporeal imagination makes others' perspectives present by abstracting from the conditions that constitute a subject's particular body. Yet Arendt's formulation of the hierarchy of spectator/actor, taste/genius places the burden of transfiguration upon others' bodies/minds if they are to be seen and heard (LK, 63). Recall my reading of the social production of necessities of cause and effect in Hobbes' political theory. Like Hobbes's subject-citizen imbricated in a sovereign body, the Arendtian judge not only subjects her will and judgment to a larger body, she also induces others to conform to its social rules. As a consequence, this spectator-judge fosters at least the appearance of increasingly sovereign individual and collective bodies. The spectator-subject who judges others' words and deeds is herself "made" through the *sensus communis* that conditions what can be said and seen. But if she cannot account for the generation of the powers and knowledges before which she becomes a subject, she is even less aware (conscientious) of how she brings their effects to bear upon others.

Judgment enables us to feel at home in the world. In contexts of ordered evil, however, we need to question the trespasses that constitute every community, home, and self. Judgment's corporeal imagination of power inhibits our experience of these limits because it does not interrogate the conditions of their political constitution. Far from rendering the spectator disinterested in relation to others she encounters, the transformation of thinking into judgment according to *sensus communis* makes her a willing, if often thoughtless, participant in the extension and elaboration of the trespasses that flow from what is commonly visible and sayable. Both spectator-judge and judged-actor comply with common conditions of communication. Neither judged nor judge will or can consider, however, what the communicable renders invisible, silent, and outside. *Sensus communis* embodies the powers and knowledges that make us subjects; it represents the limits of what our present bodies/minds can see and say. Selves and others may be changed (or imagined changed) so that we remain the same subjects, in agreement with selves whose constitution we cannot discern and whose limits we do not experience.[23] Subjects of the visible and sayable discern neither the limits of what can be seen and said, nor how they participate in the constitution of the invisible, silent, outside traced by those limits.

Again, the case of Eichmann makes my claim more concrete. Apparently judgment's maxim, "Put yourself in thought in the place of everyone else," provides the remedy we seek for Eichmann's thoughtlessness. But even on Arendt's own account it is far from clear that remaining on friendly terms with oneself, while judging in accordance with *sensus communis*, addresses thoughtlessness about conditions of power. Arendt suggests that judgment reveals the limits of what we are. But judgment does not necessarily facilitate a free and deliberate response to those limits or reveal who we might become: "By communicating one's feelings, one's pleasures and disinterested delights, one tells one's *choices* and one chooses one's company" (LK, 74). Recognizing and responding to the trespasses that inform and flow from our choices amid ordered evil is neither the demand nor the effect of judgment. Trespasses trace what is invisible, silent, and outside—the other side of what is visible and articulable—what *sensus communis* by definition takes as given. My point is not to disavow judgment (as if that were possible) but to call attention to the limits of reasonable, public judgment in the face of the thoughtlessness that founds ordered evil.

The enigmatic closing paragraphs of her *Lectures* suggest that Arendt herself recognized these limits. Politics always concerns particulars, and judgment is the faculty, as Kant put it, of "thinking the particular." But Arendt notes a mystery at the heart of this idea, even as she seems to have dispensed with such quandaries by explicating Kantian judgment: "But to *think* means to generalize, hence [judgment] is the faculty of mysteriously combining the particular and the general" (LK, 76). The mystery is dispatched with relative ease, Arendt says, "if the general is given—as a rule, a principle, a law—so that judgment merely subsumes the particular under it" (LK, 76). Mystery disappears when the requirements and effects of a code appear to be obvious and visible. However, we are faced with great difficulties if, as Kant put it, "only the particular be given for which the general has to be found" or, we might add, if it is anything but obvious what an ethical enactment of principle entails. In such contexts, Arendt finds inadequate the Kantian ideas of a compact of communicability and a law of purposiveness. Instead, she finds a "far more valuable solution" to the mystery of combining the general and particular in the Kantian notion of exemplary validity (LK, 76). Principled examples emerge through thoughtful enactment of what is invisible, silent, and outside.

In contexts of ordered evil, the thoughtful, free, and deliberate exercise of power does not require detachment from our bodies and agreement with our selves; it requires questioning their conditions of existence, especially the governing knowledges and powers that make and unmake subjects who judge and think. Thinking's engagement of what is invisible, silent, and outside enables us to discern the body active in our mind and, thereby, potentially unleashes the mind active in our body. By identifying our participation in the social production of necessities that constitute every self and home, as well as the trespasses in which this implicates us, political thinking identifies the material upon which we must work to become ethical subjects (UP, 26). Only when we begin to discern the powers and knowledges that shape our judgments as subjects can we question and possibly transfigure them.

Thinking facilitates the transfiguration of bodies/minds as it brings us to the limits of our selves, in two senses. First, thinking problematizes the political constitution of our individual bodies/minds by revealing contingencies in what appears to be essential, thus creating space for the free and deliberate exercise of power in relation to socially produced necessities. Second, as knowing subjects, we bring relations of power to bear upon ourselves and others, which reveals our need to think and act with others if we are to exceed those limits and accede to others. In this sense, thinking's enactment of what is invisible, silent, and outside constitutes a political spirituality.

Both Arendt and Foucault associate thinking with spirituality, and there are good etymological reasons for doing so (theoria, theos). But neither Arendt's nor Foucault's affiliation of thinking with the invisible and immaterial, silent and outside, counsel a return to gods, the otherworldly, or even the forgotten voice of Being. For both, thinking connotes being alive on this earth, which in its fullest sense entails experiencing the invisible in the visible, the immaterial in the material.

Thinking manifests reason's need "to come to terms with whatever may be given to our senses in everyday appearances," our need to give an account of what has occurred (LM, 100). This presents no great difficulty if we only need account for what is given in the world according to its reigning terms; for this task, knowledge and common-sense reasoning will do. Matters are altogether different, however, if reason's need transcends the boundaries of a given world (LM, 103). Then, imagination's metaphors enter the fold.[24] Metaphors, Arendt says, bridge the abyss between invisible mental activities and the world of appearances (LM, 105) by turning "the mind back to the sensory world in order to illuminate nonsensory experiences for which there are no words in any language" (LM, 106). Metaphor responds to the thinking mind's dissatisfaction: "No mental act, and least of all the act of thinking, is content with an object as it is given to it. It always transcends the sheer givenness of whatever may have aroused its attention and transforms it into what Petrus Johannis Olivi . . . called an *experimentum suitatis*, an experiment of the self with the itself" (LM, 73–74).

After surveying the metaphors various thinkers have found for their activity (for example, seeing and hearing), Arendt finds only one metaphor that could possibly illuminate this activity "in which something invisible within us deals with the invisibles of the world," namely, the sensation of being alive (LM, 123). I think Arendt seeks to articulate how thinking can be both beyond the world as it is given to us, yet still within it, if always "out of order." Metaphor bridges the gulf between the visible and invisible. "The simple fact that our mind is able to find such analogies, that the world of appearances reminds us of things nonapparent, may be seen as a kind of 'proof' that mind and body, thinking and sense experience, the invisible and visible, belong together, are 'made' for each other, as it were" (LM, 109). Here Arendt's own thinking unsettles the hierarchy she elsewhere institutes between body and mind, as well as the one-way dependence of actor upon spectators and the *sensus communis* that follows from it. Arendt's thinking suggests the power of the invisible, of "spirit," to challenge and reconstitute present common sense.

Arendt associates thinking with the "region of spirit" because it enables the present to touch the infinite. Arendt's metaphors of thinking suggest an intimate link between transgression of present limits and revelation of the limitless. Her metaphors suggest too why natality and plurality are intimately intertwined. Arendt deploys Kafka's parable "He" to conceive the interval between the no-longer and the not-yet as an "odd in-between period" we traverse as we move from action to thought and back again (BPF, 9). As in *The Life of the Mind*, Arendtian thinking is a mental activity distinct from, and not bound by, logical rules of noncontradiction and inner consistency (BPF, 14). Nonetheless, the gap opened by "alogical" thinking may hold the moment of truth (BPF, 9,14). Kafka tells us what Arendt already learned studying Augustine, namely, that the forces of past and future are interrupted by "the beginning of a beginning," a gap in time created by "his" constant fighting and making a stand against past and future.[25] The force of past and future would have neutralized or destroyed one another long ago, Arendt suspects, were they not focused on the particle or body which gives them their direction (BPF, 11). She quotes Kafka's parable:

> He has two antagonists: the first presses him from behind, from the origin. The second blocks the road ahead. He gives battle to both. To be sure, the first supports him in his fight with the second, for he wants to push him forward, and in the same way the second supports him in his fight with the first, since he drives him back. But it is only theoretically so. For it is not only the two antagonists who are there, but he himself as well, and who really knows his intentions? His dream, though, is that some time in an unguarded moment—and this would require a night darker than any night has ever been—he will jump out of the fighting line and be promoted, on account of his experience in fighting, to the position of umpire over his antagonists in their fight with each other. (BPF, 7)

Though she finds his metaphor brilliant, Arendt believes that Kafka misconceives the power of thinking because he "retains the traditional metaphor of a rectilinear temporal movement [where] 'he' has barely enough room to stand and whenever 'he' thinks of striking out on 'his' own 'he' falls into the dream of a region over and above the fighting line" (BPF, 11). Kafka misses, Arendt says, a "spatial dimension where thinking could exert itself without being forced to jump out of human time altogether" (BPF, 11). If we forgo the presumption of rectilinear time, "his" presence actually deflects the forces of past and future into a parallelogram of forces and "he" begins a diagonal force "whose origin would be the point at which the forces clash and upon which they act." By means of this diagonal force, the present and infinite touch. Arendt explains:

> The two antagonistic forces are both unlimited as to their origin, the one coming from an infinite past and the other from an infinite future; but though they have no known beginning, they have a terminal ending, the point at which they clash. The diagonal force, on the contrary, would be limited as to its origin, its starting-point being the clash of the antagonis-

> tic forces, but it would be infinite with respect to its ending by virtue of having resulted from the concerted action of two forces whose origin is infinity. This diagonal force, whose origin is known, whose direction is determined by past and future, but whose eventual end lies in infinity, is the perfect metaphor for the activity of thought. (BPF, 12)

Thus, we have another Arendtian metaphor that suggests thinking can be beyond the world as it is given to us, yet still within it, if always out of order. What meanings would Arendt have us find in her metaphor? Of course, I cannot be certain, but Arendt appears here as a transgressive thinker, as one who believes that crossing limits affords our only access to the limitless. In this case, we see that only "his" limited existence, the particular present, makes infinity accessible in human thought and action. Only a deflection, the beginning of a beginning, makes the limitless discernible. Thinking brings the infinite to bear upon the present, but only in a contingently limited sense.

A similar point can be made by reference to natality and plurality. Only as the forces of past and future bear down upon the individual body, only as each individual thoughtfully inserts her or himself at the point where infinite past and future converge, and discovers and deliberately opens a gap between these forces, does this "small non-time space" appear. This gap "can only be indicated, [it] cannot be inherited and handed down from the past" (BPF, 13). Why? Because tradition fosters uniformity of being; it paves the gap between past and future. Paradoxically, only individual natality (the particular) can reveal the plenitude of being (the infinite), and then, of course, only as finitude, as a particular deflection into infinity.

In what way is thinking that creates a gap between past and future "impartial," as Arendt claims it is (BPF, 12)? The present is impartial to the extent that it touches the infinite, but it always does so in a limited way. As I suggest in the next chapter, Foucault means something similar when he says that we only encounter the universal in its eventful singularity.

It is a truism that Hobbes seeks to purge the world of all but his own metaphorical thinking.[26] I am especially interested in the ethical political implications of this constitutive move for his and our scientific politics. The early Quakers' highly expressive, metaphorical deeds referred to a spiritual reality, a realm of latent moral meanings. In this sense, their metaphors, as "transaction[s] between contexts," shuttle them between the quotidian and the moral occult it obscures. Metaphors reveal the ethical significance of the everyday as they put pressure upon ordinary things and gestures "to release hidden meanings, to transfer their signification to another context." This moral occult, Peter Brooks claims, should not be thought of as a metaphysical system, however, but as something "closer to unconscious mind."[27] Who might we become if we sought to exemplify the early Quakers' witness?: "To be so sensitized an instrument, one upon whom everything leaves a mark, with whom everything sets up a correspondence, is not simply to be an observer of life's surface, but someone who must bring into evidence, even bring into being, a moral substance."[28]

Arendt and Foucault were at best ambivalent about psychoanalysis.[29] In the moments when their imagination of power becomes incorporeal, however, their thinking resonates with notions of the moral occult as unconscious or archaic mind. Both find life in the region of spirits: Foucault, in the invocation of yet unknown "bodies and pleasures,"; Arendt, in the conception of thinking as an exchange between the invisible within us and the invisible in the world. Likewise, for each, spirit is profoundly historical. Whether pearl-diving among the historical fragments unsettled by the break in tradition or doing genealogies of forgotten knowledges, both Arendt and Foucault engage the invisible, which predominant conceptions of rationality cast as irrational, to reveal the historical contingency of rationalities and the promise of thinking.

Thinking that opens a gap between the forces of past and future sifts through the archaic and opens itself to the unprecedented—what is often represented as mad or unintelligible by reigning rationalities. By discovering within ourselves what we once reasoned was unintelligible in others, we may discover the method in the apparent madness of the archaic and unprecedented.[30] We cannot, however, simply submit to what is invisible, silent, and outside common sense. Like "he," we must put up a fight, if a space of freedom is to be created amid the necessities of past and future. In a psychoanalytic frame, simply being overrun by these forces constitutes regression to a nonindividuated or irremediably psychotic state. To put the same point another way, an "I" cannot experience the limitless in all its expansiveness because an "I" is necessarily limited; thus, limits must not only be transgressed but also affirmed. If we simply flow with these forces in accordance with what currently and conventionally passes for tradition, however, we will also fail to begin something new. If we do not fight these forces, if we do not meet plurality with natality, then a corporeal soul will make us appear only as what we are made to be.

By contrast, an incorporeal soul actively conditions who we are becoming, though not as a sovereign being. Rather, an incorporeal soul accepts responsibility for the forces of past and future, even if it cannot be held responsible for them.[31] If I am to become who, as distinct from what, I have been made to be, I accept responsibility for the forces of past and future, not as a sovereign being who would seek to abolish them, but as a collaborative being who seeks to actively incorporate them. A positive reason exists, as well, for accepting responsibility for the forces of past and future, and fighting to open a gap within their necessity. Incorporating what was once unintelligible to my self affords me the energies and resources I need to become other than I have been made to be. Recognizing myself in the archaic and unprecedented, I find my power in the midst of the forces of past and future. Thinking in the gap between past and future creates a space for ethical political action as the exercise of freedom amidst necessity.

What is within us? And what is the relationship between what is within, beside, and above us, which common sense renders invisible, silent, and outside? Perhaps no conclusive answers exist. Finally, however, the difference between a corporeal and incorporeal imagination of power turns upon whether or not we even pose these questions. An incorporeal imagination seeks what is invisible, silent, and outside a given order because it believes that trespass is inevitable and acknowledges our limits in the face of the limitless. An incorporeal imagination seeks to recognize, name, and engage these invisible powers so that what makes us might become our own, or at least more deliberately and freely so.

For an incorporeal imagination of power, mind and body, immaterial and material, invisible and visible, "belong together" (LM, 109). Thinking may enliven the soul of a body/mind to experience conjunctions with what appears distant, the unseen and unsaid in relation to what appears immediately present. In this respect, thinking does not leave our particular body behind (as Arendt sometimes claims) but enables us to experience (and sometimes exceed) its limits, to awaken the invisible within the visible, the immaterial within the material. Thinking is an experiment with the self which leads us to (its) others. And unlike judgment, which is confined by the visible and sayable, collaborative thinking may bring us to the limits of what can be seen and said, and to the possibility of crossing and transfiguring those limits.

Political thinking that engages what is invisible, silent, and outside becomes a limit-experience in two senses. First, political thinking may reveal the limits of individual selves, both the power and bounds of individual conduct in relation to particular subject as well as the resentments our promise making may engender. By engaging the conjunction between individual conduct and invisible powers, thinking explores our participant role in the authority of political contexts without authors and headless bodies politic. Collaborative conscience may discern the invisible powers that shape our judgments as well as those social rules that are not necessary but contingent, and, thus, those limits where the free and deliberate exercise of power is possible. More concretely, to think politically is to pursue the effects and trespasses of our literal and figurative homes. To do so does not require abstracting from our particular bodies/minds and homes but experiencing their limits. At the limit of our selves, we may seek to experience the extent to which our bodies/minds are amenable to transfiguration. Thinking does this by engaging the other side of what is visible and articulable. In its boundedness to what is invisible and silent, thinking approaches that which exceeds every particular way of understanding and making the world, both within and among ourselves. Thinking what is invisible, silent, and outside, we open ourselves to plurality, the new beginning each human being signifies.

When we open ourselves to plurality, a second more affirmative experience of limits becomes possible (what I discuss in the next chapter in terms of forgiving promises). Forgiving promises are spiritual political practices that enable us to exceed (and, sometimes, to accede to different) ways of being, to reimagine the "head" of political bodies, the interrelationship of power and thinking within our own bodies/minds. Thinking may put us "out of order," problematizing what we take as given, necessary, ordinary, ordered, without and within ourselves. Experiencing the limits of our selves is not a strictly negative project, for it requires more than discerning the traces and tracings of trespass which constitute us as subjects. Forgiving promises also unleash the spirit of power in our bodies/minds, that which exceeds what we are made to be in any particular present, those energies that suggest we might become other than we are, or at least that what we are does not exhaust who we might become. Interrogating the conjunction between individual conduct and invisible powers—how we are not only constituted by, but also exercise, these governing powers—not only reveals the trespasses in which we are implicated but also may enable us to create a deliberate form and particular style in our exercise of power. This sort of forgiving promise in the face of promising resentments begins principled politics.

CHAPTER 7

A Political Ethos of Conscience

Forgiveness, the restitution of liberty . . .

Thomas Hobbes, *Leviathan*

How can we conduct ourselves ethically when we are conditioned by history and the governing powers we carry as much as others are influenced or harmed by our power effects? How might we recognize and respond to the past and present, collective and individual, harms and wounds that suffuse our relations with one another? If harm and injustices are to some degree an unavoidable effect of human living, how should we acknowledge these grievances? What does it mean to live responsibly and freely in such contexts? Throughout, I have sought to convey and convince that these questions are among the principal challenges facing contemporary ethical political thinking and practice.

Although various permutations of resentment are an unfortunately prevalent response to this challenge, resentment at our own and others' injuries might be overcome and political action assume its place. In my view, we live responsibly and freely when we put what we are in question by refusing merely and passively to reinscribe social rule. To live responsibly and freely—to act extraordinarily and to reveal who we are—requires that we problematize social rule(s). Indeed, if we desire to be free, we must assume responsibility for our trespasses. If we do not exercise power deliberately, we reinforce and expand the socially produced necessities that not only harm others but also constrict the power of our own action. Promises that ignore or obviate the constitution of political bodies generate hopeless cycles of resentment as they secure homes and make worlds. Forgiving promises, by contrast, interrupt resentment by beginning political relations in which we answer to one another for trespasses that flow from our social rule. Paradoxically, responsibility demands incalculability and unpredictability, while freedom requires that we be responsive to the harms that invariably accompany the good we would do. In short, to live ethically, we must think and act politically.

Promising resentments

Increasingly, many people experience their individual lives as fated.[1] Fate is mysterious, Arendt says, something that we receive but do not create and which we can therefore observe but never fathom (JP, 118–19).[2] Fate is a way of naming the weight of what we appear to be. Our fate emerges in the convergence and combination of past and present makings of the world; that fabricated world conditions what and who we are. Often we passively receive our identity as if we cannot affect it or, as in Arendt's reading of Kafka's *The Castle*, as if it comes from above (JP, 118). Renewed interest in tragic fate appeals to a growing awareness of our progressively circumscribed ability thoughtfully to affect the conditions of our lives. Resentment is a predominant reaction of late modern subjects to the weight of the past and the apparent foreclosing of futures, to the diminishment of action's power in the present and the prevalent strategies of responsibility designed to master our selves and world.[3] Practices of promise-making may produce resentments as they generate governing powers which at once expand and bound our agency. Our nonsovereignty also creates opportunities for the practice of freedom, but more often we react with resentment.

Resentment takes a variety of forms and engenders a variety of responses to our plight. First, when the weight of what we are governs us so severely, we may feel and claim that speaking of our responsibility toward others is no longer useful and may even be harmful. From this perspective, for instance, I might profess my innocence in relation to institutionalized forms of racism which specify the meanings and prerogatives of whiteness in manners I neither instituted nor choose. Alternatively, facing the fatefulness of our lives, we may reassert our self-fashioning potential and the plasticity of fate, whether through heroic self-assertion or willful ignorance. In this case, I might declare my own and others' capacity to defy the conditions of race, if only we have the will to do so. The irresponsibility of the first orientation, and the willful self-creation of the second orientation, take an unthinking bearing toward the human condition. In the first case, our nonsovereignty results in a renunciation of the practice of freedom, while in the second case, the practice of freedom is confounded with an assertion of sovereignty. Both orientations are, for all their obvious differences, reactive and resentful (HC, 5, 240–41). Moreover, they play a role in cycles of resentment which are exceedingly difficult to interrupt.

The first view, that responsibility is no longer a useful category, may evoke the resentful counter-assertion that surely others must be held responsible (and blameworthy) even as we acknowledge the degree to which we are unfree (at least from the perspective of a sovereign subject). From this perspective, my race, or your gender or sexuality, are so determinative of the benefits and pleasures we derive from social rule that we must be held responsible for them, even if we did not choose them. Likewise, in response to the second view—reassertion of willful self-creation—resentment is evident in our apparently ceaseless (and ultimately passive) iteration of the ways our ascribed social positions deny us the freedom of agency others celebrate. According to this perspective, you have social power, I do not; you may be free, I am not. Immobilizing guilt ("there is nothing I can possibly do to appease these people or to change my blameworthy self") or reverse resentment ("they've been complaining and receiving help for so long that now everything goes their way") are, further, common reactions to these charges which only augment cycles of resentment.

In a political culture steeped in resentment, some of us feel guilt or rancor at being accused for what we are (for instance, white or male), namely, something we did not "choose," while others of us conceive our identity in terms of the wounds we imagine to have been inflicted upon us by what we take those others to be. (Of course, many of us may assume both these positions depending upon our location at any particular moment.) In both instances, however, we seek enemies to blame for our suffering and see others only for what, not who, they are. In neither case are we likely to prove particularly adept at asking the question of how to live responsibly and freely, or at provisionally enacting answers to that question. Our difficulty formulating let alone answering these questions is symptomatic of the modern subject-citizen's ethical crisis. Our resentful rage at what we are, or at the demands made upon us by virtue of what we appear to be, forecloses promising futures (HC, 240–41). Contestants locked in a battle of escalating recriminations, far from releasing or redeeming the past, repeat and increase its weight. A corporeal imagination of power, of the fatefulness of our bodies/minds, and of how we live them, is one source of this hopeless, cyclical movement of resentment. Recognizing (instead of reacting to) the harm and wounds that permeate our relations with one another means rethinking the dispositions that incite resentment toward what we appear to be. Cultivating an incorporeal imagination of power—engaging the invisible powers among and within us—may foster the free and deliberate exercise of power in relation to socially produced necessities.

All of the preceding responses (irresponsibility, willful self-creation, blame, passivity, guilt) exhibit one of two equally problematic orientations toward fate characteristic of a corporeal imagination of power. On the one hand, we may regard and embrace what we are as given and unalterable. Indeed, some of the positions described here orient themselves by means of this certainty and are suspicious of demands to transfigure who they are. On the other hand, we may dismiss the relevance of what we are, either ignoring it or treating it as so plastic as to be susceptible to willful transcendence. In neither case, however, can we imagine exodus from our wounded existence. Both perspectives finally regard what we are as immutable, but whereas the former is subjectified by it, the latter seeks (if always unsuccessfully) to flee it. In one case we allow trespasses to define us, in the other case we flee what we are by ignoring our own and others' trespasses.

Both perspectives upon fate evince a corporeal imagination because they regard our bodies/minds as impervious to the transfigurative powers of an incorporeal soul; they neither recognize nor engage the invisible powers without and within them. As a consequence, both miss the potential for forgiveness amid promising resentments. What we are need not determine (though it will always condition) who we are. But a corporeal imagination of power overlooks (because of the limits upon what it can see and say) the practices and powers which constitute selves.

We may find an alternative to these self-defeating perspectives in a problematization of what we appear to be, which in turn reveals who we might become. Political problematization demands that we accept at least partial responsibility for what we have been made to be (JP, 109), for our participant role in the authority of political contexts.[4] I endeavor to transmute my self when I discern the artifice in what appears to be essential, when I descrie the social rules that register the meaning and significance of what I appear to be. By acting with and *against* the social rules that would determine what we are, we may engender a self and reveal who we are. Recall the collaborative, conscientious practices through which the early Quakers not only disrupted, but also reordered, social rules. A political bearing toward what we appear to be is distinct from a resentful sensibility because it renounces passivity by continually and responsively chastening otherwise thoughtless social effects. Guiding the effects of the apparent necessities of our lives, we responsibly seek and disclose our freedom. Thinking what is invisible, silent, and outside cultivates the deliberate exercise of power.

Arendt teaches that thinking is invisible, silent, and "out of order." For a thinker who associates politics with spaces of appearance, who valorizes speech and emphasizes the love of the world upon which it is founded, few things could appear less political than the otherworldly, speechless, and phantasmic. Still, Arendt worries about "the disrepute into which everything that is not visible, tangible, palpable has fallen" and our "growing inability to move, on no matter what level, in the realm of the invisible" (LM, 12). This loss of interest and dexterity is linked to a confusion of thinking with knowing. Kant's distinction between "reason" (*Vernunft*) and "intellect" (*Verstand*) inspires Arendt's elaboration of differences between thinking and knowing, meaning and cognition. When Kant discovered that we are incapable of certain, verifiable knowledge of matters that our minds nevertheless cannot help thinking about, he claimed that he "found it necessary to deny *knowledge* . . . to make room for *faith*." Arendt maintains, however, that Kant had made room not for faith but for thinking; he had not denied knowledge but separated knowledge from thinking (LM, 13–14, 57–65). She does acknowledge, however, that "the experience of the activity of thought is probably the aboriginal source of our notion of spirituality" (LM, 44). Likewise, thinking may incite spiritual political practices, more specifically, forgiving promises.

Thinking engages invisibles and is itself invisible because it withdraws from the world as we commonly perceive it (LM, 22, 51). Ordinarily, our perceptions of reality are guaranteed by worldly context: by our sense of objects; by the fact that the same objects appear to others, if from different perspectives; and, thus, by the human species sharing the same context, a world. This sense of commonness (*sensus communis*) fits each of us into the world (LM, 50). But thinking withdraws from what common sense finds close at hand. As thinking moves away from the world, external appearances become silent, and so the thinker may appear to be also.[5] Thinking leads us "out of order" as it stops all everyday activities and "inverts all ordinary relationships: what is near and appears directly to our senses is now faraway and what is distant is actually present" (LM, 85). From a commonsense perspective, however, thinking always appears at best irrelevant, at worst disorderly.

Arendt's understanding of thinking (or at least the alternative I pursue here) may prove especially well suited to the forms of ordered, ordinary evil which are my concern. "What sets men wondering is something familiar and yet normally invisible" (LM, 143). Specifically, Arendt notes that we use concepts all the time for which we seem unable to give an account because they are invisible. For example, the concept *house* is the "unseen measure" and "holds the limits of all things" pertaining to being at home. Every imagined house, even the most abstract, Arendt says, is a particular house if it is a home at all. At the same time, the recognition of any particular house presupposes this general concept and relies on what the concept signifies, namely, thinking about being housed, dwelling, having a home. "The word house is something like a frozen thought that thinking must unfreeze." Such meditation produces no definitions or rules, "though somebody who had pondered the meaning of 'house' might make his own look better" (LM, 171). Thinking seems to produce nothing but perplexity and disorientation as it unfreezes the thought that language has frozen into place. Established criteria, values, norms, and rules cannot withstand the "wind of thought"; in their place thinking leaves only mystery, quandary, predicament. But is thinking then rightly characterized as without direct political effects? Though Arendt says yes, she suggests otherwise: "To take again the example of the frozen thought inherent in the word 'house,' once you have thought about its implied meaning—dwelling, having a home, being housed—you are no longer as likely to accept for your own home whatever the fashion of the time may prescribe; but this by no means guarantees that you will be able to come up with an acceptable solution to what has become '*problematic*'" (LM, 175). Arendt is surely right that thinking does not *necessarily* resolve what has become problematic. Rather, thinking opens a space of freedom in relation to what appears necessary. Here, Arendt's thinking resonates with Foucault's critical ontology. Socrates is one of its exemplars.

The thinking activity of Foucault's Socrates affects how he cares for others as a result of caring for himself. Thinking, at least when practiced with others, is part of the practice of virtue rather than distinct from it. Foucault finds the need for training (*askēsis*) to be one of the great Socratic lessons (UP, 72). By contrast to Arendt's Socrates, whose thinking is ultimately solitary, the thinking of Foucault's Socrates is collaborative and oriented toward mutual transfiguration. In Socratic practice, Foucault identifies analogous relations between the cultivation of body, soul, and mind. Awareness of principle alone is not sufficient to establish a proper ethical constitution.[6] Rather one must exercise oneself—physically, spiritually, mentally—to enact principle. Practicing with others one learns to attend effectively to one's self, how both to exercise and transform oneself so as to become an ethical subject (UP, 73). Practice upon oneself with others is important because in telling the truth about and to myself "I constitute myself as a subject by a certain number of relationships of power, which weigh upon me and which I lay upon others" (FL, 254). Because telling the truth of oneself brings relations of power and, thus, trespasses to bear upon oneself and others, those others play an integral and active role in the transformation of oneself definitive of ethical self-constitution.

Foucault's later thinking exhibits repeated interest in *parrhesia* or practices of truth-telling. Indeed, the onus of *The Use of Pleasure* and *The Care of the Self* seems to be articulation and exploration of differences between the Greeks' and Christians' desire for the truth. Foucault recognizes a virtue in the latter by contrast to our modern selves. We saw this difference at work in the early Quakers who sought to lose their selves as determinedly as most of us seek to find our selves. If we have taken to heart Foucault's warnings about the compulsion to confess, we may find it hard to believe that he found something redeeming in Christians' confessional practices. But while both early and late Greek practices sought to master the self, Christians sought self-negation. In most Christian experience, to discover the truth of oneself and to renounce oneself are intimately related.[7] Foucault's acknowledgement that the movements encompassed by the "Reformation" represented struggles for new forms of subjectivity (SP, 213) is not an idle observation, for it alerts us to what James Bernauer has called the religious quality of Foucault's thinking.[8]

Individual conscience conceived in the mirror of the "sciences of Man" institutes the rule of our selves and others. But conscience need not be so experienced. For Foucault, "conscience" might as well open us to the limits of our self in a given subjection. The distinction between *savoir* and *connaissance* informs his understanding.[9] Savoir "is the process through which the subject finds himself modified by what he knows, or rather by the labor performed in order to know." By contrast, connaissance (a knowledge) "is the process that permits the multiplication of knowable objects, the development of their intelligibility, the understanding of their rationality, while the subject doing the investigation always remains the same" (RM, 69–70). From this perspective, *sensus communis* is a connaisance. Maintaining internal agreement between the "me and myself" of a particular subject, while "courting" and "wooing" the assent of other subject-citizens, may both obscure and avoid the trespasses that make and unmake selves in relations with others. Trespasses remain unseen when the way the selves (both myself and others) with whom I seek agreement become *what* they are does not become the object of thinking. In this case, knowledge (connaissance) displaces conscience as awareness of the limits of our selves (savoir as limit-experience) and, as a consequence, the transfigurative potentialities within any subject are made calculable and silent. The powers without me, which make me what I am, become increasingly invisible as the invisible powers within me—energies that exceed what I am made to be—are mastered to become vehicles of social rule. Such activity constitutes and enacts a corporeal soul because it does not question the governing powers and knowledges which make and unmake subjects. For Foucault, however, conscience is the awareness of "the involvement and commitment of oneself . . . within the object of one's own 'knowledge' (savoir)" (RM, 71).[10] In this way, a self approaches its limits by thinking what is made invisible, silent, and outside when a self becomes a subject.

Both Arendt and Foucault redefine thinking as an exercise of oneself in which the "essay" has an important place (BPF, 3–15; UP, 9). Thought brings its critical work to bear upon itself in an "endeavor to know how and to what extent it might be possible to think differently, instead of legitimating what is already known." Thinking is an "assay or test by which, in the game of truth, one undergoes changes, and not as the simplistic appropriation of others for the purpose of communication" (UP, 9). Thinking that seeks agreement with a self and judgment that simply complies with given conditions of communication are inadequate ways of conceiving the conjunction of the general and particular, principle and power, in contexts of ordered evil. Both processes cultivate a conception of ethics insufficiently attentive to the effects of our enactment of principle and therefore cannot do justice to contemporary conditions of power in which subjects find their selves and are related to others. Where trespass is inevitable and ubiquitous, thinking must help us get free of ourselves, just as our judgments endeavor to make a home for us in the world. Thinking that enables us to experience the limits of our selves is collaborative, but not guided by *sensus communis*. Rather, political thinking that queries the invisible, silent, outside constituting subject-citizens and their judgments is disruptive collaboration; it problematizes the ordinary relations that order evil. Political thinking oriented toward the deliberate and conscientious exercise of power requires not agreement with ourselves and others but experience of the limits of both.

Political relations are ethical when we "answer," "talk back," and "measure up to" what has happened, what we are or have done, in short, the effects of our bodies/minds in the world (HC, 26). Like Foucault's savoir, Arendt's conception of political action is founded upon awareness of the manner in which we are involved with others in the world we make and the homes we secure. Arendt says that political action "is like a second birth in which we confirm and take upon ourselves the naked fact of our original physical appearance" (HC, 176–77). She means, as I interpret her, that we act ethically and politically when we become responsive to those injurious effects of social rule that condition our bodies/minds and homes. When promises become so forgiving, promising resentments become truly promising.

Forgiving promises

When joined together, forgiving and promising are practices of overcoming. But forgiving promises are spiritual political practices of transgression, not transcendence. When our promises are forgiving, we recognize and respond to trespasses by interrupting, not by repeating, cycles of resentment. In this way forgiving promises facilitate free and responsible living in the midst of inevitable and ubiquitous trespass. Creating and sustaining ethical political relations requires forgiving and releasing trespasses, and promising to redirect how our effects bear upon the future. Arendt writes: "Without the faculty to undo what we have done and to control at least partially the processes we have let loose, we would be the victims of an automatic necessity bearing all the marks of inexorable laws" (HC, 246). Forgiving promises deflect the forces of past and future and leaven the weight of the social rules that always threaten to routinize human relations and render us predictable creatures of necessity, capable not of action but only of acting out parts that are always already scripted for us. Forgiving promises thoughtfully enact our participant role in the authority of political contexts.

The possibility of political action, Arendt maintains, depends on our continually considering and releasing one another from what we have done unknowingly or thoughtlessly (HC, 237, 241). Without forgiveness or the possibility of being forgiven our capacity to act would be consumed by our first act or, more likely, by all the activities that precede and condition us, and by the resentments promise-making engenders. Trespasses go unrecognized and unanswered when a corporeal imagination of power allows what we appear to have been made to be to consume who we might become. The result is an apparently irrevocable logic of identity and social law: my resentment at what you appear to be and your resentment of what I accuse you of being seem irredeemable because the "origin" of resentment appears determined. Without forgiveness, it would not only be difficult but impossible to remedy our own violations and those of our forebears. Without forgiveness, we are doomed to carry on the trespasses of those who came before us, and perhaps as inevitably we would be subject to the resentment and vengeance those acts provoke (HC, 237, 241). Political action and relations would be foreclosed and with them the principal way of learning who we are as opposed to what we appear to be. Promising resentments require forgiving promises if we are to live freely and responsibly.[11]

Forgiveness calls us to become responsible for who we are—for how we display the effects of what we appear to be.[12] We cannot altogether change what we are or the fact that in the course of living we trespass against others. But we can change the meaning and significance of what we are when we transmute the effects of trespasses by challenging the patterns of social rule which multiply them.[13] Forgiving promises (and promises that may evoke forgiveness) open a gap between past and future, a moment where the powers of natality and plurality appear, by making visible, then responding to, what is ordinarily invisible, silent, and outside.

How, then, does political thinking reveal the invisible, silent, outside, and, most important, how does it transfigure our bodies/minds? What in fact is collaborative thinking, and how does it help us come to see trespasses, the unknown, often unintended, but nonetheless thoughtless effects that make our bodies/minds and the collective histories of which they form a part? Arendt offers a suggestive formulation:

> I form an opinion by considering a given issue from different viewpoints. This process of representation does not blindly adopt the actual views of those who stand somewhere else, and hence look upon the world from a different perspective; this is a question neither of empathy, as though I tried to be or feel like somebody else, nor of counting noses and joining a majority *but of being and thinking in my own identity where actually I am not.* (BPF, 241)

Political thinking "imagines" other views. But what is Arendt practically endeavoring to describe? The Kantian notion of enlarged mentality, from which Arendt draws in this and related passages, has become a popular locus for efforts to conceive political judgment.[14] But political judgment may not do justice to the difficulties of political imagination. Too often the imperative and possibility of regarding matters from another's point of view are conceived without due attention to conditions of power. Though Arendt, following Kant, often invokes forgetting the body and what we are as the goal of such reflective activity, a mutual transfiguration among Arendt's and Foucault's perspectives counsels against it. Political thinking cannot escape trespass or leave our particular bodies/minds behind. When, however, political thinking helps us experience the limits of the bodies/minds of given subjects by making their invisible, silent, outside apparent, it may begin principled action by enabling thoughtful redirection of our power effects. I call this political thinking, not judgment, because it is infused by an incorporeal imagination of power. Political thinking seeks to cross the limits of what can be said and seen, the common sense of visible political bodies, both individual and collective. Read from this perspective, Arendt's formulation suggests just how difficult matters can be when we endeavor to see and hear the perspectives of other bodies/minds so that we can act together to begin principled politics. She helps illuminate political thinking by first telling us what it is not.

First, representative thinking is not empathy, "as though I tried to be or feel like somebody else." Although there may be other ways of conceiving it, empathy proceeds as if I can consciously suspend what I am to adopt an impartial viewpoint in relation to another. The fallacy that we can simply adopt another view is thoughtless because it gains another perspective without thinking. When we presume to adopt another perspective without reflection on the knowledges and powers that constitute our own bodies/minds, more often than not we simply impose the view from there upon another. More precisely, the presumption that common conditions of communication facilitate impartiality (even as only a regulative idea) takes for granted the configuration of bodies/minds, the inevitable yet contingent limits upon what can be seen and said. *Sensus communis* makes communication possible, but it also renders invisible, silent, and outside other ways of being both within and without subjects. Indeed, this process is a principal means by which ways of understanding and making the world are bolstered, and it demonstrates the productive, if not always affirmative, effects involved.

A comparable process is at work in Eichmann's obliviousness to the conditions of power that constructed his figurative and literal home, his social identity and livelihood. Perhaps most disconcerting is Eichmann's belief that he empathized with the Jews, that they were "pulling together." To be sure, Eichmann's self-perception was absurd. Could he, personally, have exemplified other ways of thinking and acting? I doubt it. But if we who would act with others are to avoid unwittingly mimicking his thoughtlessness (albeit, we can hope, in less grave forms) then political thinking must discern the generation and elaboration of the discourses that make us subjects, as well as our participation in the constitution of what we and others can see and say.

Representative thinking is not, Arendt says, a tally of viewpoints the calculation of which result in a majority view for two reasons, one plausible to most with "normative" commitments, the other more likely to provoke resistance. First, amassing multiple perspectives into a single view is an abdication of thought and evaluation because the value of a view then depends upon its strength. In such cases, power and principle are equated as matters of force. Politics as a battle of competing interests is thoughtless.

Arendt also suggests that the goal of political thinking (and, perhaps we now can say, by contrast to judgment) is neither agreement nor consensus. Judgment enacts what is given to be common, it does not question its conditions of existence. *Sensus communis* incorporates us into a general body, it does not query its political constitution. Indeed, to the extent that we do not problematize the constitution of political bodies (whether individual or collective), they appear increasingly sovereign; just as political bodies that appear headless in time become actually so. Again, Eichmann is an instructive case (if also an extreme one since I cannot speak of the effects of his deeds as trespass). According to the Arendt of *Life* and *Lectures*, Eichmann is thoughtless because he fails to recognize or remedy disagreement between himself and his internal interlocutor, as well as being unable to look at matters from others' perspectives. The suggestion seems to be that if Eichmann sought thoughtful agreement within himself while he put himself in the place of others and tried to court and woo their agreement, he would communicate with others while sustaining the plurality of the world.

In contexts of ordered evil, however, conditions of power are not adequately addressed by approaching (or, in Foucault's terms, appropriating) the other for the purposes of communication. The search for agreement (even as only a regulative ideal) fails to discern and engage the invisible, silent, and outside. In this case, commonality does not represent a full view (an aspiration toward as comprehensive an opinion as possible) but the imposition (again without attending to its contingency and ineliminable arbitrariness) of a single (sovereign) embodiment. Political commonality is confused with the ascendance of a consensual perspective. Such thinking is neither "representative" nor political because the viewing of commonality in only one aspect ultimately threatens to obliterate the world in which we appear and act politically. The political constitution of commonality depends upon the preservation of plurality. A representation of what is common which foregoes this plurality, obscuring or destroying each differentiating relationship to it, threatens to render indiscernible the powers that constitute our bodies/minds and world. Loving the world demands transgressing limits upon what can be seen and said, at least if natality and plurality are not to be lost in a sovereign being.

Arendt's alternative is the idea of "being and thinking in my own identity where actually I am not." Arendt may be read as trying to convey a precarious balance: the preservation of one's thinking capacity while incorporating the perspective of another's body/mind. Political thinking and action should not result in the obliteration of any participant's body/mind. When they do, neither thinking nor deed are political but bear a greater resemblance to making. The sovereign mastery of other perspectives is antithetical to the "answering" and "measuring up to" the perspective of another definitive of ethical political relations. Political thinking requires the alteration of both one's own body/mind and that of another, but the total loss of neither.

The effort to think from another's perspective may change who I am or how I live what I am made to be. Our bodies/minds are the sum of traces left by our habits and beliefs, and the sway of the world and its other inhabitants upon how we live them. Endeavoring to conceive another body/mind whose sense is not common to me, even if ultimately to refuse it (and no doubt I often will), entails incorporating what was previously invisible, silent, and out of order, without (and perhaps also within) my self. When an incorporeal imagination comprehends another body/mind, we envision what we are from another perspective. When we engage invisible powers among and within us, we expand what we can imagine and, perhaps, even may transfigure who we are becoming. Likewise, our responses to others may also commute what others are. As we each open a gap between past and future our collaboration may become a new beginning on the world and an alteration of the plurality of bodies/minds that sustain it and whatever political commonality we achieve. If I have actually come to conceive another body/mind, and to answer to it, my habits and beliefs, my own body/mind, may never again be lived in quite the same way. To think from the vantage of another, to respond to the perspective born of another body/mind and to measure up to the relation of my body/mind to it, may call for changing who I am becoming. Thoughtful enactment of the invisible, silent, and outside offers the world modified views and mixtures of bodies/mind, thus transfiguring what they appear to be, as well as who they are becoming.[15]

Collaborative political thinking seeks not only to change minds and opinions but also to transfigure bodies/minds and their habits. Code-oriented moralities focus upon the grounds for the authoritative claims of juridical institutions and subjects. In contexts of ordered evil, the purity of our mind is not the decisive question, and neither is the force of our reasons. At issue are the ethical political practices that cultivate deliberate style in our free activity (UP, 29, 78–79, 97). Foucault explored historical variations on the activities through which subjects participate in their ethical self-constitution. The conditions of self-practices are collaborative: not only do they require specifically political thinking, they also pursue distinctively political principles. A political ethos of conscience seeks freedom in relation to the ways we are ruled, but it also seeks to exercise power deliberately in our relations with others. This is why it is a political theoretical ethos, rather than a simply philosophical one. Traditionally, philosophy has sought to liberate the self by resisting the political and by searching for sovereign mastery over a self. Political theory, at least the novel tradition I follow here, seeks to work on and beyond the limits of selves through politics as the practice of freedom.[16]

First, ethical practices of the self require the determination of ethical substance—the constitution of this or that part of myself as the prime material of my ethical conduct (UP, 26). Foucault's own interest in sexual ethics may have obscured the general utility of his approach. His historical study of sexuality and interest in a genealogy of the desiring subject led him, for example, to examine the problematization of *aphrodisia* among fourth-century Greeks. Some have followed Foucault's lead to elaborate contemporary sexual ethics.[17] But Foucault's framework for ethical self-constitution is not relevant to "sexuality" alone, for any activity where the deliberate and free exercise of power is possible or desirable may become an ethical substance. How do we determine such ethical material? This is the task of critical ontology of our present and selves. Critical ontology as an ethical political practice seeks possibilities for the deliberate exercise of freedom within and in relation to the socially produced necessities that order ordinary evil. Not only "sexuality," but also "race," "gender," and other aspects of what we are may become substances for ethical elaboration—the prime material upon which we must work to constitute our selves as ethical subjects of our actions so as to reveal who we are becoming.

Ethical self-constitution also engages a "mode of subjection" through which I establish my relation to a principle of conduct and feel obliged to put it into practice (UP, 27). Subjectivation is the first step in the stylization of a principle's enactment. But the ethical political crisis of the subject makes this neither easy nor unambiguous. When mere subscription to a moral code is neither ethically obvious nor sufficient to guarantee ethical conduct, then a self's responsibility and freedom require the creation of a deliberate form and particular style in the exercise of power and enactment of principle. The determination of ethical conduct—the relation to principle which a self establishes and to which it feels obliged—emerges, at least in part, through thinking with others not as a thought-experiment but as a locatable political practice. Ethical conduct requires more than thinking about the limits of the self, it also demands ethical political work on those limits. One performs such work upon one's self, but the activity of others is crucial to its practice. One works upon oneself "not only in order to bring one's conduct in compliance with a given rule, but to attempt to transform oneself into the ethical subject of one's behavior" (UP, 27). Political problematization does not seek a corpus of universal and uniform rules but ways of thinking and acting which enable each of us to respond to the power relations in which we are implicated (UP, 106).

Ethical political action creates its own "telos" which "commits an individual, not only to other actions always in conformity with values and rules, but to a certain mode of being, a mode of being characteristic of an ethical subject" (UP, 28). Both Foucault and Arendt have been widely criticized for failing to provide sufficient normative criteria for the evaluation of social and political conduct. To a great extent, the success of such criticism has depended upon ignorance (in both senses) of their claim that how principles are enacted, not moral codes per se, matters most politically. If Arendt and Foucault are right that trespasses are ineluctable, then forgiving promises—forgiving and being forgiven—are the only possible responses to this situation which avoid resentment or a simply reactive meeting of one trespass with another. Forgiving promises are the only basis for relations that, if they cannot avoid trespass, maintain mutuality in awareness of trespass. When our promises are forgiving, we may not only enact existing norms but also begin principles anew.

We think and act ethically and politically, not only (or perhaps not even primarily) when we give strong arguments to justify or "woo" acceptance of our perspectives (LK, 72), but when we open ourselves to others' perspectives with a willingness to transfigure our bodies/minds and to reveal who we are becoming. Such responsiveness is a condition of the "action in concert" which generates the collaborative power needed to transfigure our trespasses and the patterns of social rule which amplify them. When we become responsive to others' claims about our effects, and when we show a willingness to transpose them, we may disrupt what we are predicted to be and redirect the social necessities that flow from given subject(ion)s. Such free yet responsible action may evoke political forgiveness.

But what, more concretely, is a forgiving promise or a promise that may evoke forgiveness? Is political forgiveness offered or expressed with a simple "I forgive you"? The formulation is inadequate because it presupposes an "I" and a "you" fully present and self-made. It denies the extent to which you and I are, and remain, pieces of fatefulness; we are subjects of trespass precisely because we are not sovereign. A "you" alone did not make trespasses permeating our relations, anymore than an "I," any "I," has the authority or power to release them. Political forgiveness is a more provisional, reciprocal release but, like any political action, it may have boundless, unexpected, even miraculous, effects (HC, 246–47, 7–11). Forgiveness is the only response to trespass that does not merely re-act but acts anew and unexpectedly. By breaking cycles of reactive resentment and beginning something new, forgiving promises open futures and, if only momentarily, free from the consequences of previous activities both the one who forgives and the one forgiven (HC, 241). Recognition of trespasses, and then a desire to reveal who as distinct from what you are, may initiate such release. This revelation of who we are, as opposed to what we might have been expected to be, may engender mutual respect, trust, and political friendship (HC, 241, 243). All three are conditions of the collaborative (not sovereign) action that begins principled politics.

The promises we make often have harmful effects. Should we be forgiven for them? What would forgiveness entail? If we recognize our trespasses and act on the desire to answer for and redress them, we may evoke forgiveness. But forgiveness will not follow from just any interruption of social rules. Interruption must be joined to the aspiration to live ethically. Passivity and thoughtlessness must give way to mindfulness of inevitable trespass and continual effort to respond to it deliberately and freely. To be forgiven, we must move to overcome our thoughtless social effects. Forgiveness is evinced by a commitment to act together, and by the valuable willingness of those who have reason to resent our trespasses to engage us nonetheless as political friends. We are then held together by the principles that emerge in the course of our action and despite the trespasses that separate while binding us together.

Beginning principles

How marvelous that men can perform courageous or just deeds even though they do not know . . . what courage and justice are.

Hannah Arendt, *The Life of the Mind*

Let us leave in their piety those who want to keep the *Aufklärung* living and intact. Such piety is of course the most touching of treasons. What we need to preserve is not what is left of the *Aufklärung* in terms of fragments; it is the very question of that event and its meaning (the question of the historicity of thinking about the universal) that must now be kept present in our minds as what must be thought.

The other face of the present that Kant encountered is the Revolution. . . . what is to be done with that will to revolution, that "enthusiasm" for the Revolution, which is quite different from the revolutionary enterprise itself. The two questions—"What is *Aufklärung*?" and "What is to be done with the will to revolution?"—together define the field of philosophical interrogation that bears on what we are in the present.

Michel Foucault, "The Art of Telling the Truth"

For Arendt and Foucault, as for Kant, revolution is an eventful sign through which meaning emerges in the "sympathy of aspiration bordering on enthusiasm" it inspires. In the spectators' enthusiasm for the French Revolution, Kant found a sign of the moral disposition of mankind. Neither Arendt nor Foucault, however, finds the most promising (or forgiving) representation of human ethical dispositions in the willful commands of neoKantian practical rationality, a compact of communicability, or a law of purposive progress. This is not because Arendt and Foucault renounce principle. For them, I shall suggest, revolution and Enlightenment signify the exemplary singularity of universal principle. Principles emerge through always limited actions that, by acknowledging their limits and attending to the trespasses this entails, open us to (though they can never encompass) the limitless (the universal). Paradoxically, only enactments of principle which affirm their limits sustain the idea of universality and guard against affirming the limited as if it were limitless.[18]

Like Kant, Arendt and Foucault suggest links between the questions "What is revolution?" and "What is enlightenment?" Understandings of revolution and enlightenment are interdependent because our response to the question of enlightenment will condition our perception of what revolutionary enthusiasm signifies. Likewise, how we remember revolution will retrace our experience of enlightenment. By way of conclusion, I offer provisional reflections upon Arendt's and Foucault's perspectives on beginning principles, revolution and enlightenment, and on ethical political action. Specifically, I explore connections between Foucault's effort to conceive the historicity of the universal (PPC, 94) and Arendt's invocation of the exemplary validity of particulars that in their very particularity reveal a principle otherwise indefinable (LK, 77). Ethical political action is "revolutionary" or transgressive when it begins principles that otherwise would remain invisible. "Transgression contains nothing negative, but affirms limited being—affirms the limitlessness into which it leaps as it opens this zone to existence for the first time" (LCP, 35). A principle's universality appears and is experienced only in particular ethical enactments.

Arendt's and Foucault's reflections upon ethics and politics are bound to appear normatively "unfounded" from any perspective that denies the possibility of a reasonable critique of political rationality. In the wake of Kant, it may appear that few hold such a position, reason and critique having become largely synonymous. But a predominant view claims that critiques of rationality presuppose an affirmation of reason's idealized content. Neither Foucault nor Arendt, however, subject thinking to this presumption. In Foucault's view, no particular rationality is exhaustive of reason. Likewise, in Arendt's view, no knowledge or common sense exhausts the invisible, silent, outside that thinking engages.

What Foucault calls an "analytics of truth" "poses the question of the conditions in which true knowledge is possible" (PPC, 95). In political theory, this tradition seeks to justify the normative ground of politics. Both Arendt and Foucault are often criticized for "failing" to accomplish this step: When they appear unaware of this failure, their views are represented as insufficiently developed; when they disavow this project, they are called "cryptonormative." For example, Seyla Benhabib criticizes Arendt for neglecting the question of "by what reason or on what ground should I respect the other as my equal?" Benhabib calls Arendt a reluctant modernist in part because she does not directly address the normative foundations of her own commitments, though Benhabib finds an "anthropological universalism" grounding Arendt's thought. Benhabib's interpretation, however, casts Arendt as far more of a secular (by contrast to postsecular) thinker than I believe she was.

Benhabib is surely right that Arendt, following Augustine, renounces the "sin" of believing that we are the ground of our own being, that we are self-made. I am less certain, however, that Arendt would follow Benhabib in limiting the mystery of our natality to our dependence upon other human beings and nature.[19] As Foucault infamously put it, "Man" (anthropological universalism) is a recent invention, and, perhaps, if he died human beings and the world they inhabit would be better for it. In my view, Arendt, like Foucault, believes that negative theology, not anthropodicy, is the best way to care for the world.[20] This is why we may (of course, we need not necessarily) read them as postsecular thinkers. Finally, Arendt and Foucault reject the reign of all sovereign absolutes on earth, whether God or Man.[21] For them, ordinary evil (trespass) originates when we conceive and live the limited as if it were limitless. To a degree, this habit is unavoidable; finite beings cannot encompass the infinite; and we must affirm the limited if we are to love, and not despise, the world. Our challenge, then, is to experience traces of the limitless within our limits. At least we must do so if we are to do justice to the trespasses entailed by our finitude.

To seek to do justice in the face of ineluctable trespass is to recognize an intrinsic relationship between the actualization of our natality and the plurality of the world. The imperative here is existential, but not of the simple factual sort that Benhabib claims. Arendt is not saying that people simply do affirm plurality (Benhabib says that Arendt answers a *quaestio juris* with a *quaestio facti*).[22] Arendt means, I think, that if we do not affirm plurality by attending to our trespasses, we will not actualize our natality; if we do not freely respond to our trespasses, we will appear only as what we are made to be, not as who we might become. Natality and plurality are intrinsically related insofar as both require recognition that we (and others) could be other than we are. Actualizing our natality requires opening our selves to plurality without and within us, but not (as Arendt argued by reference to Socrates) because I must remain on friendly terms with my self (whose constitution I do not question). Rather, assuming responsibility for my trespasses seeks to let others be as it enables me to become other than I am made to be, which is to say, capable of practicing freedom amid necessity.[23]

Although the interrelationship of natality and plurality is constitutive of Arendt's political theory, anthropological universalism's "limitless" is too limited. Ultimately, the tradition of an analytics of truth remembers revolutionary enthusiasm as a sign of the moral disposition of mankind grounded in a historically transcendent (if weakly so) universality.[24] As a result, this tradition of rationality and ethics, if contrary to its best intentions, cultivates a monotheistic political ethos: it treats the limited as limitless (creates a Mortal God) by effacing its own limits and trespasses. In contexts of ordered evil, living ethically and acting politically requires acknowledging the obdurate fact of trespass. Ethical politics calls for an understanding of (and between) enlightenment and enthusiasm other than that fostered by monotheos.

Foucault contrasts an analytics of truth (which seeks to "identify the universal structures of all knowledge or all possible moral action") with critical ontology. Critical ontology "treats the instances of discourse that articulate what we think, say, and do as so many historical events" (FR, 46). By thinking the historicity of the universal, critical ontology does not renounce universal principle but perpetually seeks the limits of our aspirations to encompass the limitless. Critical ontology of our present selves engages two questions: What is the present? and, Of what is revolution a sign (PPC, 95)? In this case, revolution becomes a sign of our capacity to disrupt and reorder governing forms of power and knowledge to begin something new—to think, say, and do other than we are made to think, say, and do. The condition of such transgression is an experience of the limits of our present, as well as the spirit to move beyond them. Political enthusiasts experience invisible powers both as forces delimiting what can be seen and said (like the forces of past and future in Arendt's reading of Kafka's parable) and also as energies exceeding such contingent limits (like the deflection "He" creates amidst these forces by which the infinite touches a particular present).

New beginnings are not unprincipled, though they do contain a necessary element of arbitrariness. Beginning principles are free and principled in nonconventional meanings of those terms. Like sovereign promises, the forgiving promises of entheos begin principle. Unlike monotheos, however, they also engage the trespasses traced in every beginning. Entheos makes trespasses visible and responds to them by conceiving law as rapport rather than as command, by maintaining the inseparability of power and principle, by emphasizing ethical relations rather than normative codes, and by problematizing what has become normalized.

Forgiving promises are principled practices. But they are also intrinsically political, and they respond to trespasses without being imported from "outside" action and imposed upon it from "above" (HC, 236–37). All other ways of dealing with trespass and the unpredictability and irreversibility of action allow making to consume action. Sovereign (as opposed to enthusiastic) promises thoughtlessly master and violate freedom and human plurality. The assumption of rulership—that some must rule and others be ruled—is the hallmark of all efforts to escape the frailty of human affairs and the contingencies of action (HC, 222). "Moral irresponsibility" and trespass are inherent in a world where there are a plurality of agents (HC, 220). Action always has effects that were never intended and which, once begun, cannot be undone (we can respond to the effects of what we have done, but not undo them altogether). Sovereign promises meet these conditions by seeking (though never achieving) absolute mastery over them. Sovereign governance and its subjects meet one trespass with another but they can deny this mutual trespass because they render invisible and inarticulate the trespasses they trace. By contrast, forgiving promises seek to respond ethically and politically to this invisible, silent, outside.

Throughout this book, I have concentrated on trespasses inherent in securing homes and making worlds. Moreover, I have argued that predominant conceptions of rationality and ethics tend not only to overlook ordered, ordinary evil, but also often, however unwittingly, to reinforce and extend trespasses. Even if we are persuaded that the pursuit of sovereign mastery and the subsumption of action by making are dangerous, questions still remain. How should we evaluate political thinking and action that reject ruling, or at least seek to make the contestation and transfiguration of ruling their central task? What do such political thinking and action seek to accomplish? What do they begin and achieve? Together, Arendt and Foucault help us approach answers to these questions.[25] On my reading, their location of principles in specific political practices and ethical relations helps us understand how principles are begun and, most important, how principles accrue meaning that matters.

According to Arendt's genealogy, Plato was first to introduce a gulf between beginning and achieving, two aspects of action which the Greek understanding took to be intimately connected. Whether or not Arendt is right about the Greek understanding, the coexistence of beginning and achieving is crucial to her understanding of political action. Though action is always begun by individuals, its achievement—both its effects and meanings—depend upon the actions of others (OR, 174), upon both their political enthusiasm and everyday promises. In short, political action is collaborative, not sovereign. An actor can neither entirely foresee nor control the effects of her or his action, the process she or he began. Plato introduces a distinction between beginning and achieving with the hope that the beginner will remain master of what he set in motion (HC, 222). Action, as deliberate collaborative activity, comes to play no part in beginning and, as a result, action becomes a matter of making. Likewise, sovereign promises conceive beginning as ruling over what one has executed, while action becomes a matter of executing orders begun or commanded by another (HC, 223). Quite simply, ruling promises assume the place of action. Thus founded, governance colonizes the political. With this "redefinition" of action, Arendt says, "the most elementary and authentic understanding of human freedom disappear[s] from political philosophy" (HC, 225).

When freedom is equated with sovereign mastery, and power with oppression or domination (BPF, 162), freedom appears to be a matter of will in an inward domain rather than of action that creates political relations (BPF, 146). This tendency may be accentuated in "modern" popularly authorized states where subjects experience their conscience as individual and subjective. But Arendt finds broader significance in our difficulty conceiving freedom "summed up [by] the contradiction between our consciousness and conscience, telling us that we are free and hence responsible, and our everyday experience in the outer world, in which we orient ourselves according to the principle of causality" (BPF, 143). Here, Arendt confronts what I have called the problem of political theodicy: How can subjects who do not freely make themselves, who are subject by and to "causal necessities," nonetheless act freely? What can free action mean amid socially produced necessities?

Where Hobbes's political theodicy imagines and encourages subjects to freely will what they are made to be, Arendt rejects the equation of freedom with sovereignty (whether individual or political), locating freedom neither in will nor in choice. Instead, freedom is the capacity "to call something into being which did not exist before, which was not given, not even as an object of cognition or imagination, and which therefore, strictly speaking, could not be known" (BPF, 151). From such passages we might conclude that Arendt champions the action of a voluntarist subject who transcends the weight of socially made necessities (a subject who jumps out of the fighting-line as dreamt of by Kafka's "He"). But Arendt does not deny the conditioning, even determinative, affect of motive and aim (and the conditions that condition them) upon action.

While will follows the commands of judgment and common sense necessities, action is free to the extent that it is able to exceed the commands of common sense. Such free action does not depend upon strength or weakness, as does the will, but upon the "inspiration" of principle. Here we approach the heart of Arendt's political spirituality.

> Principles do not operate from within the self as motives do . . . but inspire, as it were, from without; and they are much too general to prescribe particular goals, although every particular aim can be judged in the light of its principle once the act has been started. For, unlike judgment of the intellect which precedes action, and unlike the command of the will which initiates it, the inspiring principle becomes fully manifest only in the performing act itself. . . .In distinction from its goal, the principle of an action can be repeated time and again, it is inexhaustible, and in distinction from its motive, the validity of a principle is universal, it is not bound to any particular person or any particular group. However, the manifestation of principles comes about only through action, they are manifest in the world as long as action lasts but no longer (BPF, 152).

Principles are invisible prior to action, or in its absence. The universality of principle is singular and exemplary, evinced only in action and only so long as it lasts. As a consequence, Arendt says, "virtuosity" is the criteria for evaluating the performance of every action. Virtuosity is not antithetical to universal principle, however, as some have concluded, but the only means of its appearance and enactment.

Typically, universal principles are believed to command obedience. In Arendt's view, this monotheistic understanding of principle confuses freedom with a matter of will and neglects the intrinsic relationship between principle and power as free capacity. In the former case, freedom is too easily confounded with willing what we are made to be, especially when what our intellect and will command expresses reigning forms of rationality. Freedom as a matter of what I-will and I-know is bound to necessity, even if willingly and knowingly so (for example, in the laws and decisions we obey because they appear, and may be, democratically legitimate). By contrast, Arendt maintains, freedom is manifest only when our actions surpass aim, motive, and all the other factors that externally condition persons. "The power that meets these circumstances, that liberates, as it were, willing and knowing from their bondage to necessity is the I-can. Only where the I-will and the I-can coincide does freedom come to pass" (BPF, 160). Willing what we are made and known to be approaches freedom only when it becomes joined to the capacity to will and know otherwise, when what I-will is related to free capacity and *not only* necessity. I say "not only necessity" because, even on Arendt's account, external conditions, our aims and motives, cannot be transcended altogether. But we are free when we deliberately exercise power in relation to the necessities that condition us; when we are thoughtful, not thoughtless. In this sense, our freedom is manifest in how we enact principle. A political actor's body/mind evinces an "incorporeal soul" when she or he enacts principles that would otherwise remain invisible.

Historically, philosophy and political theory have sought to master action, to gain sovereignty over its unpredictability and irreversibility. Simply put, thinking has too often imposed principles upon politics that have turned it into a matter of ruling rather than free action. The imposition of governing principles upon free action is especially problematic in contexts of ordinary evil where all ways of understanding and making the world involve trespass against others. Governing rationalities and rules order ordinary evil. According to a social ontology of trespass, even norms which are communicatively rational from one perspective may entail trespass and, as a (train of) consequence, could solidify into forms of domination from another perspective.[26] In contexts of ordered evil, forgiving promises respond to the sovereign effects of founding promises. For an enthusiastic political ethos, principles emerge through the free exercise of power amid socially made necessities and the trespasses flowing from them. How principles are enacted concerns how we exercise power and with what effects upon our selves and others. An unavoidable element of arbitrariness—of limits upon the limitless—inheres in every action, even founding actions with which all apparently agree. Every beginning of principle is arbitrary in a number of respects. We have encountered these contingencies and their effects before.

The political death of God signifies the absence of a preordained order to which the founding of individual and collective political bodies can refer to gain authority. Every way of understanding and making the world is from another perspective an unmaking. To augment and amend founding promises, to make them our own, does not necessarily engage, recognize, and overcome the trespasses they begin and continue, or the resentments they rouse. At times, overcoming trespasses may require "revolutionary action," that is to say, beginning principles anew by contesting the location of invisible powers and the representation of authority. In this case, ethical political action does not affirm the founding promise but the capacity for forgiving promises founding represents.

Relatedly, an element of arbitrariness rests in the delimiting of possibilities every beginning establishes. To say that a founding delimits possibilities is not to say that it is therefore a bad or unprincipled founding. Because the founding cannot enact a preordained order, we acknowledge that an element of arbitrariness inheres within this delimitation of possibilities. Matters might have been different, they are not necessarily as they are, and, what is more, trespasses adhere in every way of understanding and making a world. What bodies/minds can know, say, and do is conditioned by what is knowable and sayable. When we fail to engage what a political founding renders invisible, silent, and out of order, however, what is socially made appears necessary and what is conventional seems essential. Governing forms of power and rationality render unimaginable and, thus, apparently impossible other, presently unknown and unseen ways of thinking, saying, and doing. Perhaps this arbitrariness would not matter were it not for the trespasses it inevitably involves.

Finally, every beginning is arbitrary in another, more mysterious, sense. A new beginning cannot be predicted, demanded, or commanded. Principles become manifest in action, miraculous and without precedent. Action is its own origin, and a matter of "spirit."

> It is the very nature of a beginning to carry with itself a measure of complete arbitrariness. Not only is it not bound into a reliable chain of cause and effect, a chain in which each effect immediately turns into the cause for future developments, the beginning has, as it were, nothing whatsoever to hold onto; it is as though it came out of nowhere in time and space. For a moment, the moment of beginning, it is as though the beginner had abolished the sequence of temporality itself, or as though the actors were thrown out of the temporal order and its continuity (OR, 206).

But the beginning is saved from total arbitrariness by the principle within it (OR, 212–13), and by the fact that we need others to carry through what we begin (BPF, 165–66). When human beings act together, something, often invisible to them, brings and binds them together, namely, the principle inherent in their action. The principle elicits why they gather and stay together. Principle inspires their deeds but remains apparent only so long as their action lasts. In other words, principles remain principled, as opposed to becoming merely normalizing norms, only so long as action "problematizes" them.

But from where and what does principled and, thus, free action emerge? As we might expect, given Arendt's emphasis on action's miraculous character, she imagines this human power as a matter of faith rather than will. Human beings can perform miracles; they do so whenever they interrupt a natural series of events or automatic process in whose context free action constitutes the wholly unexpected (BPF, 168). But in, or before what, does one have faith? Following Augustine, if not theologically, Arendt seems to locate faith in the human capacity to begin.[27] "Man does not possess freedom so much as he, or better his coming into the world, is equated with the appearance of freedom in the universe. . . . Because he *is* a beginning, man can begin; to be human and to be free are one and the same" (BPF, 167). The source of this beginning is not what is already known and visible, but the invisible, silent, and outside. More precisely, free action evinces an incorporeal soul in that it begins and carries through the invisible in the visible, the immaterial in the material, which thinking allows us to experience as pressing upon the present and as "belonging together." "It is the very nature of every new beginning that it breaks into the world as an 'infinite improbability,' and yet it is precisely this infinitely improbable which actually constitutes the very texture of everything we call real" (BPF, 169).

Arendt seeks to remember the miraculous character of what we take to be necessary and ordinary, "to illustrate that what we call real in ordinary experience has mostly come into existence through coincidences that are stranger than fiction" (BPF, 170). But because what is socially made conditions its human makers, we are inclined to miss the miraculous, to will what we are made to be, to forget that we can act otherwise and begin again. This tendency becomes all the more pronounced when we confuse freedom with sovereignty, regarding freedom as a matter of will rather than of action. This confusion spells danger and potential disaster, in Arendt's view, because "it is disaster, not salvation, which always happens automatically and therefore always must appear to be irresistible" (BPF, 170). Perhaps the claim sounds at once mysterious and hyperbolic. But Arendt conveys a too often forgotten truism: principles exist only when they are enacted. The enactment of principle is always singular, if not always exemplary. "Political institutions, no matter how well or badly designed depend for continued existence upon acting men; their conservation is achieved by the same means that brought them into being" (BPF, 153)—which is another way of saying that how principles are enacted makes all the difference.

Arendt and Foucault have similar views about the status and location of principle. Foucault emphasizes the historicity of thinking the universal, its eventful singularity, the ethical relations through which it is enacted rather than the code to which it makes reference. Likewise, Arendt emphasizes an act's exemplary validity over and above its communicability or purposiveness. In my view, both do so because of their shared concern for what I have called trespass and ordered evil. This concern leads each to the conviction that how principles are enacted matters most politically. The "inspirations" for this principle are various.

First, in contexts of ordered evil, the normative always tends to become normalizing. If governing ways involve trespass, then questioning and reconstituting social rules is often the course of free and deliberate action. Problematization guards against principles becoming merely normalizing norms. Foucault's efforts to awaken our concern for ethics-oriented rather than code-oriented moralities correlates with the distinction between savoir and connaissance which informed his alternative understanding of conscience. Ethics addresses our simultaneously free and necessary relations with others. As in the Greek practices Foucault studied, ethics speaks to precisely those conducts in which we are called upon to exercise our rights, our power, our authority, and our liberty (UP, 23). Our free action conditions whether we flow with or against social necessities and how their rules bear upon others and our selves. Such relations call for a stylization of freedom, rather than a justification of moral codes, for at least two reasons. Many forms of trespass cannot be addressed through interdictions without having recourse to forms of governance that threaten to turn liberation away from freedom and toward domination. But even were this not the case, code-oriented moralities tend to normalize principle because rather than continually questioning proper conduct they express a desire to find the true ground of our being (UP, 243). I suppose this might not matter if this move did not precipitate the very trespasses that found ordered evil. Only by stylizing freedom can we address the trespasses entailed by our finitude. Ethical political action does not renounce principle, but it is vigilant against confounding principle and normalizing norms.

Principles only appear—assume meaning and value which matter—through action; this is the second inspiration for Arendt and Foucault's belief in principle. Principles such as freedom, equality, reciprocity, and responsibility cannot finally be defined. But actions that exemplify principles can lead and guide us to their meaning and value. I take this to be Arendt's meaning in the epigraph to this section. Similarly, Foucault maintains that ethical enactment makes the meaning of a code matter. For example, the Greeks affirmed codes of marriage, freedom, responsibility. The meaning and value they attributed to these principles, however, and the way they enacted them, often could not have been more different from our own. Likewise, Hobbes affirmed equality, freedom, magnanimity, reciprocity, responsibility, yet his imagination of their enactment could not have been more different from that of the early Quakers.

Third, Arendt emphasizes exemplary validity, and Foucault ethical relations as opposed to normative codes, because in contexts of ordinary and ordered evil, not our intentions, but the effects of our actions matter most. Trespasses flow from makings and unmakings as they constitute and condition us. Forgiving promises respond to these effects by seeking to begin anew. Principles acquire meaning and actuality not in our professed purpose (intention), or even in the reasons we can give for them (justifications), but in the effects of our actions, in what our ethical relations perform. For instance, our conception of, and commitment to, freedom and responsibility are evinced by the example our actions provide. In politics, it is not what we profess to believe, or the reasons we can give for our purposes, but our actions and effects that are decisive.

Matter is fateful because of our spirit, not in spite of it. Our particular ways of being are necessarily limited; we are finite, not infinite. Our spirit shapes this finitude, even if we can neither see nor altogether master these invisible powers. Our bodies/minds, our power effects and thinking, are inextricably bound. But we can begin space for the exercise of freedom within and upon this necessity, just as surely as we can thoughtlessly affirm it. The decisive issue is whether we recognize and engage invisible powers, or ignore them while thoughtlessly exercising them. We cannot will a different past, but we can change its meaning for us. We can achieve that change neither by recognizing the intrinsic worth of the past nor by simply desiring or deciding not to be burdened by it. We do not renew the past's meaning by abstracting from our own and others' interests in past actions, or by forgetting without "healing" our wounds. Abstracting from the past always threatens to become wishful thinking blithely ignorant of the social effects at stake in the past and its present incarnations. Forgetting past harms, in the absence of ethical political action, similarly ignores the weight (both material and psychological) of what we have been made to be. These responses promise a return of the repressed, a repetition of the past, not a metamorphosis.[28]

Living ethically entails acting politically, and to act politically is to seek to live ethically. Meaningful changes in perspective require political action; they require us to make alterations in our bodies/minds and how we live them. By making forgiving promises that rechannel social rule, we transpose the past's significance and transmute the way we live in the present and face the future.

Recognizing trespasses and transfiguring their effects may yield promising futures. By this I do not mean fixed futures, for that would be to close the future, to specify what we will be at the expense of who we might become. Who we are will always carry traces of social rule, even when we have interrupted it, just as Kafka's "He" cannot escape, but only deflect, the forces of past and future. What we are can never be left completely behind. Forgiveness, then, is the twin of promising for a very good reason: not only to protect political actors from the contingencies that lead to broken promises but also to protect political actors from the ill-effects of promises kept. Promising secures homes and makes worlds. Since making a beginning can never be free of arbitrariness and trespass, promising is always an occasion for forgiveness. When forgiving promises do appear, we may feel gratitude for the inspiration they enact and wonder at the mysteries they exemplify.

If we are to avoid sacrificing our freedom to socially produced necessities, we must gauge, as best we can, how effects coming from the past and pressing upon the present bear upon the future. This is my provisional answer to the question of what it means to live freely and responsibly today. To be free is to act unpredictably, to upset expectations based on what you appear to be in order to reveal who you are becoming. To be incalculable is to act responsibly because we thereby abate the deadening weight of harm and wounds; we arrest rather than replicate unjust pasts. Facing the future in such moments, it may indeed appear promising and forgiving.

Under pressure to conform, whether under a totalitarian regime or the relatively benign requirements of social rule, Arendt believes that most people comply. But not everyone does. Herein lies the meaning and significance of ethical political action, for each ethical political action memorializes our human capacity to act incalculably, to interrupt social rules, to resist wrong and harmdoing, and to assuage their effects. After recounting one of the few stories we have of a German (Sergeant Anton Schmidt) who risked his life and ultimately died to save the lives of his (once) fellow-citizens, Arendt writes: "For the lessons of such stories is simple and within everyone's grasp. Politically speaking, it is that under conditions of terror most people will comply but *some people will not*. . . . Humanly speaking, no more is required, and no more can reasonably be asked, for this planet to remain a place fit for human habitation" (E, 233). In Arendt's view, and in the face of the necessities of our fate, such hopeful stories of action exemplify and embody more about the spirit of courage, justice, and freedom than any code will ever command.

Notes

Introduction

1. Nietzsche, Freud, Weber, Adorno, Horkheimer, in addition to Arendt and Foucault, are among many prominent explorers of this theme.

2. Mark Rosenthal, *Anselm Keifer* (Chicago: Prestel-Verlag, 1987), p. 18; also see John C. Gilmour, *Fire on the Earth: Anselm Kiefer and the Postmodern World* (Philadelphia: Temple University Press, 1990).

3. Simone Weil, *Oppression and Liberty*, trans. Arthur Wills and John Petri (Amherst: University of Massachusetts Press, 1973), p. 59.

4. Peter Brooks, "The Melodramatic Imagination," *Partisan Review* 39(2) (Winter 1972): 195–212 (henceforth cited parenthetically in the text). I am grateful to George Shulman for bringing this essay to my attention.

5. Transgression expresses the impulse toward transcendence in contexts where only negative theology is possible.

6. I am quoting Marc P. Lalonde, "Power/Knowledge and Liberation: Foucault as a Parabolic Thinker," *Journal of the American Academy of Religion* 61(1) (Spring 1993): 81–100, 92, who is drawing upon John Dominic Crossan's *The Dark Interval: Towards a Theology of Story* (Allen, Tex.: Argus, 1975).

7. Foucault's faith in transgression signifies hope; Arendt affirms faith and hope in contradistinction to the Greek tradition with which she is usually associated (HC, 247).

8. Sheldon S. Wolin, *Hobbes and the Epic Tradition of Political Theory* (Los Angeles: University of California, William Andrews Clark Memorial Library, 1970).

9. Chapter 3 introduces the alternative political theologies I associate with monotheos and entheos.

10. I am roughly following M. M. Bakhtin, *The Dialogic Imagination*, ed. Michael Holquist, trans. Caryl Emerson and Michael Holquist (Austin: University of Texas Press, 1981), pp. 3–40, 259–371. I cannot here pursue a fuller exploration of the contrast between an epic and novel tradition of political theory.

Part I. The Contemporary Imagination of Power

1. It is of course problematic to employ an undifferentiated plural pronoun when discussing harm and wrongdoing, advantages and disadvantages. The concepts presuppose assymetry and, thus, different degrees of power and agency in relation to any particular "we." Addressing these assymetries, ethically and politically, is precisely my concern. The "we" to which I refer includes all those who have some measure of power and agency, that is to say, those who are not wholly dominated. I am theorizing situations from the perspective of those who have some measure of agency that implicates them, however unwittingly, in harm to others; those who, like myself, exercise relatively pronounced social effects as a consequence of their race, class, education, and the like. To be sure, even an un(der)employed U.S. citizen who purchases a "Nike" product made by women workers in another part of the world under laws that are illegal in the United States, stands in a position of advantage to those women, or at least is implicated in their harm. Nonetheless, I always have in mind the former, relatively more privileged cases when I invite identification with "we."

2. I find imbrication an appropriate word for subject-citizens' relations to social rule and one another because it captures the convergence of distinct, individual bodies into a collective body, as in the frontispiece to Hobbes's *Leviathan*. I have this image in mind throughout but address it explicitly in chapter 2.

3. "My Hobbes" is the product of a mutual transfiguration among his views and those of Foucault and Arendt (see the introduction for the protocols of reading as mutual transfiguration among diverse, sometimes divergent, perspectives). Throughout this book I defend my reading of Hobbes and argue that I have captured some of the meaning he may have for us in the present. Though I think I am "right" about Hobbes, I acknowledge that others may read him differently in ways that they, too, can defend. Finally, readers must judge which interpretation they find most compelling (i.e., most responsive to Hobbes's texts and most meaningful in the present).

Chapter 1. Makings, Trespasses, and Ordinary Evil

1. Only Arendt uses the term trespass (see note 17 below), but I show how the concept is relevant to Hobbes' and Foucault's thinking as well.

2. The quoted phrase that is not Hobbes's comes from Sheldon S. Wolin's *Politics and Vision* (Boston: Little Brown, 1960), p. 244.

3. The capacity for science is not equal, a fact not coincidental to its political utility.

4. See Michael Oakeshott's "Introduction to Leviathan," *Hobbes on Civil Association* (Berkeley: University of California Press, 1975), p. 35, on the competition inherent in the pursuit of felicity.

5. In addition to Arendt, see C. B. MacPherson, *Possessive Individualism* (Oxford: Oxford University Press, 1964), pp. 9–106; Jürgen Habermas, *Theory and Practice* (Boston: Beacon, 1974), pp. 41–81 (which I discuss below); and Seyla Benhabib, *Situating the Self* (New York: Routledge, 1992), pp. 152–58.

6. Arendt makes a comparable distinction. She argues that humans are conditioned beings, but this is not the same as saying that there is a "human nature" per se (HC, 9–10). I shall say more about this distinction when I discuss how we are made and unmade.

7. Reading Hobbes cultivates appreciation for the materialization of matter, but I am sure that reading Judtih Butler's *Bodies That Matter* (New York: Routledge, 1993) affirmed my sense of its significance.

8. Of course, Nietzsche is unsurpassed on this theme, but Hobbes recognized it, too.

9. Marx allegorizes the bourgeosie as those who can buy what they are not; see "Economic and Philosophical Manuscripts," in *The Marx-Engels Reader*, ed. Robert Tucker (New York: Norton, 1978), pp. 93–94, 101–5.

10. For another perspective on Hobbes as a theorist of making and unmaking, see Richard Flathman, *Thomas Hobbes: Skepticism, Individuality, and Chastened Politics* (Beverly Hills, Calif.: Sage, 1993), p. 1.

11. I realize that this doctrine is what "Hobbesian" has come to signify, but resting our focus there obscures thornier dilemmas that Hobbes would have us face and in which we are all implicated. My point is that this reading of Hobbes is something like a defense mechanism against ethical problems. Trespass stands at one end of a continuum, war and domination at the other. Trespasses and the resentments they provoke may foster a will to dominate and resist domination which results in intransigent social conflict and, potentially, violence.

12. Though Hobbes distinguishes mind and body, he conceives the former as expressive of the latter. Thus, I deploy the notion of body/mind. In chapter 2, I begin my challenge to Hobbes's "purely" corporeal articulation of this configuration.

13. Hobbes's famous phrase about our perpetual and restless desire for power occurs in "Of the difference of Manners," a fact of which the significance has not been sufficiently appreciated.

14. And war prevails not only when there are actual battles, "but in a tract of time, wherein the Will to contend by Battell is sufficiently known" (L, 13:185–86).

15. One of my primary objectives in this book is to begin querying the assumptions about power, and its relationship to principle, at the root of this perception.

16. Arendt and Hobbes do proffer very different conceptions of politics, and much of my argument will turn on that difference. But many interpreters of Arendt ignore her pessimistic social ontology in the interest of a utopian political ontology. In my view, that interpretive strategy obscures contemporary ethical dilemmas and diminishes what Arendt has to teach us about them. I think Arendt can be read as sharing Hobbes's social ontology *and* as proffering an affirmative, if tragic, way of living responsibly and freely within it. This reading distinguishes Arendt from Habermas and most communicative ethicists, and places her closer to Foucault.

17. As Arendt elaborates the concept, to trespass is to miss, fail, or go astray, rather than to sin (HC, 240). It does not apply to the extremity of crime and willed evil (HC, 239).

18. This is an extremely loose characterization of a historical transformation about which much good history has been written; for example, see Buchanon Sharp, *In Contempt of All Authority: Rural Artisans and Riot in the West of England, 1586–1660*

(Berkeley: University of California Press, 1980); Keith Lindley, *Fenland Riots and the English Revolution* (London: Heinemann, 1982).

19. Conceiving evil as radical and ignoring its banal or ordinary forms is hopeless in two senses: no longer productive of hope and destructive of the hopefulness that is possible.

20. Henry David Thoreau, "Civil Disobedience," in *Walden and Other Writings* (New York: Modern Library, 1981), p. 637.

21. Thoreau, "Civil Disobedience," p. 640. Arguably, our time poses greater difficulties than Thoreau's because in a headless body politic it is not easy to identify actual foes, far-off or near; indeed, it is not even clear whether it is any longer useful to think in terms of "enemies." Chantal Mouffe, following Carl Schmitt, however, gives reasons for concluding otherwise; see *The Return of the Political* (London: Verso, 1993).

22. On invisible and incorporeal powers and battles, see Gilles Deleuze, *The Logic of Sense* (New York: Columbia University Press, 1993), pp. 4–11, 94–108, 127–53, 210–23; and Foucault, LCP, 169–76. For an ingenious illumination of the neglected importance of surfaces, see C. Fred Alford, "Socrates' Cloak," in *The Man Who Couldn't Lie* (Huntington, W.V.: University Editions, 1995), pp. 21–27.

23. See E. R. Dodds, *The Greeks and the Irrational* (Berkeley: University of California Press, 1951), pp. 186, 199. Aubrey tells us that Hobbes translated Euripides' *Medea* for his high school teacher. Medea must have made quite an impression upon him, for she is a central figure in each of his accounts of the causes tending toward the dissolution of commonwealths. I discuss the figure of Medea in Hobbes's political theory in chapter 4.

24. Paul Ricoeur, *The Symbolism of Evil* (Boston: Beacon Press, 1967), pp. 151–57.

25. See Ernest Baker, *The Structure of Evil* (New York: George Braziller, 1968).

26. For example, see William E. Connolly's *Political Theory and Modernity* (New York: Basil Blackwell, 1987), pp. 16–40, and his *Identity\Difference* (Ithaca, N.Y.: Cornell University Press, 1991), pp. 68–73.

27. I say *partly* mistaken because Hobbes does advocate "reasoning alone" and self-interrogation as ways of coming to terms with "evil," even so transposed. Unlike Connolly, I don't think that Hobbes proffers an ontotheological solution or that he thinks one is available to us. To be sure, if subject-citizens submit to socially produced order as if it were so ordained, Hobbes would be pleased. George Kateb thinks that Hobbes believes most persons incapable of living with anything less certain, more mysterious, or contingent; see "Hobbes and the Irrationality of Politics," *Political Theory* 17(3) (August 1989): 358–59.

28. For a useful survey, see Kenneth Surin, *Theology and the Problem of Evil* (New York: Basil Blackwell, 1986).

29. For a political reading of such myths, see Sheldon S. Wolin, "Postmodern Politics and the Absence of Myth," *Social Research* 52(2) (Summer 1985): 217–39.

30. See Elaine Pagels, *Adam, Eve, and the Serpent* (New York: Vintage, 1989).

31. In this vein, Hobbes is often regarded as an early theorist of anthropodicy, but though to a degree this is an apt portrayal, it should not be overemphasized. Hobbes will deploy the techniques of anthropodicy—for example, he pathologizes religious enthusiasts as mad—to the extent that they are useful but not because they emanate from some deep ontological or theological source. Finally, Hobbes's is a political the-

odicy. That is to say, Hobbes seeks to explain the apparently incomprehensible and often seemingly unjust and irrational necessities of political authority and power to citizens so that they willingly become its subjects.

Reflection on trespasses calls for neither theodicy nor anthropodicy but, perhaps, for something between the two. Theorizing ordinary evil shares terrain with anthropodicy insofar as it explores how human suffering follows from and is amenable by human activity. But some readers may find remnants of "gods" and "powers invisible" and thus theodicy in such reflections, insofar as space is reserved for contingency and even mystery. Following William Connolly, we might call such thinking "postsecular"; see *The Ethos of Pluralization* (Minneapolis: University of Minnesota Press, 1995). Recognition of the ubiquity and inevitability of trespass makes such theoretical vision more tragic than utopian. Anthropodicy most always reasserts the promise of human artifice and thus is always tempted to ignore or deny its trespasses. Political, not scientific, activity redeems trespasses. And politics is fundamentally tragic; it offers no guarantees.

32. *Shorter Oxford English Dictionary*.

33. For a reading of such a body politic see chapters 2 and 3.

34. Here I follow William E. Connolly, *Identity\Difference*, pp. 1–2.

35. In the introduction to *Leviathan*, Hobbes names man both "Matter" and "Artificer" (p. 82).

36. I attribute no intrinsic character to "race," "gender," and other attributes used for identification but regard their meaning and significance as the effect of struggles over and within social rule.

37. The problem with Hobbes's "solution" is that it increases rather than alleviates wounding, exacerbating resentment and war while professing to chasten them.

38. See L, 12:169, on the perpetual search for causes and for control over their effects, as well as the escalating anxiety this produces. Such anxiety often produces fear of and speculation about "invisible powers."

39. For the function of sovereign theories, see DP, 188, 208, 222–24; HSI, 144; PK, 95, 103–5, 139.

40. Foucault's writings are continuous, but on the matter of power important differences emerge: between writings prior to "Nietzsche, Genealogy, History" (LCP, 139–64) and *Discipline and Punish* (what I call "early"); from the latter through the first volume of *The History of Sexuality* ("middle"); and his final writings after the latter ("last" or "later"). Foucault comes to recognize the inadequacy of his formulation of power in terms of "war" because it is still "negative" and tends to conceive the subject exclusively as a target rather than as an agent of power. This recognition explains Foucault's turn to ethics in the last works and, as I argue, to the question of what it means and entails to be a thinking agent of power.

41. These phrases are drawn from Michael Shapiro's *Reading the Postmodern Polity* (Minneapolis: University of Minnesota Press, 1993), p. 2, but they are exemplary, not unique to it.

42. Kateb, "Irrationality of Politics," and Flathman, *Thomas Hobbes*, are recent interpretations that emphasize this aspect of Hobbes's political theory.

43. As I shall argue, Hobbes's political theory does place some hope in concealing or

moderating making, unmaking, and trespass by depoliticizing social relations and the differences that emerge within them, and by detheologizing discourses of power.

44. Hobbes's challenge is to find ways of regulating political discourse which can manage battles so as to secure order. Moreover, social conflict can be productive, for its regulation develops the administrative powers of the state (as, among others, Marx argued in "On the Jewish Question").

45. On Hegel, see Habermas, *The Philosophical Discourse of Modernity* (Cambridge, Mass.: MIT Press, 1987), pp. 23–44; on Hegel and Marx, see Habermas, *Knowledge and Human Interests* (Boston: Beacon, 1971), pp. 1–63; on Marx and Weber, see Habermas, *The Theory of Communicative Action*, vols. 1 and 2 (Boston: Beacon, 1984), esp. 2:301–403.

46. Habermas, *Theory and Practice*, p. 65.

47. For an analogous critique of Foucault, see Habermas, *Philosophical Discourse of Modernity*, pp. 238–93.

48. Compare my preceeding discussion with Habermas, *Theory and Practice*, pp. 50–51, 64–65.

49. Hobbes characterizes the "state of nature" as hypothetical, and the "laws" of the continually mutating bodies he describes are the product of artifice as much as nature. Russel Hardin ("Hobbesian Political Order," *Political Theory* 19[2] [May 1991]: 156–80) makes a comparable argument from a game-theoretic perspective. In chapter 2, I compare communicative rationality and rational choice theory as conceptions of public reason.

50. See *Communication and the Evolution of Society*, trans. Robert McCarthy (Boston: Beacon Press, 1979), esp. pp. 1–129; *Moral Consciousness and Communicative Action*, trans. Christian Lenhardt and Shierry Weber Nicholson (Cambridge, Mass.: MIT Press, 1990), pp. 117–211.

51. For succinct elaborations of this claim, see William E. Connolly, "Beyond Good and Evil: The Ethical Sensibility of Michel Foucault," *Political Theory* 21(3) (August 1993): 376, and Michael Kelley, *Critique and Power: Recasting the Foucault/Habermas Debate* (Cambridge, Mass.: MIT Press, 1994), pp. 390–391.

52. In chapter 2, I argue that Habermas's account of communicative rationality is compatible with the Hobbesian conception of "public reason" which Arendt and Foucault, rightly I think, wish to contest.

53. See CSPF for this distinction, which I discuss in chapter 3. For an illustrative but by no means the sole example of those who speak of power's "productivity" while imaging domination, see Iris Young, *Justice and the Politics of Difference* (Princeton, N.J.: Princeton University Press, 1990), pp. 39–65. Domination remains a typical mode of power between "western" and "nonwestern" states and, as a result, also within the latter.

54. Herschel Baker, *The Wars of Truth: Studies in the Decay of Christian Humanism in the Earlier Seventeenth Century* (Cambridge, Mass.: Harvard University Press, 1952).

Chapter 2. Subject-Citizens and Corporeal Souls

1. A classic account is Ernest Kantorowicz, *The King's Two Bodies* (Princeton, N.J.: Princeton University Press, 1957).

2. Hobbes analogizes the motion of the limbs of the "Artificial Animal" that Leviathan is to "Engines that move themselves by springs and wheeles as doth a watch" (L, Intro: p. 81). In this respect, we may read Hobbes as a theorist of hybridity, of the mixing of organic bodies and machines. On the production of hybrids among "moderns," see Bruno Latour, *We Have Never Been Modern* (Cambridge, Mass.: Harvard University Press, 1993), pp. 13–48.

3. Steven Shapin and Simon Schaffer do make quite a bit of this in Hobbes' relation to Boyle; see *Leviathan and the Air-pump* (Princeton, N.J.: Princeton University Press, 1985), pp. 80–154. But I think Latour is right that they neglect its full political significance (*We Have Never Been Modern*, pp. 24–27), though I read that significance differently than Latour.

4. "Knowing together" follows Hobbes's preliminary definition of conscience (L, 7:132). For the "politics of conscience" see chapter 4.

5. Otto Gierke also found the soul to be a particularly apt metaphor for Hobbes's conception of sovereign power as "a physically perceptible Ruler-personality, which is to be found everywhere"; see *Natural Law and the Theory of Society, 1500–1800* (Cambridge: Cambridge University Press, 1950), p. 60.

6. Foucault's reflections on "confession" as a mode of discourse and configuration of power/knowledge suggest why Hobbes might have perceived no threat to order in encouraging the people to speak up about their grievances. In the course of speaking to and through governing powers, the one who speaks is transformed; through speech, power takes effect, not only in the one who receives these words, but also in the one who speaks them (HSI, 62).

7. Justice is the keeping of covenants. Through covenants individuals incur obligations, the most important being those specifying obedience to governing powers and an ethic for regarding their fellow subject-citizens (e.g., see L, 15:201–2; L, 14:189–94; L, 18:228–39).

8. L, 21:264. Of course, the sovereign state has the "right" to regulate all of these activities (L, 24:294–302).

9. Compare Foucault, HSI, 136, 141, and see the next section, "Governing powers."

10. Sheldon S. Wolin, "Hobbes and the Culture of Despotism," in *Thomas Hobbes and Political Theory*, ed. Mary G. Dietz (Lawrence: University Press Kansas, 1990), p. 27. The next two paragraphs are indebted to Wolin's essay.

11. I am indebted to conversations with Carl G. Estabrook for calling this inversion of tradition to my attention.

12. Judith Butler makes a similar point from a Lacanian-Derridean perspective: "What is 'forced' by the symbolic is a citation of its law that reiterates and consolidates the ruse of its own force"; see *Bodies That Matter* (New York: Routledge, 1993), p. 15.

13. For a useful and, in this context, revealing comparison of rational choice theory and communicative rationality, see James Johnson, "Habermas on Action," *Political Theory* 19(2) (May 1991): 181–201. Johnson concludes with the "utopian" wish that the insights of game theorists and critical theorists might be "encompassed by even a more comprehensive concept of rationality" (196).

14. Foucault cites Mably. It is true that he refers here to the first moment in the transformation of punitive practice (the play of representations and signs) which is

eventually overcome; but Mably's suggestion about the soul, and Foucault's characterization of his own project, suggest the relevance and complexity of the body/soul/mind relation to Foucault's story throughout.

15. To be sure corporeal power is ascendant (DP, 130–31), but this is due in part to power's constitution of subject-citizens' corporeal souls, which become increasingly invisible and apparently noncorporeal. Hence my claim that there is no straightforward answer to this question.

16. Foucault does not call this soul *corporeal*, but, as I argue later, this is because he misses crucial aspects of modern productive powers, in part because of his inattention to the role sovereignty plays in their production.

17. Compare Hobbes's "silence of the laws" (L, 21) and see this chapter's next section.

18. See note 1, Part I.

19. Of most relevance here are Nancy Fraser, *Unruly Practices* (Minneapolis: University of Minnesota, 1989), pp. 17–34; J. Habermas, *Philosophical Discourse of Modernity* (Cambridge, Mass.: MIT Press, 1987), pp. 238–93; and essays by Taylor, Walzer, and Said in *Foucault: A Critical Reader*, ed. David Couzens Hoy (New York: Basil Blackwell, 1986).

20. His late turn to the question of individual conduct and "practices of the self" is a sign of this transfiguration. Foucault's last writings may be read as an effort to recover the affirmative, potentially transfigurative relationship of "body," "soul," and "mind," thereby to offer a more adequate account of the subject's active participation in corporeal powers. His late works begin to overcome more fully the Hobbesian corporeal imagination of power. I discuss these later developments in chapters 3, 6, and 7.

21. In contrast to Fraser and Habermas, for instance.

22. What Foucault observed of Hegel is also true of Hobbes: there is much that we must learn from Hobbes before, and if, we are to escape him.

23. As I note in chapter 6, we can recognize this inadequacy only now, in the new space opened by *Discipline and Punish*.

24. In chapter 6, I offer a critique of the common sense constituted as individuals become imbricated in one sovereign body.

25. I shall say more about the "authors" of sovereignty in chapter 3.

26. Richard Flathman, *Thomas Hobbes: Skepticism, Individuality, and Chastened Politics* (Beverly Hills, Calif.: Sage, 1993), p. 2.

27. I focus upon Flathman's, Kateb's, and Chabot's interpretations of Hobbes's skeptical teaching because these three recent interpretations avoid finding in Hobbes's political theory an absolutist state which abolishes individual conscience. Nonetheless, though I admire their readings, I largely disagree with the positive political and ethical teachings they draw from it. In other words, I think they get Hobbes's political theology right but fail to see its problems and their contemporary significance. The secondary literature on Hobbes is voluminous. Though I do not position my reading within this totality, the detailed reading of Hobbes I offer should indicate what my perspective would be on any other particular reading. Finally, this is a work of political theory, not a history of political thought.

28. According to Kateb, Hobbes "sees the social utility of the belief that people suffer because they deserve to, [but] also insists on their creaturely innocence in the face of unfathomable and afflictive power. . . . Suffering is everywhere, and no one and no

creature deserves it. Nature is what it is, and its maker's mind is beyond our knowing" ("Hobbes and the Irrationality of Politics," *Political Theory* 17[3] [August 1989]: 360, 359). Kateb's Hobbes counsels contemplative submission before the sublimity of nature, but I think Kateb fails to see that this nature often appears only as the collective project(ion) of the sovereign collectivity he loathes ("Irrationality of Politics," 381–88). The "monster" Leviathan-state generates the "modern" image of nature which is thus socially produced a hybrid.

29. This moral can be drawn from one possible reading of Job, the reading Hobbes prefers (L, 31:398–99).

30. Dana Chabot, "Thomas Hobbes: Skeptical Moralist," *American Political Science Review* 89(2) (June 1995): 407, 408–9. Kateb says little about Hobbes's science, whereas Flathman emphasizes its prudential character (27–50). For this reason, their "Hobbes" seems less interested in the domestication and discipline of conscience and more welcoming of free individuality than does Chabot's. Regardless, I shall argue that individuality and conscience are parasitic upon governing powers and knowledges for their freedom. But the more free individuality becomes subject to governmentality the less it is able to account for it (see chapter 4).

31. There are resonances, as Alexander Hamilton recognized (*Federalist*, no. 4), between the powers of monarchy and those of an administrative state; for an elaboration of this theme, see Sheldon S. Wolin, *Presence of the Past* (Baltimore: Johns Hopkins University Press, 1989), pp. 82–136.

32. "Any hopes you might have would prove vain for the mere sight of him [Leviathan] would stagger you" (Job, 41:1–2).

Chapter 3. Recovering Political Enthusiasm For Invisible Powers

1. According to the *Encyclopedia of Religion*, ed. Mircea Eliade (New York: Macmillan, 1987), 4:455, the attributes associated with traditional discourses of the soul are evinced in some contemporary languages of the self. I believe that both Arendt and Foucault draw upon this resonance.

Though Arendt is often believed to depreciate the self, her concept of natality places individuality at the center of her thinking, and the miraculous character of the action, which makes natality apparent, plays upon the resonances between self and soul. Timothy Roach, "Enspirited Words and Deeds: Christian Metaphors Implicit in Arendt's Concept of Personal Action," in *Amor Mundi: Explorations in the Faith and Thought of Hannah Arendt*, ed. J. W. Bernauer, S.J. (Boston: Martinus Nijhoff, 1987), pp. 59–80, explores this relationship from one angle; James Bernauer, "The Faith of Hannah Arendt: Amor Mundi and Its Critique—Assimilation of Religious Experience," in *Amor Mundi*, pp. 1–28, pushes Arendt's apparent opposition between care of the self and care for the world in interesting directions.

Foucault's turn to classical and Christian sources sets in motion even more explicit movement between languages and practices of the soul and self. James Bernauer offers a remarkable exploration of the negative theological and religious aspects of Foucault's work in *Michel Foucault's Force of Flight: Towards an Ethics for Thought* (Atlantic Highlands, N.J.: Humanities Press, 1990). My interests are postsecular, which is to say I explore the ethical political possibilities of what religious discourses mean by the powers they call spirit in the world and selves. As I suggest in the introduction, in this case, the principal experiential reference is transgression rather than transcendence.

2. See Max Weber, *Economy and Society*, ed. Guenther Roth and Claus Wittich (Berkeley: University of California Press, 1978), p. 411; Bruno Latour, *We Have Never Been Modern* (Cambridge, Mass.: Harvard University Press, 1993), pp. 32–35. In chapters 4 and 5, I argue that the representation and resolution of political theological disputes in the seventeenth and eighteenth centuries continue to contract our political imaginations today.

3. In Hobbes's time, its emanations appeared among those who were disparagingly labeled religious enthusiasts and deemed prone to madness albeit of a holy sort. I have adopted and adapted the concept of entheos from Norman O. Brown; see "Apocalypse: The Place of Mystery in the Life of the Mind," in *Apocalypse And/Or Metamorphosis* (Berkeley: University of California Press, 1991), p. 6 and chap. 4.

4. As we shall see in chapter 5, the political monotheism of the *Federalist* did not dislodge the biblical belief that order was a function of power; it merely transferred that function from the deity to the laws of nature (Sheldon S. Wolin, *Presence of the Past* [Baltimore: Johns Hopkins University Press, 1989], pp. 73, 110). Hobbes's science of politics, inspired by political theology, Wolin writes, appropriated the "most available model of omnipotence and omniscience, the creator-god of the Old Testament, and [reversed] his order: instead of God creating man as his subject, man creates a collective being of incomparable power to whom he is perfectly subject ("Hobbes and the Culture of Despotism," in *Thomas Hobbes and Political Theory*, ed. Mary G. Dietz [Lawrence: University Press Kansas, 1990], p. 19).

5. Tracy B. Strong, "How to Write Scripture: Words, Authority, and Politics in Thomas Hobbes," *Critical Inquiry* 20(1) (Autumn 1993): 131 (henceforth cited parenthetically in the text).

6. Heart and conscience were often used synonymously in seventeenth-century popular religious discourse.

7. Latour, *We Have Never Been Modern*, pp. 13–48.

8. Compare Strong on geometry ("How to Write Scripture," 145) to my discussion in chapter 2.

9. Strong, "How to Write Scripture," 176, quoting Wittgenstein.

10. We saw in chapter 2 how the making of corporeal souls would generate the appearance of such necessity.

11. I more fully explain this phenomenon in chapter 4.

12. Strong clearly casts the contest as between papists and Protestants, for he does not mention the controversies among Protestants, and he aligns Silver (perhaps rightly) with "regimes of interpretation" (the Schoolmen?) and Hobbes and himself with Luther, Calvin, and the ordinary (178). From the perspective of religious enthusiasts, however, the latter represent disciplines of reading and a conception of the ordinary which is less than common, that is to say, which is inattentive to the exclusions upon which the common is predicated. The enthusiasts represent outcasts whose impulse (as I argue more fully in chapter 4) is less anarchic more impelled by a desire to

reconstitute the common by attending to the exclusions or trespasses that inevitably found it.

13. Geoffrey F. Nuttall, *The Holy Spirit in Puritan Faith and Experience* (Oxford: Basil Blackwell, 1947), p. 22 (henceforth cited parenthetically in the text).

14. I challenge the legitimacy of doing so, however, in chapter 4.

15. The phrase "practical mysticism" is Luella M. Wright's; see *The Literary Life of the Early Friends, 1650–1725* (New York: Columbia University Press, 1932), pp. 15, 27, 32, 229–38.

16. In this sense, they read Jesus' teaching of forgiveness much as Arendt does (HC, 239); see chapter 7.

17. Fox's *Journal* quoted in Nuttall, *Holy Spirit*, p. 45.

18. As Foucault provisionally defines spiritual practices, they refer "to a subject's acceding to a certain mode of being and to the transformations which the subject must make of himself to accede to this mode of being" (CSPF, 14).

19. I say more about the political culture of resentment in chapter 7.

20. Latour, *We Have Never Been Modern*, p. 37.

21. Baron De Montesquieu, *The Spirit of the Laws*, vol. 1, trans. Thomas Nugent (New York: Hafner Press, 1949), pp. 76, 149–52.

22. "Liberty [and thus power] is the ontological condition of ethics. But ethics is the deliberate form assumed by liberty" (CSPF, 4). Likewise, for Arendt, principled action exceeds, if it cannot transcend, necessity. I develop this point in chapter 7.

23. As I suggest in chapter 7, degrees of political problematization affect whether "codes" are normalizing or principled.

24. This is the meaning I find created through a mutual transfiguration among her writings and those of Hobbes and Foucault.

25. HC, 8. Plurality emerges from "natality," the new and unique beginning that Arendt claims each person represents, and action is the medium through which natality, this capacity for bringing something unprecedented into the world, can be expressed and plurality recognized (see HC, 8–9, 177–78).

26. For the precariousness of the distinction between what and who we appear to be, see HC, 179–81; also Nietzsche, *On the Genealogy of Morals* (New York: Vintage, 1967), p. 45. Arendt herself sometimes speaks as if we can know what (though not who) someone is (HC, 179); this is a common interpretation of her view of the relationship between what and who we are. But the question "what is man?" Arendt says, can be settled only within the framework of a divinely revealed answer, that is, it is humanly unknowable (HC, 10–11). Arendt notes the all too human tendency to believe that we know what someone is, particularly when faced with the difficulty of saying who someone is (HC, 179, 186). Relatedly "unique personal identities" tend to become subsumed under identities constituted by social rules.

Part II. A Genealogy of the Modern Subject-Citizen

1. I do not claim to chart new territory in the history of political thought; I seek only to consider contemporary ethical political predicaments in the light of this history.

2. I must leave a full development of this connection for another time.

Chapter 4. The Politics of Conscience

1. Virtually every interpretation of Hobbes that I know of shares his judgment of religious enthusiasts. J. G. A. Pocock's "Thomas Hobbes: Atheist or Enthusiast?" *History of Political Thought* 11(4) (Winter 1990): 737–49 is no exception, though George Shulman's work is; see "Hobbes, Puritans, and Promethean Politics," *Political Theory* 16(3) (August, 1988): 426–33. For general background, see James Farr, "Political Science and the Enlightenment of Enthusiasm," *American Political Science Review* 82(1) (March 1988): 51–69.

2. See chapter 3 for a discussion of Arendt's political commonality among "organized multitudes," constituted at once by plurality and commonality.

3. In 1965 Michael Walzer judged "English sectarians," though "interesting," not "the crucial innovators in English political history"; see *The Revolution of the Saints* (Cambridge, Mass.: Harvard University Press, 1965), p. 21. Since that time prevalent concerns about the relationship between discipline and normalization in radical politics suggest it may be time for a reappraisal.

4. O. L. Dick, ed., *Brief Lives* (Ann Arbor: University of Michigan Press, 1957), p. 150.

5. E. R. Dodds, *The Greeks and the Irrational* (Berkeley: University of California Press, 1951), pp. 186, 199.

6. See chapter 2 for a discussion of Hobbes's science of sovereign governance, and see chapter 3 for his mixing of what we ordinarily oppose.

7. "If there were nothing else that bewrayed their madenesse; yet the very arrogating such inspiration to themselves, is argument enough" (L, 8:141). Of course, such "madness" was a commonplace of English political discourse at the time, by no means the coinage of religious and political radicals alone; see William Lamont, *Godly Rule: Politics and Religion, 1603–1660* (New York: St. Martin's, 1969).

8. Today, analogous critiques are sometimes made of Arendt and Foucault.

9. George Shulman is excellent on Hobbes turning Promethean powers back upon Puritan radicals in "Hobbes, Puritans, and Promethean Politics," 436–40.

10. Moreover, the Quakers believed that the spirit was in everyman, converted and unconverted alike, and thus are not so easily cast as modern Manicheans with a polarized view of the universe who cast opponents as mortal enemies linked with supernatural evil. For a useful overview of this apocalyptic tradition, see Paul Christianson, *Reformers in Babylon: English Apocalyptic Visions from the Reformation to the Eve of the Civil War* (Toronto: University of Toronto Press, 1978).

11. Richard Bauman, *Let Your Words Be Few: Symbolism of Speaking and Silence among Seventeenth-Century Quakers* (London: Cambridge University Press, 1983), p. 129.

12. George Bataille, *Erotism: Death and Sensuality*, trans. Mary Dalwood (San Francisco: City Lights Books, 1986), p. 249 (henceforth cited parenthetically in the text).

13. There are resonances here with the later Foucault, and I develop this interpretation in the book's third section. Foucault himself seemed to view the spiritual movements associated with the Reformation in this light, namely, as a revolt against the excessive codification of moral experience (UP, 30).

14. In chapter 6, I explore this theme in contemporary contexts by reference to what is ordinarily "invisible, silent, and outside."

15. Unless otherwise noted, the discussion and quotations in this section draw upon Bauman, *Let Your Words Be Few*, pp. 95–119.

16. More precisely at issue is how we engage the constative or invisible element in every performative. I revisit this issue in chapter 5.

17. Quoted in Arnold Lloyd, *Quaker Social History, 1669–1738* (London: Longmans, Green, 1950), p. 28.

18. I lay out the details of this interpretation in chapters 2 and 3.

19. In the next chapter, "Hobbes's America," I consider in greater detail how individuals' social rule imbricates them in a sovereign state. In chapter 6, I address new problems of freedom and responsibility in the contemporary context.

20. See chapter 3, "Headless Bodies," for a discussion of the "religious sentiment" infusing the Mortal God.

21. Spinoza's *Ethics* seems to me a meditation upon the difference between self-debasement and self-negation.

22. Arguably the roots of this conversion were present in their orientation toward transcendence rather than transgression. At times, also, early Quakers simply inverted Hobbes's corporeal imagination, opposing body/spirit and mind, rather than challenging the opposition.

Chapter 5. Hobbes's America

1. See Benedict Anderson, *Imagined Communities* (New York: Verso, 1991).

2. More precisely, only a particular form of revolutionary spirit infuses "America"; on this theme, see Sacvan Bercovitch, *The American Jeremiad* (Madison: University of Wisconsin Press, 1978), and *The Rites of Assent* (New York: Routledge, 1993). I explore a different understanding of revolutionary spirit in chapter 7.

3. For examples of other perspectives on Hobbes's relationship to the American founding, see George Mace, *Locke, Hobbes, and the Federalist Papers* (Carbondale: Southern Illinois University Press, 1979); Frank M. Coleman, *Hobbes and America: Exploring the Constitutional Foundations* (Toronto: University of Toronto Press, 1977).

4. See Hanna Pitkin, *The Concept of Representation* (Berkeley: University of California Press, 1967), pp. 14–37; L, 16:217–22; and my discussion in chapter 2 of the shift between *De Cive* and *Leviathan*.

5. Edmund Morgan, *Inventing the People: The Rise of Popular Sovereignty in England and America* (New York: Norton, 1988), pp. 13–15 (henceforth cited parenthetically in the text). The obviousness of "common sense" and the necessity of what "we know" is precisely what I want to query.

6. For an elaboration of the radical potential of democracy, see Hanna Fenichel Pitkin and Sara M. Shumer, "On Participation," *democracy* 2(4) (Fall 1982): 43–54.

7. See A. S. P. Woodhouse, ed., *Puritanism and Liberty* (London: Everyman, 1992), pp. 342–67.

8. I discussed the invisibility of the authors of popular sovereignty from another, related, perspective in chapter 3.

9. See William Appleman Williams, *Empire as a Way of Life* (Oxford: Oxford University Press, 1980).

10. In my view, Morgan underestimates Hamilton's contribution and judges his national fiscal policy as far more incidental to the constitutional regime than it in fact was. See Sheldon S. Wolin, *Presence of the Past* (Baltimore: Johns Hopkins University Press, 1989), pp. 95–99, and my discussion in the following pages.

11. Tocqueville's "democratic form of despotism" is a different sort of tyranny, which I shall consider later.

12. Suzette Hemberger, "Creatures of the Constitution: The Federalist Constitution and the Shaping of American Politics" (Ph.D. diss., Princeton University, 1994), p. 4 (henceforth cited parenthetically in the text). I have found Hemberger's text especially useful and illustrative because there are numerous points of convergence between what she argues for in the American context and my more general theoretical argument. Other relevant works include Herbert J. Storing, ed., *The Anti-Federalist* (Chicago: University of Chicago Press, 1981), and *What the Anti-Federalists Were For* (Chicago: University of Chicago Press, 1981); Gordon Wood, *The Creation of the American Republic* (Chapel Hill: University of North Carolina Press, 1969); Douglass Adair, *Fame and the Founding Fathers*, ed. Trevor Colbourn (New York: Norton, 1974); David Epstein, *The Political Theory of "The Federalist"* (Chicago: University of Chicago Press, 1984); Merrill Jensen, *The Articles of Confederation* (Madison: University of Wisconsin Press, 1940).

13. Implicit here is the question of what constitutes a political space or body. See chapter 3 for reflections upon this theme.

14. Unfortunately, the assimilation of internal dissension and foreign threat remains a popular trope of the American political unconscious.

15. Wolin, *Presence of the Past*, p. 11.

16. The proceedings of the federal convention were kept secret, one indication among many that the framers expected that the Constitution would change public opinion while they made no provisions for popular opinion changing the Constitution.

17. On the antipolitical culture of the U.S. Constitution, see Wolin, *Presence of the Past*, pp. 8–31, 82–99.

18. Ibid., p. 11.

19. Ibid., p. 12.

20. Seyla Benhabib, "Deliberative Rationality and Models of Democratic Legitimacy," *Constellations* 1(1) (April 1994): 26–52, 28.

21. Claude Lefort, *The Political Forms of Modern Society* (Cambridge, Mass.: MIT Press, 1986), p. 279 (henceforth cited parenthetically in the text).

22. Ernesto Laclau and Chantal Mouffe's *Hegemony and Socialist Strategy* (New York: Verso, 1985) is an influential work that elaborates this view along lines similar to Lefort's.

23. Wolin, *Presence of the Past*, pp. 28, 27.

24. I am reminded of a colleague whose class bemoaned the inefficacy of the federal government at exactly the moment when that same government, in a matter of days, amassed troops and arms in the Persian Gulf with the apparently unanimous approval of "the people."

25. See Wolin, *Presence of the Past*, pp. 151–79.

26. Alexis de Tocqueville, *Democracy in America* (Garden City, NY: Doubleday, 1969), pp. 255, 669.

27. Bonnie Honig, *Political Theory and the Displacement of Politics* (Ithaca, N.Y.: Cornell University Press, 1993), p. 114.

28. Ibid., p. 103.

29. Alan Keenan, "Promises, Promises," *Political Theory* 22(2) (May 1994): 297–322, 316, 309.

30. Jacques Derrida, "Declarations of Independence," *New Political Science* 15 (1986): 8–9, 11.

31. I discuss the arbitrariness of beginnings and the ineliminable interdependence of principle and power in chapter 7.

32. Honig, *Displacement of Politics*, p. 114, my emphasis.

33. Derrida also questions the embodiment of "God." In this vein he invokes the name of the state ("Declarations of Independence," p. 12) which he goes on to query in "Otobiographies"; see *The Ear of the Other* (Lincoln: University of Nebraska Press, 1988), pp. 29–38. I elaborate this reading in "Nietzsche: Servant of Nazism, Critic of Nazism," *Review of Politics* 57(3) (Summer 1995): 559–62.

34. Honig acknowledges the difficulty of distinguishing divine command and secular law, which is what recommends Derrida to her. From my perspective, however, her account binds me too forcefully to the beginning of "America" as a sovereign unity, even as she acknowledges its lack of pure legitimacy and underscores its resistability.

Part III. Living Ethically, Acting Politically

Chapter 6. Seeking the Limits of Our Selves

1. To my knowledge, however, Foucault never deploys the phraseology of construction.

2. Judith Butler, "Foucault and the Paradox of Bodily Inscriptions," *Journal of Philosophy* (November 1989): 601–7, 604 (henceforth cited parenthetically in the text). But see also her *Gender Trouble* (New York: Routledge, 1990), p. 29.

3. Judith Butler, *Bodies That Matter* (New York: Routledge, 1993), pp. 34–35.

4. Butler, *Gender Trouble*, pp. 106, 93.

5. For this critique of the middle Foucault, see chapters 2 and 3.

6. Perhaps Butler would not see the analogy, for she questions whether "Foucault's effort to work the notions of discourse and materiality through one another fail to account for . . . what is excluded," and asks, "what has to be excluded for those economies to function as self-sustaining systems?" (*Bodies That Matter*, p. 35). But Foucault's "single drama" of inscription (like Butler's narration of the vicissitudes of the law) is problematic not because it makes ontological projections about bodies but because it cannot conceive politics as anything other than resistance to the law. Neither Foucault nor Butler can avoid making ontological presumptions. Even when Foucault notoriously invokes a "different economy of bodies and pleasures," he grants the body no more determinant ontological status than Butler herself does, which is to say, both presume that no regime of the articulable and visible exhausts being. In my view,

Foucault and Butler make similar ont*a*logical projections, to use William Connolly's term. On this and on the unavoidability of making such presumptions about being, see William E. Connolly, "Beyond Good and Evil: The Ethical Sensibility of Michel Foucault," *Political Theory* 21(3) (August 1993).

7. Butler, *Bodies That Matter*, p. 53.

8. To be sure, we often seek to disentangle the two, for the sake of our conscience, but often with little effect. For instance, I may have opposed the Persian Gulf war, but I still pay among the lowest gasoline prices in the world. The former does not totally explain the latter, but neither are they entirely unrelated.

9. Recall that Hobbes's proclamation of our restless desire for power occurs in "Of the Difference of Manners."

10. The situation is analogous to Greek practices of the self which stylized freedom, and thus converted power, in order to expand freedom qualitatively (UP, 97–98).

11. I have already suggested an answer to the question of desire, namely, we might desire to deliberately exercise the powers we inevitably bear because our freedom depends upon it. I elaborate this point here, though its thorough development must await another project.

12. See the Putney Debates in A. S. P. Woodhouse, ed., *Puritanism and Liberty* (London: Everyman, 1992), pp. 1–124.

13. Foucault explicitly says that his claim is not that all relations in the army are "gay." Indeed, the dichotomy of gay and non-gay cannot do justice to the complexity of relations. Perspectives such as this suggest why Foucault has been such a logical resource for theorizing "queer" identities; see, for example, David Halperin, *Saint Foucault* (New York: Oxford University Press, 1995).

14. We encountered the distinction between divine command and secular law in chapter 5; whether we recognize and enact the difference between them depends, in Foucault's terms, upon an aesthetics of existence or, in my terms, upon whether and how we name and engage invisible powers.

15. For example, "From Antiquity to Christianity, we pass from morality that was essentially the search for a personal ethics to a morality as obedience to a system of rules. And if I was interested in Antiquity it was because, for a whole series of reasons, the idea of morality as obedience to a code is now disappearing, has already disappeared. And to this absence of morality corresponds, must correspond, the search for an aesthetics of existence" (PPC, 49). I am uncertain whether Foucault means that the appeal to a moral code is no longer intellectually sustainable and ethically affirmable, or whether it is disappearing altogether. The latter claim seems unwarranted by the current dynamics of intellectual and cultural life. Throughout this book I emphasize the indeterminacy and insufficiency of normal conformity to a code for the pursuit of ethical conduct in contexts of ordered, ordinary evil.

16. In the contemporary context the stylizations associated with various politics of identity corresponds to the first position, whereas an aspiration toward and celebration of free individuality corresponds to the latter position. In my view, what interests both Foucault and Arendt are the possibilities for the practice of responsibility and freedom in the space political action opens up between these opposing strategies and types.

17. These failures are magnified, in turn, by the stories we have of individuals who

did interrogate and transform the conditions and effects of their exercise of power. I discuss the case of Anton Schmidt in chapter 7.

18. As Arendt renders it, the commitment thinking induces is existential, not transcendental (not even weakly so).

19. In this context, Arendt assumes that thinking, like conscience, is solitary.

20. More specifically, Richard Bauman discusses the difficulties many contemporaries had reading Quakers' performances because they were at once over- and underdetermined (*Let Your Words Be Few* [London: Cambridge University Press, 1983], pp. 84–94).

21. In this light, we can read my discussion of the frontispiece of *Leviathan* in chapters 2 and 3 as a description of the constitution of the sensus communis of sovereign individual and collective bodies.

22. Benhabib disagrees; see *The Reluctant Modernism of Hannah Arendt* (Beverly Hills, Calif.: Sage, 1996), pp. 193–99.

23. In the next chapter I imagine an alternative, mutually transfigurative encounter.

24. Hobbes's professed war upon metaphorical thinking is related to its engagement of the invisible.

25. Joanna Vecchariarelli Scott and Judith Chelius Stark, eds., *Love and Saint Augustine* (Chicago: University of Chicago Press, 1996), esp. pp. 45–57.

26. For complexities attending this claim, see Sheldon S. Wolin, *Hobbes and the Epic Tradition of Political Theory* (Los Angeles: University of California, William Andrews Clark Memorial Library, 1970); Leo Strauss, *The Political Philosophy of Hobbes: Its Basis and Genesis*, trans. Elsa M. Sinclair (Chicago: University of Chicago Press, 1952); and, most recently, Quentin Skinner, *Reason and Rhetoric in the Philosophy of Hobbes* (Cambridge: Cambridge University Press, 1996).

27. Peter Brooks, "The Melodramatic Imagination," *Partisan Review* 39(2) (Winter 1972): 199–200.

28. Ibid., 212.

29. James Bernauer notes resonances between the early Foucault's work on Binswinger, which inspired Foucault's claim that dreams reveal the essential meaning of human being to be a radical liberty, and his later ecstatic thinking (Michel Foucault's *Force of Flight* [Atlantic Highlands, N.J.: Humanities Press, 1990], 175). John Rajchman's *Truth and Eros: Foucault, Lacan, and the Question of Ethics* (New York: Routledge, 1991) is also suggestive in this regard. Likewise, Frederick Dolan has explored resonances between Lacan and Arendt in "Political Action and the Unconscious: Arendt and Lacan on Decentering the Subject" *Political Theory* 23(2) (May 1995): 330–352. Along these lines, however, I am most indebted to Jonathan Lear's *Love and Its Place in Nature: A Philosophical Interpretation of Freudian Psychoanalysis* (New York: Noonday Press, 1990). There are plenty of reasons to prefer a Lacanian unconscious, but Dolan brings out an important reason why we might not—namely, it instrumentalizes action. To my mind, the same cannot be said of Lear's reflections upon love and the unconscious. Moreover, his elaboration of love as a force of nature resonates nicely with the Quakers' practical mysticism, as well as with what Bernauer names Foucault's worldly mysticism (*Forces of Flight*, p. 178).

30. I draw here upon Lear, *Love and Its Place in Nature*, pp. 183–222.

31. On Lear's distinction between accepting responsibility versus finding oneself responsible see chapter 7, note 23.

Chapter 7. A Political Ethos of Conscience

1. Thus the resurgence of interest in tragedy, albeit a few decades ago George Steiner wrote of its death, even as he hoped for its reincarnation. In my view, awareness of the inevitability and ubiquity of trespass calls for a tragic rather than a utopian political outlook, for mindfulness of the complexities and ambiguities of our condition rather than visions of a final "redemptive" solution. Among the recent treatments of tragedy noteworthy from a political theoretical perspective are Martha Nussbaum, *The Fragility of Goodness* (Cambridge: Cambridge University Press, 1986); J. Peter Euben, *The Tragedy of Political Theory* (Princeton: Princeton University Press, 1990); C. Fred Alford, *The Psychoanalytic Theory of Greek Tragedy* (New Haven: Yale University Press, 1992); Bernard Williams, *Shame and Necessity* (Berkeley: University of California Press, 1993).

2. On the hostility evoked by differences appearing as given, "dark and mysterious" within cultures that conceive of equality as social (rather than political) and are committed to mastery, see OT, 300–301, 54–55. Arendt's antipathy toward "naturalizing" social characteristics and her astute sense of the dangers of doing so are especially pronounced in *Antisemitism* (e.g., OT, 79–88).

3. For example, see William E. Connolly, *Identity\Difference* (Ithaca, N.Y.: Cornell University Press, 1991), pp. 16–35, 95–122, 158–97, *Political Theory and Modernity* (New York: Basil Blackwell, 1987), pp. 1–15, 137–75; Bonnie Honig, *Political Theory and the Displacement of Politics* (Ithaca, N.Y.: Cornell University Press, 1993), pp. 42–75; Wendy Brown, "Wounded Attachments," *Political Theory* 21(3) (August 1993): 402, and *States of Injury* (Princeton: Princeton University Press, 1995).

4. Compare Foucault on regimen as a practice of problematization (UP, 101–2).

5. The early Quakers' silent ecstatic practices certainly defied ordinary standards of judgment, but can we be certain that they were thoughtless?

6. Compare Foucault's claim to the early Quakers' challenge to orthodox Puritans.

7. "About the Beginning of the Hermeneutics of the Self: Two Lectures at Dartmouth," *Political Theory* 21(2) (May 1993): 198–227, 221. Gnostic and American experiences are obvious exceptions to this generalization about Christians. See chapter 5 and Harold Bloom, *The American Religion* (New York: Touchstone, 1992).

8. *Michel Foucault's Force of Flight* (Atlantic Highlands, N.J.: Humanities Press, 1990), pp. 158–84, 180.

9. The distinction is analogous though not equivalent to Arendt's distinction between thinking and knowing.

10. Thus, for example, the reasonable subject-citizen is involved in the knowledge that differentiates him or her from the "mad" religious enthusiast and the trespasses this entails.

11. For Arendt, assuming responsibility for the conditions that condition us and others is fundamental to ethical political relations: "For insofar as man is more than a mere creature of nature, more than a mere product of Divine creativity, insofar will he be called to account for the things which men do to men in the world which they themselves condition" (JP, 109).

12. Arendt appears to deny that what we are has any effect upon who we are. But her understanding of the conditioning effect of the world of human artifice upon the web of

human relationships (our words and deeds) complicates this radical distinction (HC, 9–11, 182–83, 204). Her own writings suggest that who we are revealed to be through political action can never altogether leave behind what we are. Additionally, reflection upon the force of social imperatives suggests that ignoring what we have been made to be does not protect but imperils who we might become. For further development of these points, see chapter 3.

13. To say that we should challenge social rules is not to say that we should never decide to affirm them. Affirmation can be a form of interruption so long as it departs from thoughtless repetition.

14. See BPF, 197–226; Seyla Benhabib, *Situating the Self* (New York: Routledge, 1992), pp. 121–44; Ronald Beiner, *Political Judgment* (Chicago: University Chicago Press, 1983); and chapter 6.

15. For deployment of these concepts to a specific case of political activity, see my "Forgiving Trespasses, Promising Futures," in *Feminist Interpretations of Hannah Arendt*, ed. Bonnie Honig (University Park: Penn State University Press, 1995), pp. 337–56.

16. For a novel tradition of political theory, see my introduction.

17. See, for example, David Halperin, *Saint Foucault* (New York: Oxford University Press, 1995); Mark Blasius, *Gay and Lesbian Politics* (Philadelphia: Temple University Press, 1994).

18. This may be why both Arendt and Foucault find Socrates a more principled example than Plato. The "historical Socrates" at once affirmed a will to truth and justice while proclaiming ignorance of what truth and justice actually are. Indeed, only by disavowing possession of truth or justice does Socrates sustain the distinction between truth and untruth, justice and injustice. Plato's desire (at least on one reading) to possess truth and justice threatens to confound the limited with the limitless and thus altogether to lose the distinction. An interesting correlate of this dictinction is found in contemporary theological reflection upon the idol and the icon; see Jean-Luc Marion, *God without Being*, trans. Thomas A. Carlson (Chicago: University of Chicago Press, 1991), pp. 1–52.

19. Seyla Benhabib, *The Reluctant Modernism of Hannah Arendt* (Beverly Hills, Calif.: Sage, 1996), pp. 193–98, esp. 195–97.

20. Is *The Human Condition* a philosophical anthropology? What are we to make of the fact that Arendt regards the problem of what humans are as a theological question (HC, 11)?

21. For a development of this theme in Foucault, see James Bernauer, S.J., "The Prisons of Man: An Introduction to Foucault's Negative Theology," *International Philosophical Quarterly* 27(4)(108) (December 1987): 365–80, and his *Michel Foucault's Force of Flight*.

22. Benhabib, *Reluctant Modernism*, p. 196.

23. Though Arendt and Foucault might balk, an interesting parallel can be drawn with psychoanalysis. In response to the question of why I should assume responsibility for my instinctual life even though, like Oedipus's fate, I did not literally make it, Jonathan Lear answers: "Accepting responsibility is constitutive of the process of individuation, the process by which I become an I" (*Love and Its Place in Nature* [New York: Noonday, 1990], pp. 195–96). Neither Arendt nor Foucault adequately addresses the

politics of desire (what makes us desire to act freely or not?), but neither does justificatory political theory. In this regard, psychoanalytic discourse still seems among the most promising courses, especially as it seeks to incorporate rather than to abolish archaic mental life.

24. I find Benhabib's contextual unversalism more compelling ethically than Habermas's universal pragmatics, but I still find it insufficiently attentive to the trespasses that follow from even the good we would do.

25. Only a beginning to this revaluation of the relationship between power and principle can be made here.

26. Habermas's vision of erecting a "democratic dam against colonializing encroachment of system imperatives on areas of the lifeworld" ("Further Reflections on the Public Sphere," in *Habermas and the Public Sphere*, ed. Craig Calhoun [Cambridge, Mass.: MIT Press, 1992], p. 444) adequately addresses this issue only if the "social-integrative power of solidarity" necessarily flows *against* rather than *with* system's imperatives. To determine whether or not communicative action challenges more instrumental powers, it is not sufficient to identify "anonymous yet intelligible rules" of self-reflexive argumentation (Seyla Benhabib, "Deliberative Rationality and Models of Democratic Legitimacy," *Constellations* 1[1] [April 1994]: 26–52, 28). Some may experience the communicatively derived commands of the lifeworld as a source of trespass, in part, but not only, because of the facilitative role communicative action can play in relation to economic and administrative systems. In his more recent work, *Between Facts and Norms: Contributions to a Discourse Theory of Law and Democracy*, trans. William Rehg (Cambridge, Mass.: MIT Press, 1996), Habermas opens a bit more space within his theorizing for criticizing the disciplinary tendencies of communicative action.

27. In addition to the recently published translation of Arendt's dissertation, *Love and Saint Augustine*, also see Jean Bethke Elshtain's *Augustine and the Limits of Politics* (Notre Dame, Ind.: University of Notre Dame Press, 1996): 69–87. I find resonances between my argument and her discussion of evil as mimesis in contrast to generativity.

28. For an example of the former, see David Ingram, "The Postmodern Kantianism of Arendt and Lyotard," *Review of Metaphysics* 42 (September 1988): 67–77, and, of the latter, Wendy Brown, "Wounded Attachments," 400–408. Brown's emphasis on the politics of desire and will-to-freedom is welcome, but to my mind she moves too quickly to "getting over" our wounds (though *States of Injuries*, pp. 96–134, shows awareness of the problem). After all, even Zarathustra was tempted and instructed by resentment to the end (*The Portable Nietzsche* [New York: Penguin, 1954], pp. 250–53, 309–10, 438–39).

Index

C O N T E S T A T I O N S

CORNELL STUDIES IN POLITICAL THEORY

A series edited by
WILLIAM E. CONNOLLY

Skepticism, Belief, and the Modern: Maimonides to Nietzsche
by Aryeh Botwinick

Rethinking Generosity: Critical Theory and the Politics of Caritas
by Romand Coles

The Other Heidegger
by Fred Dallmayr

Allegories of America: Narratives, Metaphysics, Politics
by Frederick M. Dolan

united states
by Thomas L. Dumm

Intimacy and Spectacle: Liberal Theory as Political Education
by Stephen L. Esquith

Political Theory and the Displacement of Politics
by Bonnie Honig

The Self at Liberty: Political Argument and the Arts of Government
by Duncan Ivison

The Inner Ocean: Individualism and Democratic Culture
by George Kateb

The Anxiety of Freedom: Imagination and Individuality in Locke's Political Thought
by Uday Singh Mehta

Living Ethically, Acting Politically
by Melissa A. Orlie

The Art of Being Free: Taking Liberties with Tocqueville, Marx, and Arendt
by Mark Reinhardt

Political Theory for Mortals: Shades of Justice, Images of Death
by John E. Seery

Signifying Woman: Culture and Chaos in Rousseau, Burke, and Mill
by Linda M. G. Zerilli

Melissa A. Orlie is Associate Professor of Political Science, Criticism and Interpretive Theory, and Women's Studies at the University of Illinois, Urbana-Champaign.